Fostering Wellbeing through Collective Writing Practices

This book explores the transformative power of collaborative writing sessions in fostering wellbeing among academics. In this collection, the second of two volumes, the editors bring together diverse voices from around the globe, offering insights into how Shut Up & Write! (SUAW) sessions are revolutionising academic practice and nurturing healthier, more connected scholarly communities.

From remote scholars finding connection to working-class academics addressing unfinished business, this book illuminates the multifaceted benefits of SUAW. It delves into how these sessions build resilience, cultivate passion, boost productivity, and nurture academic identity. The contributors share personal narratives, practical strategies, and critical reflections on how SUAW initiatives are reshaping academic culture.

This is essential reading for academics, doctoral students, and university administrators seeking innovative approaches to enhance wellbeing in higher education. It offers a compelling case for integrating SUAW into academic life, demonstrating its potential to combat isolation, foster supportive networks, and promote a more balanced approach to scholarly work.

Narelle Lemon is a Professor and Vice Chancellor Professorial Research Fellow at Edith Cowan University, Australia, where she leads the Wellbeing and Education Research Community, and is an interdisciplinary scholar across arts, education, and positive psychology. She is also Creative Director of Explore & Create Co.

Aaron Bolzle is Co-Founder of Writing Partners and President of its flagship initiative, Shut Up & Write!. He also serves as an Innovation Fellow at the Cambridge University ThinkLab, where he collaborates on community-focused initiatives that support connection and wellbeing. Bolzle's work centers on creating inclusive, thriving global writing communities that foster belonging, resilience, and sustainable practice. Under his leadership, Shut Up & Write! has expanded to hundreds of cities and universities in over 60 countries.

Malaika Santa Cruz served as a key early team member at Shut Up & Write!, growing the community back when Shut Up & Write! was only a few thousand members across eight chapter cities. A decade later, her operational expertise and dedication to fostering meaningful partnerships has been pivotal in maintaining the inclusive culture as Shut Up & Write! has expanded to hundreds of cities and universities worldwide.

Rennie Saunders is the founder and CEO of Shut Up & Write!, a global organisation that hosts free writing events for authors worldwide. What began as a personal quest to find creative community in San Francisco has grown into a movement supporting nearly 100,000 writers across 53 countries. A lifelong science fiction enthusiast who wrote his first story at age 12, Rennie is passionate about providing writers with the resources, community, and accountability they need to succeed.

Wellbeing and Self-care in Higher Education
Editor: Narelle Lemon

Passion and Purpose in the Humanities
Exploring the Worlds of Early Career Researchers
Edited by Marcus Bussey, Camila Mozzini-Alister, Bingxin Wang and Samantha Willcocks

Supporting and Promoting Wellbeing in the Higher Education Sector
Practices in Action
Edited by Angela Dobele and Lisa Farrell

Understanding Wellbeing in Higher Education of the Global South
Contextually Sensitive and Culturally Responsive Perspectives
Edited by Youmen Chaaban, Abdellatif Sellami and Igor Michaleczek

The Making Academic
Perspectives on Expressive Practice and Wellbeing in Higher Education
Edited by Narelle Lemon, Sharon McDonough and Mark Selkrig

Creating Wellbeing
The Role of Making Practices in Academic Contexts
Edited by Narelle Lemon, Sharon McDonough, and Mark Selkrig

Cultivating Wellbeing and Community through Writing in Academia
Shifting the Culture with Shut Up & Write!
Edited by Narelle Lemon and Aaron Bolzle with Malaika Santa Cruz and Rennie Saunders

Fostering Wellbeing through Collective Writing Practices
Shut Up & Write! in Higher Education Settings
Edited by Narelle Lemon and Aaron Bolzle with Malaika Santa Cruz and Rennie Saunders

For more information about this series, please visit: www.routledge.com/Wellbeing-and-Self-care-in-Higher-Education/book-series/WSCHE

Fostering Wellbeing through Collective Writing Practices
Shut Up & Write! in Higher Education Settings

Edited by Narelle Lemon and Aaron Bolzle with Malaika Santa Cruz and Rennie Saunders

Designed cover image: Getty Images

First published 2026
by Routledge
4 Park Square, Milton Park, Abingdon, Oxon OX14 4RN

and by Routledge
605 Third Avenue, New York, NY 10158

Routledge is an imprint of the Taylor & Francis Group, an informa business

© 2026 selection and editorial matter, Narelle Lemon, Aaron Bolzle, Malaika Santa Cruz, and Rennie Saunders; individual chapters, the contributors

The right of Narelle Lemon, Aaron Bolzle, Malaika Santa Cruz, and Rennie Saunders to be identified as the authors of the editorial material, and of the authors for their individual chapters, has been asserted in accordance with sections 77 and 78 of the Copyright, Designs and Patents Act 1988.

All rights reserved. No part of this book may be reprinted or reproduced or utilised in any form or by any electronic, mechanical, or other means, now known or hereafter invented, including photocopying and recording, or in any information storage or retrieval system, without permission in writing from the publishers.

Trademark notice: Product or corporate names may be trademarks or registered trademarks, and are used only for identification and explanation without intent to infringe.

British Library Cataloguing-in-Publication Data
A catalogue record for this book is available from the British Library

ISBN: 978-1-041-05989-9 (hbk)
ISBN: 978-1-041-05985-1 (pbk)
ISBN: 978-1-003-63332-7 (ebk)

DOI: 10.4324/9781003633327

Typeset in Galliard
by SPi Technologies India Pvt Ltd (Straive)

Contents

List of Figures	xi
List of Tables	xiii
Contributors' Biographies	xiv
Forward: Cultivating Wellbeing through Shared Writing Practices	xxix
Series Preface	xlii
Acknowledgements	xlv

PART I
Foundations of Community and Wellbeing   1

1 Shut Up & Write! A Dialogue on Community, Wellbeing, and Purpose   3
NARELLE LEMON, AARON BOLZLE, AND MALAIKA SANTA CRUZ

2 From Isolation to Connection: How Online Shut Up & Write! Fosters Wellbeing for Remote Scholars   25
STEPHANIE MILFORD

3 Moreton Bay Fridays: Creating Community in a Regional University Campus through Convivial Co-located Quiet Writing   33
DEANNA GRANT-SMITH, KATIE MCINTYRE, KAREN HANDS, DAVID SCHMIDTKE, RORY MULCAHY, AND MARGARIETHA DE VILLIERS SCHEEPERS

4 Shut Up and Write! Online: Affective Atmospheres and Postdigital Pedagogies of Care   41
MIRIAM REYNOLDSON AND ANNA FARAGO

PART II
Doctoral and Graduate Student Experiences   49

5 Everyday Tales of an Online 'Shut Up & Write! (SU&W) PhD Research Community'   51
MARGARET (MEG) DAVIS, SANDRA CROAKER, NATALIE LINDSAY, AND BRONWYN CHARLES

6 From Procrastination to Productivity: Developing Collegial Interconnectedness through Belonging, Being and Becoming   58
JACQUI PETERS, RACHEL FINNERAN, PENNIE WHITE, AND KATRINA MACDONALD

7 And See What Comes to You in the Silence: Reflecting on the Restorative Potential of "Shut Up and Write!"   66
HAIDEE HICKS

8 Beyond the Individual: Reflections on Writing, Identity, and Wellbeing in Academia   73
GILLIAN KIMUNDI

PART III
Creative and Collaborative Approaches   81

9 Changing the Script: Collective and Creative Possibilities   83
TIMOTHY CLARK

10 Shut Up and Write!, Connect, and Support: Bridging the Gap to Support Rural Postgraduate Students   91
DANIEL P WADSWORTH, DAVID DUNCAN, STACEY WHITELAW, KATE MCCUBBERY, REBECCA TERLICH, ALEXANDRA POTTER, MICHELLE GOSSNER, ISHWAR KOIRALA, ERIN HARCOURT, JOLENE A COX, AND DYLAN POULUS

11 The Therapeutic Power of Writing: Exploring the Mental Health Benefits for Writers and Readers   99
REAGAN FLEMING

12 Academic Identity Development in the Context of Online Writing Groups: Increasing Resilience and Wellbeing   106
JASON MURPHY AND LISA HODGE

PART IV
Technology and Innovation   115

13 Times to Shut Up, Times to Sing Out: How Technology
   Fosters Productivity and Wellbeing   117
   YVONNE WOOD AND ALISON TALMAGE

14 'We are All in this Together' The Role of Collaborative
   Writing Sessions in Developing Doctoral Candidates'
   Confidence to Engage in the Academic Publication Process   126
   LUCY HALL AND PAULA VILLEGAS

15 A Luxurious Commodity: Reflections on 'Shut Up and
   Write!' for Part-time, Taught, Postgraduate Students   134
   MARK WIDDOWFIELD

PART V
Maximising Impact and Effectiveness   141

16 Shut Up and Write!, Not Work: Personal Reflections and
   Strategies Towards Maximising SUAW Wellbeing Benefits   143
   STEPHANIE RICHEY AND CAYLEE TIERNEY

17 Unlocking Writing: Using Creative Tasks to Prepare
   the Ground   150
   CLAIRE SAUNDERS

PART VI
Identity, Care, and Resistance   159

18 Nurturing Academic Mothers: Reconstructing Academic
   Identity During and After Career Interruptions through
   a Writing Community   161
   BELINDA PAULOVICH, EMMA FISHER, EMMA GRACE, ABIRAMI THIRUMANICKAM,
   AND JULIE-ANN HULIN

19 Choosing Affective over Effective Collaboration in Academic
   Writing: Pathways to Mentorship, Collaborative Wellbeing,
   and Self-Care through Scholarly Personal Narrative   168
   SYED ALI NASIR ZAIDI AND FINNEY CHERIAN

20 'Performing' the Good Neoliberal Academic: Using Critical Autoethnography to Interrogate Dominant Higher Education Audit Cultures 177
KATARINA TUINAMUANA, RAFAAN DALIRI-NGAMETUA, WADE NAYLOR, MELISSA CAIN, LUKE ROWE, DEBRA J. PHILLIPS, JASON Y.L WONG, HELEN SHEEHAN, MARIE WHITE, RENEE MORRISON, CHRISTOPHER DUNCAN, AND SHU CHAO

21 Benefits of Shut Up and Write! for Inclusion 186
JONATHAN O'DONNELL, ROSEMARY (ROSEY) CHANG, AND AMIE O'SHEA

Figures

1.1	Geeking out on SUAW and the heart of its impact on wellbeing (Longarm selfie exploration series, November 2024, Cambridge)	7
2.1	Writing from the Edge – The Kimberley Coastline as a Backdrop to Shut Up & Write!	28
3.1	The mandala as visual metaphor for Moreton Bay Fridays	35
4.1	SUAW Zoom patchwork 2025 (Artist: Anna Farago)	42
5.1	Early days of SU&W, Kuranda North Queensland: October 2021 (Left to Right: Sandra, Natalie, Bronwyn, Margaret)	52
6.1	Being, belonging, and becoming (Adapted from Accurs, n.d.)	62
7.1	"Disappearing" every Saturday to attend the SUAW group. Image includes ten Pomodoro timers, each set to 25 minutes	68
8.1	Like glimpses through a canopy, my sense of purpose is slowly emerging	74
9.1	A space for thinking and talking on a SUAW wellbeing walk	85
10.1	The Manna gum tree branches represent the connection, growth, and flourishing found across our virtual SUAW sessions. Students exchange discussions, ideas, and research assets across branches, representing the 'fruit' of new thinking and community supported by our virtual SUAW sessions (© Manna Institute/Bright Pilots)	92
11.1	Books	100
12.1	The contradiction of universities (Photo credit: Benjamin Lehman)	108
13.1	The Threads and Thoughts that Connect our Community of Practice in Action	123
14.1	Structure of the individual writing output	127
15.1	A representation of the interplay between time, Shut Up and Write!, space, and reflection	135
16.1	Finding the write path (created by Caylee)	144
17.1	*Water Ripple* by Linus Nylund on Unsplash	151
18.1	Our SUAW group can be visualised as an organic Venn diagram containing our five group members. We are united by a central link of shared experiences of parenthood and the demands of academic careers, while also being enclosed and supported by our surrounding SUAW community	166

19.1	Affective and effective writing practices reciprocate mutual self-care and well-being	169
20.1	ACU SUAW group	178
21.1	The toadstool-style stools	187

Tables

13.1 Mapping the Integration of Webber's (2016) Community of Practice Model and the Social Construction of Technology Model (Pinch & Bijker, 1986) in *Research Accelerator* Shut Up and Write! Sessions 119
14.1 Hopes gained 129
21.1 Adaptation and implementation strategies for Shut Up & Write!® and sit down & write! (Reproduced from Micsinszki & Yeung, 2021) 192

Contributors' Biographies

Aaron Bolzle is Co-Founder of Writing Partners and President of its flagship initiative, Shut Up & Write! He also serves as an Innovation Fellow at the Cambridge University ThinkLab, where he collaborates on community-focused initiatives that support connection and wellbeing. Bolzle's work centres on creating inclusive, thriving global writing communities that foster belonging, resilience, and sustainable practice. Under his leadership, Shut Up & Write! has expanded to hundreds of cities and universities in over 60 countries.

Melissa Cain is Associate Professor in the National School of Education at Australian Catholic University, and a Senior Fellow of the Higher Education Academy. Melissa teaches and researches in the fields of Inclusive Education and Creative Arts education and supervises Higher Degree Research students in these areas. Melissa's current research centres on facilitating full access to the Australian Curriculum (academic, social, emotional, and physical) for students with disability and supporting students with blindness and low vision in mainstream schools. Melissa has extended this focus to an area that is currently unaddressed – the impact of cultural, religious, and spiritual conceptions of disability on the advance of inclusive education. She also explores the experiences of students studying units fully asynchronously online.

Dr Rosemary (Rosey) Chang is a researcher developer, educator, and writer. As a lecturer in the Researcher Development Academy at Deakin University, Rosemary creates curriculum and initiatives to cultivate conditions for graduate researchers to thrive and flourish. After research on learning with emerging technologies, Rosemary has published on researcher and academic development, practice-based education, contemplative studies, and mindful writing practice. A common thread through her research is learning and development, and her focus is now on the experience and development of graduate researchers.

Dr Shu Chao is a Lecturer in the National School of Education at Australian Catholic University. Shu teaches in the fields of educational psychology and digital technologies in education. Shu's research includes gender equity in

ICT education and initial teacher education, and she is currently exploring the role of ethics in initial teacher education.

Bronwyn Charles is an academic and social worker based on the Gold Coast, Queensland, Australia. Bronwyn is currently studying her PhD at James Cook University Townsville and is also a casual lecturer at Griffith University, Gold Coast, Australia. Bronwyn's PhD project is exploring how social workers respond to sudden, unexpected death in hospital emergency departments. Bronwyn is interested in the role of community, kindness, and connection to support productivity. Bronwyn was inspired by the 'Shut Up and Write!' model to combat isolation as a distance student. Moving into academia from social work practice she has found that the 'Shut Up and Write!' model brought many unexpected outcomes of close friendships, increased opportunities to develop academic skills and knowledge, and application of theory to her personal circumstances. Bronwyn hopes to support practitioner social workers to develop identity and skills in research and academic writing. Bronwyn is passionate about social work practice and its impact on creating a more socially just world.

Finney Cherian is an Associate Professor at the Faculty of Education at the University of Windsor. He teaches undergraduate and graduate courses in literacy and Instructional design and his research interests are social justice, critical literacy and preservice teacher education. Dr. Cherian earned his PhD from the University of Toronto.

Dr Timothy Clark is Director of Research for the School of Education and Childhood at the University of the West of England (UWE). Tim's research focuses on aspects of doctoral pedagogy and researcher development. His recent research projects include studies investigating the pedagogic role of doctoral progression assessment and the affordances of arts-based research for the doctorate in education (EdD). He has also conducted a range of work exploring doctoral students' methodological decision-making and learning and recently co-edited a book focusing on 'lessons from doctoral studies' for which 14 EdD graduates wrote a chapter.

Dr Jolene A Cox is a Research Fellow and Research Theme Leader for Societal Health and Wellbeing at the Centre for Human Factors and Sociotechnical Systems, University of the Sunshine Coast. She is also a Research Affiliate at the Manna Institute for rural and regional mental health. Jolene's research focuses on the application of complex systems science theories and methods to address societal health concerns. Her research interest is driven by her passion to support the mental health and wellbeing of others.

Sandra Croaker is a Lecturer in Social Work at James Cook University, Townsville, Australia. Sandra is in the final stages of her PhD research. As part of her learning journey, she engaged in the 'Shut Up and Write!' group and found a passion for learning more about strategies to support herself and others through the highs and lows of the PhD journey.

Dr Rafaan Daliri-Ngametua (FHEA) is a Lecturer and Researcher in Education at Australian Catholic University (ACU)'s National School of Education, Queensland. Previously a classroom teacher and academic at The University of Queensland (UQ), she holds a PhD from that institution, where her research explored the datafication of assessment and learning. Rafaan's expertise spans education policy, governance, datafication, teachers' work, assessment, and student voice. She is a member of the Pedagogy, Education and Praxis (PEP) network and is currently partnering with the Queensland Teachers' Union on a project supporting teacher autonomy. Her work is internationally recognised and has appeared in leading journals and media outlets. Guided by a strong sense of social justice, Rafaan believes education should be a creative, reflective engagement with the world, aiming to "learn to live well, in a world worth living in."

Margaret (Meg) Davis is a retired social worker with extensive community experience in regional North Queensland. She was awarded her PhD (March 2025) by James Cook University North Queensland, Australia for her study which explored the resettlement experiences of former refugee women from diverse African countries into North Queensland and which included recommendations for regional resettlement policy and implications for social work and human services practice.

Christopher Duncan is an Associate Lecturer (Indigenous) in the National School of Education at Australian Catholic University and has a background in secondary education. His research interests include Indigenous university students' wellbeing and Indigenous histories. Christopher is an Aboriginal Australian academic who currently teaches in Indigenous Education and is also completing his PhD thesis based in Sydney, Australia, and which focusses on the degree progression and completion of Indigenous Secondary Education preservice teachers.

David Duncan is a PhD candidate at the University of the Sunshine Coast (UniSC) and a Manna Institute scholarship holder. David's PhD research, exploring a whole-of-university approach to student mental health and wellbeing, complements his professional practice as UniSC's Student Health Coordinator, responsible for student health and wellbeing strategy. David is a member of Manna Institute's HDR Community of Practice and a Fellow of the Australian Health Promotion Association, reflecting his commitment to advancing public health and health promotion practice.

Anna Farago is an artist, researcher, and teacher whose investigations are animated by feminist art histories, craft traditions, the intergenerational transmission of knowledge, and experience of place. Central to her practice is an exploration of ecosystems. Her work poses questions around ways in which we sustain material traditions, the intersection of personal and collective memory, and processes of constructing and reconstructing belonging.

Contributors' Biographies xvii

Rachel Finneran completed her PhD at Deakin University in 2022 and is currently a casual research fellow at Deakin University, working on a range of projects. Rachel is interested in the sociology of education and student voice. Her PhD explored the relationship between the policy and practice of student voice in Victoria and highlighted how class, schooling, and affect mediate student voice enactment.

Dr Emma Fisher is a lecturer and researcher at Swinburne University of Technology and a director and graphic designer at Cordial Creative. She holds over 25 years' experience in industry, working on local and international communication design projects and has taught at undergraduate and postgraduate levels since 2004 in a wide range of graphic design and professional practice subjects. Emma completed her PhD on practitioners' research engagement in the Australian communication design profession in 2015 and conducts ongoing research into employability and portfolio literacy issues for design graduates.

Reagan Fleming works as a Media Content Editor by day and is a master's student by night. She loves reading Asian-American literature, books about writing, and the occasional romance novel. Her writing spans from concert reviews and poetry to essays and movie listicles, and her work has been featured in a university literary magazine and on FilmAesthete.com. When not writing, she watercolors portraits of her favorite television and movie characters, which often reignites her creativity for the written word. She resides in Tulsa, Oklahoma with her pup, Harper.

Alberto Garcia is an Academic Skills Librarian at Wolfson College, University of Cambridge.

Nysha Chantel Givans, a first-generation university attendee, is the daughter of a single Jamaican mother and proudly embraces her working-class heritage. She is pursuing a Professional Doctorate in Education at the University of Wolverhampton. Her research focuses on how marginalised groups from lower socio-economic backgrounds navigate barriers within education.

Michelle Gossner is a PhD candidate at CQUniversity. With a background in education and psychology, she has a keen interest in child and adolescent development. Her research focuses on understanding and addressing the diverse factors that influence the wellbeing and educational outcomes of young people. She is also a member of the Manna Institute Higher Degree Research (HDR) Community of Practice.

Dr Emma Grace is a Senior Lecturer in Inclusive Education at Flinders University and a qualified Speech-Language Pathologist. Her PhD, funded by an NHMRC Cerebral Palsy Alliance Research Foundation Postgraduate Scholarship and awarded 3rd prize globally in the Pursuit Award, investigated effects of peer e-mentoring on participation in online conversations for adolescents with communication disability. Building on this work,

Emma now evaluates real-world communication interventions and supports, including technology-supported phonics for early reading and multimodal communication approaches for individuals with communication disability.

Deanna Grant-Smith is Professor and Management Discipline Lead in the School of Business and Creative Industries at the University of the Sunshine Coast. Based on its Moreton Bay campus, she researches decent work and the opportunities for exploitation and potential for diminished wellbeing associated with unpaid internships, emerging models of employment, and multilevel marketing business models.

Dr Lucy Hall is an Effective Learner Advisor at Heriot-Watt University and a lecturer in English Literature at the Open University. She also worked as the Postgraduate Student Developer at the University of St Andrews from 2021 to 2024.

Karen Hands is a Senior Lecturer and Discipline Lead in Creative Industries in the School of Business and Creative Industries at the University of the Sunshine Coast. Based at its Moreton Bay campus, Karen's research focuses on arts and cultural policy, specifically examining how policy shapes the conditions of creative/cultural workers and the creative cultural labour market.

Erin Harcourt is a PhD candidate at Federation University and a member of Manna Institute's HDR Community of Practice (CoP). Erin's research focuses on identifying patients at risk of developing psychological issues associated with Post Intensive Care Syndrome (PICS). Her PhD will explore a comprehensive range of bio/psycho/social risk and protective factors, and how they are associated with the possibility of developing anxiety, depression, and Post Traumatic Stress Disorder (PTSD) after a stay in the Intensive Care Unit (ICU).

Haidee Hicks is a Lecturer in Social Work at RMIT University in Melbourne, Australia, where she is Deputy Program Manager and coordinates the Honours program. She finds great joy in participating in SUAW communities and recently facilitated a writing retreat in her program. Haidee's research interests focus on international students, research pedagogies, and students' learning during work-integrated learning (WIL) placements. Current publications relate to social work students' experience of group supervision and collaborative autoethnographic research that explores academics' self-care and wellbeing practices. Other research interests focus on doctoral education in Australia and the ways in which social workers respond in post-disaster recovery contexts.

Lisa Hodge, PhD, is an Associate Professor and Head of School for Social Work at the Institute of Health & Management (IHM), and Adjunct Research Fellow, Swinburne University of Technology, Melbourne,

Australia. Her research focuses on a number of areas: mental health, including in the areas of higher education; soldier recovery after physical and mental health injury; and eating disorders. Lisa has a background as a counsellor and uses creative expression in both her research and practice.

Dr Julie-Ann Hulin is an Early-Mid Career research-only academic at Flinders University, specialising in gene regulation, epigenetics, cancer, and stem cell biology. Her research explores molecular target identification and validation in cancer and regenerative medicine, which broadly encompasses analysis of signalling pathways in disease states in order to identify potential therapeutic targets. Julie-Ann's research has received funding from the Flinders Foundation, Cancer Council SA and Tour de Cure. She is establishing her independent research profile and is co-founder of Academics Down Under with Dr Belinda Paulovich.

Gillian Kimundi is a final-year graduate researcher in Finance at Deakin Business School (Melbourne, Australia). Her research focuses on the interconnections amongst financial institutions, and related implications on financial markets. She has experience in academia, has contributed to banking sector policy research in Kenya, and has facilitated multiple professional trainings for organisations in data science. She is a faculty representative for her fellow graduate researchers at the Business and Law School. Her journey through policy work, academic research, and advocacy have deepened her appreciation for community engagement and belonging as vital components of academic success and meaningful work. Outside of her professional interests, Gillian enjoys a good cup of coffee and cinema.

Ishwar Koirala is an educator, researcher, and writer based in Sydney, Australia. He is a Doctoral Candidate at the School of Science and Technology, University of New England and Manna Institute. With over 15 years of teaching experience, he currently serves as a lecturer at Canberra College of Management and Technology, Sydney. His research focuses on mental health and wellbeing, coping and resilience, international students' experiences, learner differences, and strategies for enhancing learning engagement.

Professor Narelle Lemon is a Vice Chancellor Professoriate Research Fellow at Edith Cowan University, Perth, Australia. She is Lead of the Wellbeing and Education Research Community (WE). Previous to moving to Perth, Narelle was Associate Dean Education in the School of Social Sciences, Media, Film and Education at Swinburne University of Technology, Melbourne, and she is best known for her work in Pedagogy of Belonging. Narelle is an interdisciplinary scholar across the fields of arts, education, and positive psychology. Her research expertise is in fostering wellbeing literacy in the contexts of K-12 schools, initial teacher education, higher education, and community education. Narelle focuses on capacity-building in wellbeing and self-care of proactive action across diverse areas of evidence-based wellbeing science in order to flourish. Narelle blogs, posts, grams and podcasts as a part of her networked scholar practices. She is currently leading an international project called the "Citizen Wellbeing Scientist" capturing multimodal everyday actions of self-care (https://www.exploreandcreateco.com/citizen-wellbeing-scientist).

Natalie Lindsay is a social work PhD scholar and practitioner in the child protection space and a Clinical Teaching Associate with the College of Medicine at James Cook University. She also has experience as a sessional social work educator who is keenly interested in the experiences of international students in Australian social work education and placements. Natalie is a co-founder of Social Workers for Climate Action, an alliance of social work practitioners, students, educators, and researchers concerned about the impacts of climate change on human wellbeing and committed to taking climate action. She is a keen cyclist and interested in sustainable transport frameworks, eco-social work, narrative theory in research and practice, feminist social work, and valuing the everyday lived experience of women in both research and practice. Natalie values connection and collaboration in all spheres of her life.

Dr Katrina MacDonald is a Senior Lecturer in Educational Leadership in the School of Education, Deakin University. Her research and teaching interests are in educational leadership, social justice, school reform, intersectionality, spatiality, and the sociology of education through a practice lens (feminist, Bourdieu, practice architectures). Katrina is an assistant editor for the *International Journal of Leadership in Education*. She is a former anthropologist, archaeologist, and primary and secondary teacher in Victoria, Australia. Her most recent book is: *Socially Just Educational Leadership in Unjust Times: A Bourdieusian Study of Social Justice Educational Leadership Practices.*

Kate McCubbery is a PhD candidate at Southern Cross University and also a Manna Institute scholarship holder. Kate is an active participant in the Manna Institute's HDR Community of Practice. Her research is involved in exploring the impacts of changing environmental conditions on mental health. Kate's PhD project investigates how mental health and mental wellbeing in rural and regional communities are impacted by relationships with the natural environment and the experience of negative emotional responses to environmental change.

Katie McIntyre is a Research Fellow at The Centre for Humanitarian Leadership, Deakin University. Katie completed her PhD, examining Joyful Leadership, in the School of Business and Creative Industries at the University of the Sunshine Coast and continues to work on a number of projects at the university. Based at its Moreton Bay campus, Katie's research focused on various areas, including the role of emotions and leadership and the impact on employee wellbeing and engagement, which was the topic of her PhD research. In addition, Katie has several academic and industry publications related to leadership, social impact, and the non-profit sector.

Contributors' Biographies   xxi

Dr Stephanie Milford is a psychologist and postdoctoral research fellow with the ARC Centre of Excellence for the Digital Child. Her research explores digital parenting, parental self-efficacy, and family wellbeing. She commenced her PhD with Edith Cowan University while living in Broome, WA, and brings valuable lived experience from remote and regional contexts, including the Kimberley and the Wheatbelt regions in Western Australia. Stephanie is passionate about integrating wellbeing into everyday routines, including academic life.

Renee Morrison is a Lecturer at the University of Sunshine Coast. Her research investigates the relationship between digital practices and discursive practices. Specifically (but not exclusively), Renee's work considers how online technologies are being used in education and how they may be better used to enhance pedagogy, promote learning, as well as a more just society. A focus on understanding the role of technology in constructing versions of 'truth' and 'knowledge' is also present in her research. Renee is interested in problematising asymmetries in power and knowledge, and ensuring that discourse is a resource, not an obstacle for digital learning.

Rory Mulcahy is an Associate Professor at University of Sunchsine Coast the School of Business and Creative Industries. His research focuses on topics such as consumer vulnerability, emotions, technology, and sustainability. He has collaborated with various organisations, including government, NGO's, and start-ups. He has published his works in various journals, including Journal of Service Research, European Journal of Marketing, and Industrial Marketing Management, among others.

Jason Murphy, PhD, is a Business Analyst at the College of Design and Social Context, RMIT University, Melbourne. His research interests are in sociology, the practice of writing, and social inequality. He is an active supporter of writing groups that are based on the Shut up and Write! methodology and he has attended, coordinated and supported these groups for over a decade.

Wade Naylor, MInstP, was formerly an Associate Professor of Theoretical Physics at Osaka University (2010–2015). After a six-year career interruption to become a high school physics teacher, from 2022, Wade has been a lecturer in Physics, Mathematics & STEM education at Australian Catholic University (ACU). Wade's research interests lie in Physics Education Research (PER) and research into 'misconceptions' in physics and mathematics. He is also a visiting senior researcher at the Physics Department, University of Johannesburg (UJ). He also researches into the experiences of international academic staff.

Jonathan O'Donnell devoted himself to making life better for academics. Right now, he is doing so at Deakin University in Melbourne, Australia. For most of my career, he has been dedicated to helping both HASS and STEM academics to find funding for their research. His recent PhD examined academics that had crowdfunded their research, looking at the tension between university structures and individual actions, particularly when those actions seek to mobilise friends, family, colleagues and the general public in a new and innovative way. For the last decade, along with his colleague Tseen Khoo, he has managed the Research Whisperer blog, which is on the subject of doing research in academia. Under that umbrella, they have been running Shut Up and Write! sessions at their respective universities.

Amie O'Shea is a Senior Lecturer in the School of Health & Social Development at Deakin University. Her research interests are gender, sexuality, and disability with a focus on multiply marginalised groups experiencing intersectional disadvantage. Amie co-convenes a weekly Shut Up and Write! session for queer Deakin staff and students.

Dr Belinda Paulovich is a Lecturer in Communication Design at Swinburne University of Technology and is a member of Swinburne's Centre for Design Innovation. Her research investigates the role of co-design and communication design in improving health, wellbeing, and social outcomes across the lifespan. Belinda is the co-founder of Academics Down Under, a professional and social networking group for academics from Australia and New Zealand. She connects academics across institutions through her role as facilitator of the Academics Down Under Shut Up and Write! group.

Dr Jacqui Peters is a Senior Lecturer in Health and Physical Education in the School of Education at Deakin University. A long-time health and physical education teacher in primary and secondary schools, Jacqui has also been in an academic role at the University of Melbourne prior to taking up her position at Deakin University in 2009, where she teaches mainly into the secondary undergraduate Bachelor of Health and Physical Education. She has a keen interest in researching the student experience, teacher identity, teacher practice, transition to teaching, curriculum, assessment, and pedagogy. Her PhD focused on exploring physical educators' theorisation of their practice.

Dr Thinh Ngoc Pham is a Lecturer in the School of Psychology and Neuroscience at the University of Glasgow, UK. His research interests lie primarily in thinking skills, social psychology, cross-cultural psychology, psychology of bilingualism and multilingualism, and pedagogy, using an array of quantitative and qualitative methods.

Debra J. Phillips is a Lecturer in Education at Australian Catholic University. Her interdisciplinary doctorate, which examined suicidality through narrative inquiry, provided background for research into teachers' mental health. Her research is underpinned by theology, sociology, psychology, and visual arts. Dr Phillips promotes the ethical parameters that guide research in mental ill-health and seeks to develop collaborative, narrative style practices in teaching, research, and writing. Dr Phillips comes from a background of school-based teaching practice across education sectors, and has experience of postgraduate study in education, gender studies, narrative, and theology. Dr Phillips is also a practicing artist.

Alexandra Potter is a PhD candidate at the University of New England and a Manna Institute scholarship holder. Her doctoral research explores the lived experiences of suicide among mental health professionals, informed by both academic inquiry and personal experience. With a background in mental health practice and policy, her work examines professional identity, stigma, and systemic responses to suicide. She is committed to integrating lived experience into research and advancing trauma-informed, relational approaches to suicide prevention and mental health reform.

Dr Dylan Poulus is a Researcher and Lecturer at Southern Cross University and Manna Institute Foundation Postdoctoral Fellow, specialising in esports psychology and mental health. His work explores the psychological demands of competitive gaming, including stress, coping, and performance. Dylan collaborates with students, academics, and industry stakeholders to advance research that informs policy, practice, and education in the rapidly evolving esports landscape.

Dr Aspasia Stacey Rabba is a Lecturer and Educational and Developmental Psychologist at Monash University, and Honorary Research Fellow at La Trobe University. She has nearly 15 years of experience supporting individuals with neurodevelopmental conditions. In 2020, she received the Australian Psychological Society, Psychology of Intellectual Disability and Autism, excellent thesis award for her PhD. Her research interests include the intersectionality of autism with mental illness, assessment and diagnosis, inclusive practices, equity in healthcare, and the educational experiences of neurodivergent individuals. Dr Rabba lives in Melbourne, Australia. Beyond her vast academic and clinical work, she is also the proud mother of two young boys, Nicholas (8 years old) and Zacharias (6 years old), who were both born during her PhD – 19 months apart. She submitted her PhD the same day Zacharias turned two. Dr Rabba aspires to mentor and support other women to achieve their dreams (both personal and professional).

Miriam Reynoldson is a Melbourne-based digital learning specialist, designer, and teacher who works with universities and vocational education providers. She feels like an imposter in both higher education and Technical and Further Education (TAFE), and she considers that a strength: no part of the adult education landscape is more important or more impressive than any other. Her doctoral research explores the value of lifelong, life-wide digital learning through personal narrative.

Stephanie Richey is a Lecturer in the Bachelor of Education (Primary) at the University of Tasmania (UTAS). She enjoys the rich cross-discipline collegiality and close-knit community of her regional campus. Stephanie completed both her Bachelor of Education (First Class Honours) and her PhD at UTAS. She is passionate about access to languages education for everyone, especially students, and her research focuses on Anglophone English speakers' motivation for, and attitudes towards, learning additional languages. Stephanie's other key research area is in the field of Scholarship of Teaching and Learning (SoTL), primarily focusing on enhancing higher education student participation, engagement, and retention.

Luke Rowe is a Senior Lecturer at Australian Catholic University with a PhD in the learning sciences from the University of Melbourne. He specialises in the science of learning, evidence-based teaching, digital technologies in education, and social dynamics in group learning. As an early career researcher, his interests include metacognition, self-regulated learning, human and artificial intelligence, and psychometrics, using quantitative methods and Bayesian statistics.

Malaika Santa Cruz served as a key early team member at Shut Up & Write!, growing the community back when Shut Up & Write! was only a few thousand members across eight chapter cities. A decade later, her operational expertise and dedication to fostering meaningful partnerships has been pivotal in maintaining the inclusive culture as Shut Up & Write! has expanded to hundreds of cities and universities worldwide.

Claire Saunders is Associate Dean, Students and Teaching in the Faculty of Wellbeing, Education and Language Studies at The Open University (OU). Having begun her career as a primary school teacher, Claire has worked in Higher Education for 20 years, supporting new and practising teachers in both FE and HE, including leadership of the Postgraduate Certificate in Learning and Teaching in Higher Education at Solent University. From 2020 to 2023, Claire was the Director of Praxis (Centre for Scholarship and Innovation) at the OU and is active in national and international Scholarship of Teaching and Learning networks. Her research interests relate to the ways in which universities can build sustainable writing cultures. She also works extensively with appreciative inquiry approaches to envisioning and implementing change in learning and teaching.

Rennie Saunders is the founder and CEO of Shut Up & Write!, a global organisation that hosts free writing events for authors worldwide. What began as a personal quest to find creative community in San Francisco has grown into a movement supporting nearly 100,000 writers across 53 countries. A lifelong science fiction enthusiast who wrote his first story at age 12, Rennie is passionate about providing writers with the resources, community, and accountability they need to succeed.

Helen Sheehan is a Lecturer and Course Coordinator in the National School of Education at Australian Catholic University. Her teaching areas include Secondary English pedagogy, educational psychology, and assessment. Helen's research examines the influences on student achievement motivation, sense of belonging, and classroom relationality. In particular, Helen's research examines the factors that foster, and those that thwart, students' motivation, sense of belonging, and their sense of connection to peers and teachers.

Margarietha de Villiers Scheepers is an Associate Professor of Entrepreneurship and Innovation Management and the Associate Dean Research in the School of Business and Creative Industries at the University of the Sunshine Coast. Her research interests focus on entrepreneurial decision-making in different contexts, specifically innovation within existing and new business contexts, including the antecedents of corporate entrepreneurship, digital innovation, and how individuals attract resources (social, human and capital) as they progress their start-ups using effectuation.

David Schmidtke is a Lecturer in Marketing in the School of Business and Creative Industries at the University of the Sunshine Coast. Based at its Moreton Bay campus, David's research is focused on social impact. Specific research interests include social marketing, transformative consumer research, young consumers, impoverished consumers, and sustainable development goals.

Alison Talmage is a Registered Music Therapist, teacher, and clinical supervisor with special interests in neurological rehabilitation, child development, and holistic wellbeing. A doctoral candidate in Waipapa Taumata Rau | University of Auckland School of Music and Centre for Brain Research, she has recently submitted her thesis, an interdisciplinary practice-based action research study of therapeutic choirs for adults with acquired neurogenic communication challenges. Alison has been a member of the Research Accelerator (RA) community since 2022 and believes that there is no such thing as a bad singer, encouraging song and joy in the RA community. She is a past editor of the *New Zealand Journal of Music Therapy* and a past member of the Music Therapy New Zealand Council and Registration Board.

Rebecca Terlich is a PhD candidate at the University of Southern Queensland, and Manna Institute scholarship holder. Her research is focused on the early identification of neurodevelopmental disabilities and mental health concerns in primary school settings. She has a background in early childhood education, is a disability advocate, and has multiple invisible disabilities herself. She is also the parent of three children with multiple invisible disabilities. Rebecca is passionate about improving the school environment to better understand and support the inclusion of all students.

Dr Abirami Thirumanickam is a certified practicing speech-language pathologist, and Lecturer in the School of Health and Social Development at Deakin University. Her research focuses on critical areas within disability, accessibility, and inclusion, specifically Augmentative and Alternative Communication (AAC), communication access needs, and the ethical considerations of assistive technologies. Abi's research on accessible gaming interventions: Minecraft™ project, has garnered global interest, attracting attention from academia, industry, and the broader community, leading to her participation in radio interviews, televised presentations, podcasts, and contributions to scholarly publications.

Dr Caylee Tierney has been involved in various forms of collaborative writing and manifestations of SUAW while working across academic and professional roles at the University of Tasmania and as a creative writer. Her current research focuses on writing and publishing children's fantasy fiction, and she writes YA fantasy and romance fiction.

Katarina Tuinamuana is Senior Lecturer in Education at the Australian Catholic University, Sydney, New South Wales. Her expertise is in the sociological and cultural-political dimensions of education, including discourses of global policy production processes and local cultures of practice, global movements of 'progressive' and standardised curriculum approaches, participatory action research, and critical autoethnographic writing as critical inquiry. Her recent work focuses on decolonising time in higher education, diversifying the teaching workforce through widening access programs, and racial literacy in teacher education.

Dr Paula Villegas is an Associate Lecturer in Academic English and TESOL at the University of St Andrews and also the Academic English Service Director. Her research focuses on flipped learning, online learning, and academic literacies.

Dr Daniel P Wadsworth is a Senior Lecturer in the School of Health at the University of the Sunshine Coast (UniSC), and a Foundation Postdoctoral Fellow at Manna Institute for rural and regional mental health, where his research is grounded in the healthy ageing of older adults and wellbeing across the lifespan. Dan is passionate about supporting emerging research leaders, and currently co-leads the Manna Institute Health and Wellbeing in Later Life research stream, and the Manna Institute HDR Student Community of Practice, providing virtual connection and support to rural and regional postgraduate students across Australia. He further co-leads the Early- and Mid-Career Academic Network at UniSC.

Dr Pennie White is a passionate educator and researcher with leadership expertise in professional learning, capacity-building, innovative curriculum development, transformation in digital education, and inclusive practice. As Lecturer, Deakin Learning Futures, Pennie supports excellence in teaching and learning in higher education through capacity building in learning design, including a constructively aligned curriculum, active and innovation learning environments, and authentic assessment that empowers students and enriches the quality of the learning experiences and outcomes. Her research expertise in the field of education includes professional learning, innovative pedagogy, digital technology, and inclusion.

Dr Marie White is a Lecturer in the School of Education at Queensland University of Technology (QUT). Marie has a background in early childhood education and care with experience in teaching and leadership spanning more than 20 years. Marie's doctoral research examined the experiences of leaders in early childhood education and care. Marie's research, combined with her extensive work in the field, informs her ongoing program of research focusing on leadership and the early childhood workforce. Marie coordinates the QUT Master of Teaching (Early Childhood) and leads teacher education units on child development and professional experience as well as Continuing Professional Education courses focused on educational leadership in early childhood education and care.

Stacey Whitelaw is a Scholarly Teaching Fellow at Federation University and PhD Candidate with Federation Australia and Manna Institute for rural and regional mental health. As part of Manna Institute, Stacey is a regular participant in the Manna Institute HDR Community of Practice seminars and Shut-Up and Write! groups. Stacey's research focus is on understanding delays in autism assessment and improving diagnostic timelines for potentially late-diagnosed autistic adolescents and adults, with a dual focus on regional, rural, and remote locations and gender-based differences in diagnostic timing.

Mark Widdowfield is a Diagnostic Radiographer and Lecturer at the University of Sunderland, UK. He is currently the Programme Leader for the PGCE and MEd. (Health Professions). A Senior Fellow of AdvanceHE (SFHEA), Mark's current teaching includes educational theory and practice within the health professions and research methods. Mark first came across Shut up and Write! during his (protracted, and soon to end) doctoral journey and, in experiencing its impact, is keen to implement it across a variety of curricula. Mark has a keen professional interest in curriculum development and decolonising the curriculum, particularly within Health Education.

Yvonne Wood is a Senior Lecturer and Work-Integrated Learning Leader at Te Wānanga Aronui O Tāmaki Makau Rau | Auckland University of Technology (AUT) in Kura Hākinakina the School of Sport and Recreation engaged in teaching and research. A Senior Fellow of the Higher Education Academy (SFHEA), Yvonne focuses on the nexus between tertiary teaching and research, with a passion for Work-Integrated Learning (WIL), blended learning and curriculum development – so much so that she is also a doctoral candidate at Te Whare Wānanga o Waikato | University of Waikato exploring students' perceptions of WIL learning experiences. Prior to entering academia, she combined her sense of fun and creativity with strategic roles to deliver excellent customer service in dynamic hospitality environments.

Jason Y.L. Wong is Senior Lecturer at the National School of Education, Australian Catholic University and has a background in primary and secondary school teaching. His research interests are in global mobility experiences of pre-service teachers and host communities, and active learning and teaching pedagogies in health and physical education.

Syed Ali Nasir Zaidi has taught as a lecturer and specialises in Cognition and Learning at the University of Windsor, Canada. Zaidi is focused currently on mentor–mentee relationships in the pre-service teacher education program at the University of Windsor. Apart from being an editorial board member for two international educational research journals based in Turkey, he teaches English writing courses to educational assistants, early childhood educators, and nursing, computer science, business, and robotics' students at St Clair College for Applied Arts and Technology, Windsor, Ontario.

Forward: Cultivating Wellbeing through Shared Writing Practices

Introduction

In cafés and libraries, classrooms and homes, across university campuses and beyond geographical boundaries, a quiet revolution has been taking place in academic writing culture. What began as a simple concept in the San Francisco Bay Area –writers gathering in cafés to write together – has evolved into a global movement that transforms not just how academics write, but how they connect, thrive, and sustain themselves in an increasingly demanding higher education landscape.

Shut Up & Write! (SUAW) turns writing from a solitary experience into a social one, with a straightforward premise: meet up with others, write in focused sessions, and discover the power of communal writing. Yet as the 21 chapters in this collection reveal, SUAW has become far more than a productivity technique. It has emerged as a wellbeing intervention, a community-building practice, and a form of resistance against the isolating and often dehumanising aspects of contemporary academic culture.

This book represents the first comprehensive examination of SUAW as a wellbeing practice within higher education. While existing literature has documented writing groups as productivity tools or pedagogical interventions, this collection breaks new ground by positioning SUAW as a multifaceted approach to academic flourishing. The voices gathered here – from doctoral students in remote Australian towns to established academics navigating neoliberal audit cultures – demonstrate that SUAW creates something unprecedented in academic settings: spaces where productivity and wellbeing are not competing priorities but mutually reinforcing aspects of scholarly life.

The Wellbeing Imperative

The timing of this collection is not coincidental. Higher education globally faces a wellbeing crisis, with academics reporting unprecedented levels of stress, isolation, and burnout. Traditional approaches that shame academics into productivity – the original "shut up and write" mentality – have proven insufficient and often harmful. The COVID-19 pandemic further exposed the fragility of academic communities and the essential human need for connection, even in the midst of intellectual work.

Against this backdrop, SUAW has quietly flourished as an alternative approach – one that recognises academics as whole human beings with complex lives, competing demands, and fundamental needs for community and belonging. The contributors to this volume demonstrate how SUAW sessions have become sanctuaries of care within institutions often characterised by competition and isolation.

Beyond Productivity: A Holistic Vision

While SUAW sessions do enhance writing productivity – and many chapters document impressive outputs in terms of completed manuscripts, theses, and publications – this collection argues for understanding these outcomes as byproducts of something more fundamental: the creation of conditions where academics can reconnect with their authentic scholarly selves. The chapters reveal SUAW as:

- **A community-building practice** that transcends institutional and disciplinary boundaries, creating "third spaces" where hierarchies flatten and genuine collegial relationships flourish
- **An identity formation space** where academics, particularly those from marginalised groups, can develop and maintain scholarly identities despite systemic barriers
- **A resistance practice** against neoliberal academic cultures that reduce scholars to metrics and outputs, instead affirming the relational and creative dimensions of intellectual work
- **A care practice** that normalises vulnerability, celebrates small achievements, and creates environments where academics can bring their whole selves to their scholarly work

The Chapters: A Tapestry of Experience

The 21 chapters in this collection span six thematic areas, each illuminating different aspects of SUAW's transformative potential:

Part I establishes the foundational understanding of SUAW as community-building and wellbeing practice, exploring how online and in-person sessions create supportive environments that prioritise care alongside productivity.

Part II centers the experiences of doctoral and graduate students, revealing how SUAW supports emerging scholars through the particular challenges of academic identity formation, imposter syndrome, and the isolation of research work.

Part III examines creative and collaborative approaches within SUAW, showing how these sessions can become spaces for innovation, cross-disciplinary connection, and therapeutic writing practices.

Part IV explores the technological dimensions of SUAW, particularly how online platforms have expanded access and created new possibilities for inclusive academic communities.

Part V focuses on strategies for maximising SUAW's impact, offering practical guidance for facilitators and participants seeking to enhance the wellbeing benefits of their sessions.

Part VI positions SUAW within broader conversations about academic identity, care ethics, and resistance to harmful institutional cultures, revealing its potential as a tool for systemic change.

A Global Perspective

The geographical and institutional diversity represented in these chapters – from Australian regional universities to UK institutions, from North American contexts to international collaborations – demonstrates SUAW's remarkable adaptability across cultural and systemic differences. Yet common themes emerge: the human need for connection; the importance of belonging in academic success; and the transformative power of writing together rather than alone.

For Whom This Book Is Written

This collection speaks to multiple audiences. Academic practitioners will find practical strategies for establishing and sustaining SUAW programs that prioritise wellbeing alongside productivity. Institutional leaders will discover evidence for supporting collaborative writing initiatives as strategic investments in academic culture and staff wellbeing. Researchers interested in writing pedagogy, academic culture, and higher education will find new theoretical frameworks for understanding the social dimensions of academic work.

Most importantly, this book is written for the countless academics who have experienced the isolation, pressure, and disconnection that characterise much of contemporary higher education. It offers evidence that alternatives exist – that it is possible to create academic communities characterised by care, creativity, and mutual support.

An Invitation to Transform

As you read these chapters, you are invited not merely to learn about SUAW but to imagine how its principles might transform your own academic practice and institutional culture. The evidence presented here suggests that when academics gather with the simple intention of writing together, something profound occurs: the rediscovery of why scholarly work matters; the rebuilding of communities that sustain intellectual curiosity; and the recognition that academic wellbeing is not a luxury but a necessity for meaningful scholarship.

xxxii *Forward*

The quiet revolution documented in these pages offers hope for higher education's future – one where academics thrive not despite their humanity but because of it, where productivity emerges from wellbeing rather than undermining it, and where the act of shutting up and writing together becomes a practice of opening up to the transformative possibilities of academic community.

Introducing each chapter

SUAW transforms isolated academic writing into a communal practice that enhances wellbeing by creating supportive environments where writers connect through shared intentionality rather than shared interests. Through dialogic inquiry we (Lemon, Bolzle and Santa Cruz) as SUAW practitioners reveal how these structured writing communities foster belonging across institutional boundaries, provide meaningful purpose, and model alternative academic cultures that prioritise both productivity and wellbeing as mutually reinforcing rather than competing priorities. SUAW represents a form of resistance to "care-less" academic cultures by establishing an "ethic of care" where vulnerability is normalised, failure acknowledged, and success collectively celebrated – demonstrating how care can become a lived practice within academia rather than merely an aspirational value.

This chapter explores how online SUAW sessions transformed the wellbeing of a remote PhD student in Broome, Western Australia, where extreme geographic isolation had created profound academic disconnection and writing challenges. Through personal narrative, Milford illustrates how virtual SUAW sessions provided not just structured writing time using the Pomodoro technique, but also, more importantly, a vital sense of belonging and community that normalised academic struggles, fostered resilience, and developed her scholarly identity despite the physical distance from academic peers. The author's experience demonstrates how online writing communities can significantly enhance remote scholars' wellbeing by providing the accountability, emotional support, and professional connections that combat isolation – transforming the PhD journey from one of disconnection and stagnation into one of belonging, progress, and improved mental health.

This chapter examines how a co-located SUAW group at a regional university satellite campus creates a convivial space that fosters wellbeing through community-building, mutual support, and shared purpose. The authors (Grant-Smith, McIntyre, Hands, Schmitke, Mulcahy, and de Villiers Scheepers) present six practical strategies for creating vibrant writing communities grounded in communicative democracy: establishing regular meeting spaces; creating shared rituals; using storytelling to build empathy; fostering physical spaces for self-care and care of others; celebrating progress rather than perfection; and strengthening connections through shared meals. Their experience demonstrates how SUAW can transform academic isolation into connection, creating spaces where wellbeing and productivity mutually reinforce each other.

Forward xxxiii

Through personal reflections, Reynoldson and Farago explore how online Shut Up & Write! sessions create a unique "postdigital pedagogy of care" that significantly enhances doctoral candidates' wellbeing despite geographical separation. The authors demonstrate how Zoom SUAW sessions layer multiple spaces and temporalities, forming powerful affective atmospheres where participants can develop their academic identities while sharing both silent writing time and meaningful conversations that address the isolation, overwhelm, and imposter syndrome common to the doctoral journey. These virtual writing communities support wellbeing by enabling graduate researchers to build reciprocal relationships where they exchange not only technical insights but also emotional support – providing a vital counter to the loneliness of academic work and creating decentralised "atmospheres of solidarity and support" that help sustain their complex adult lives alongside their scholarly ambitions.

Through reflective vignettes, Davis, Croaker, Lindsay, and Charles illustrate how their feminist-informed online Shut Up & Write! group creates a powerful wellbeing community that helps women navigate the unique challenges of pursuing PhD research while managing competing demands of employment, relationships, and caregiving responsibilities. Their experience demonstrates how the group's flexible, supportive structure counters feelings of inadequacy and isolation by providing not only motivational accountability for writing but also a space where members can be their "whole selves" through shared experiences, laughter, frustration, and mutual encouragement. The authors reveal how this female-centered writing community, grounded in feminist principles, serves as both a practical writing tool and a powerful wellbeing resource that makes academic knowledge production more accessible by transforming the isolating PhD experience into a collaborative journey where women feel "visible and capable" rather than "invisible and inept" in academia.

This chapter by Peters, Finneran, White, and MacDonald explores how a consistent, collegial Shut Up & Write! group created a transformative space of "belonging, being, and becoming" that significantly enhanced the wellbeing of four early career researchers navigating their emerging academic identities. Through co-authored autoethnography, the authors reveal how their weekly sessions transcended mere writing productivity to become a sanctuary where they could safely express vulnerability, share challenges, celebrate achievements, and develop "colleague friendships" that countered the isolation often experienced in neoliberal university environments. Their experience demonstrates how SUAW can foster interconnectedness and wellbeing by creating a judgment-free space where academics can authentically develop their writer identities while experiencing joy, compassion, and support – illustrated powerfully in their collaborative artwork depicting hands forming a supportive circle that represents their transformation "from procrastination to productivity" through meaningful collegial relationships.

Hicks explores the restorative potential of Shut Up & Write! (SUAW) as a practice that nurtures wellbeing through silent writing communities across doctoral studies, academic writing retreats, and student learning contexts. Through personal narratives, she illuminates how SUAW creates paradoxical "silent collegiality" that fosters self-compassion, reduces anxiety, and invites writers to disappear into restorative silence where they can listen deeply to their thoughts and develop empathy for fellow writers, ultimately transforming the writing experience beyond productivity metrics into a holistic wellbeing practice.

Kimundi explores how Shut Up & Write! sessions transformed her PhD journey from a focus on individual achievement to seeing her contributions as part of a broader ecosystem of knowledge creation. Through these communal writing spaces, Kimundi discovered that writing is not merely a means to an end but a shared scholarly practice that helped clarify her research identity, overcome imposter syndrome, and develop a sense of relatedness that supported her wellbeing and purpose as a researcher.

Through creative non-fiction scripts and personal reflections, this chapter explores how Shut Up & Write! sessions foster wellbeing through their transformative "in-between spaces" where talking, walking, and creative experimentation complement the structured writing periods. Clark illustrates how SUAW creates "imaginative spaces" that enhance wellbeing by shifting academic writing from a solitary, pressure-filled task to a social, collaborative process where wellbeing walks in green spaces, creative writing experiments, and collegial conversations generate unexpected breakthroughs and renewed confidence. The collective writing environments help academics navigate identity challenges, overcome writing blocks, and develop more joyful relationships with their writing – ultimately "changing the script" of academic writing to embrace it as a potentially transformative experience rather than merely a product-focused obligation.

The following chapter examines how virtual Shut Up & Write! sessions within the Manna Institute's Higher Degree by Research Community of Practice have uniquely addressed the isolation and wellbeing challenges faced by rural postgraduate students in Australia. Wadsworth and colleagues demonstrate how their flexible, peer-led approach extends beyond traditional writing productivity to create psychologically safe environments where rural students can connect across geographical distances, share knowledge, and develop meaningful academic communities previously unavailable to them. Drawing on reflections from multiple rural postgraduate students, the authors illustrate how these virtual sessions have transformed the often-isolating postgraduate experience into a collaborative journey characterised by belonging, support, and academic growth – addressing critical gaps in rural research capacity while simultaneously supporting student wellbeing through connection and identity formation.

Fleming explores how Shut Up & Write! sessions provide significant mental health benefits by creating structured time for writers to engage in creative expression and build supportive communities amidst busy schedules. Drawing on research showing that writing about emotional experiences improves physical and mental health, the author shares personal experiences of how attending weekly SUAW sessions as a graduate student working full-time has allowed her to maintain creative writing practice, connect with diverse writers, and experience the psychological benefits of accountability and encouragement. The chapter illustrates how SUAW creates a unique wellbeing space where writers of various ages and backgrounds can validate each other's voices, transform isolation into connection, and experience the therapeutic power of writing – demonstrating that the act of writing is not just productive but also healing for both the writer and eventual readers.

Drawing on interviews with 19 researchers who attended online writing groups during COVID-19 lockdowns, Murphy and Hodge examine how these virtual communities foster wellbeing and resilience in academia despite the crisis of increasing work demands and financial insecurity. Murphy and Hodge reveal how online SUAW groups provide psychological security, reduce feelings of depression and isolation, and create supportive environments where participants can freely exchange social and cultural capital without the hierarchy typically present in university contexts. Their Bourdieusian analysis demonstrates that, despite the shift to virtual formats, these writing communities continue to nurture academic identity development and enhance wellbeing by offering companionship, structured writing time through the Pomodoro technique, increased accessibility for participants with disabilities or geographical constraints, and opportunities for meaningful connection where researchers can confidently seek advice and share challenges in ways they might not feel comfortable doing with supervisors.

This chapter by Wood and Talmage explores how technology transforms virtual Shut Up & Write! sessions from solitary writing experiences into vibrant social events that enhance both productivity and wellbeing. Through the lens of Community of Practice Maturity and Social Construction of Technology models, the authors demonstrate how their discipline-diverse "Research Accelerator" community developed flexible technological approaches (Zoom, Welo, WhatsApp) that support not just writing productivity but also deep human connection, peer support, and creative wellbeing activities like music sharing, movement breaks, and humor. The chapter reveals how intentionally designed virtual SUAW spaces can foster strong communities where members feel a genuine sense of belonging – illustrated by a participant who describes the group as "my study group, my research community, my tribe" – creating sustainable environments where both periods of "shutting up" and "singing out" contribute to members' scholarly success and emotional wellbeing.

Hall and Villegas demonstrate how structured SUAW sessions following input workshops create supportive communities that significantly enhance doctoral candidates' wellbeing by addressing feelings of isolation and lack of confidence in the academic publication process. By fostering a pedagogy of care within a collaborative writing environment, participants experience increased motivation, productivity, and a sense of belonging that transforms the typically solitary writing experience into a shared journey. The authors' feminist pedagogical approach not only empowers doctoral researchers to navigate publication challenges but also creates a safe, communicative space where participants can freely ask questions, share vulnerabilities, and celebrate progress – ultimately improving both their writing output and emotional wellbeing in what participants described as a supportive rather than "depressing" writing environment.

Widdowfield's chapter explores how Shut Up & Write! sessions provide an essential "luxurious commodity" – quiet time and space – for part-time postgraduate students navigating multiple responsibilities and assessment anxiety. Drawing on experiences implementing SUAW with healthcare professionals pursuing further education, he demonstrates how these structured sessions enhance wellbeing by removing barriers related to finding suitable time and space for writing, fostering a supportive community through shared experience, and reducing anxiety through immediate feedback opportunities. The creation of this dedicated writing environment not only helps students manage competing demands and digital distractions but also transforms the traditional hierarchical teacher–student relationship into a more collegial one where both parties benefit from the shared commitment to scholarly activity – ultimately making the challenging writing process more enjoyable and accessible for those who might otherwise struggle to engage effectively with their assessments.

Richey and Tierney explore how honoring true writing tasks during Shut Up & Write! sessions—rather than using this time for urgent but less personally meaningful work – significantly enhances wellbeing through increased satisfaction, goal achievement, and sense of belonging. By implementing four key strategies (prioritising important over urgent tasks, completing pre-work before sessions, setting visible intentions, and taking leadership roles), participants can transform SUAW from merely completing tasks to a practice that fosters genuine writing progress, deeper academic community connections, and improved overall wellbeing in the demanding academic environment.

Saunders illustrates how Writing Kitchen, a monthly online SUAW group that incorporates creative tasks before writing sessions, creates a powerful space for wellbeing that addresses the emotional and identity aspects of academic writing. Through concrete examples of poetry, haiku, and creative writing exercises, the author demonstrates how these tasks help participants transition from other spaces into writing, overcome negative writing emotions, and deeply examine their identities as writers – creating what Fleuret and Atkinson call a "space of wellbeing" where vulnerability, community, and personal growth flourish. By acknowledging the profound connection between writing and identity, Writing Kitchen not only makes the writing process more accessible but also allows participants to navigate the emotional complexities of academic writing, transforming isolation and insecurity into connection and confidence as they reflect that they've "gone somewhere on the journey together; our identities are more secure and our writing is the better for it."

Through personal narratives, this chapter explores how a multi-institutional Shut Up & Write! group served as a vital "counter-space" for five academic mothers – Paulovich, Fisher, Grace, Thirumanickam, and Hulin – who were navigating the challenges of reconstructing their academic identities following career interruptions due to parental leave. The authors reveal how their SUAW community significantly enhanced their wellbeing by providing not only structured writing time that increased productivity, but, more importantly, a supportive environment where they could share common experiences, build cross-disciplinary networks, find renewed purpose, and feel less isolated in balancing competing demands of academia and motherhood. By prioritising dedicated weekly sessions, celebrating small achievements, and creating space for informal discussions about the challenges of academic motherhood, the group transformed individual struggles into collective strength, demonstrating how SUAW can serve as a powerful wellbeing tool that helps academic mothers maintain their professional identities while navigating significant life transitions.

This chapter by Zaidi and Cherian explores how academic writing mentorship can prioritise affective (emotional) approaches alongside effective (technical) strategies to promote student wellbeing and self-care. The authors propose a Reflexive Craft-Focused Learning Relationships (RCFLR) model that integrates Scholarly Personal Narrative methodology, advocating for collaborative writing practices that begin with "Shut Up and Write" followed by "Don't Shut Up and Share" to foster both technical expertise and soulful literacy development.

Tuinamuana and colleagues reveal how their Shut Up & Write! collective transformed from a productivity-focused exercise into a powerful wellbeing sanctuary that helped academics resist the dehumanising effects of neoliberal audit cultures in higher education. Through collaborative autoethnography, the authors demonstrate how SUAW sessions fostered essential wellbeing factors – reclaiming researcher identities, nurturing collegial relationships, and creating spaces for authentic scholarship where participants felt "bolstered and truly heard" amid isolating academic pressures. Their experience shows how SUAW can function as both "a comforting quilt and a suit of armor," enabling academics to protect their wellbeing by forging meaningful connections, overcoming imposter syndrome, resisting performative metrics-driven scholarship, and embracing a more relational, purpose-driven approach to academic writing that prioritises people over productivity.

O'Donnell, Chang, and O'Shea examine how thoughtful design choices in Shut Up & Write! programs can significantly enhance wellbeing through fostering inclusion, belonging, and community – particularly for marginalised groups in academia. Their analysis reveals that decisions about who can attend, when and where sessions occur, how they're facilitated, and what norms are established directly impact participants' sense of psychological safety and ability to bring their "whole selves" to the writing process. By purposefully considering accessibility needs and creating tailored experiences for specific communities (such as queer-identified or neurodivergent academics), SUAW facilitators can transform writing sessions into powerful wellbeing spaces that counter isolation, build meaningful social connections, and create a sense of belonging that extends beyond mere writing productivity.

Conclusion: From Silence to Song, From Isolation to Community

As we reach the end of this collection, a powerful paradox emerges from the pages: a practice called "Shut Up & Write!" has, in fact, given academics their voices back. The silence that characterises SUAW sessions – the focused, communal quiet of writers at work – has created the conditions for a different kind of speaking, one that celebrates vulnerability, acknowledges struggle, and affirms the deeply human dimensions of scholarly work.

The Transformation of Academic Writing Culture

The 21 chapters in this volume document nothing less than a grassroots transformation of academic writing culture. What began as individual attempts to overcome procrastination and increase productivity has evolved into a movement that challenges fundamental assumptions about how scholarly work should be conducted, how academic communities should function, and what it means to thrive as a scholar in the 21st century.

The evidence is overwhelming: SUAW works not because it forces academics to be more productive, but because it creates conditions where they can reconnect with their authentic scholarly selves. Participants consistently report that while they came for the writing, they stayed for the community. This finding points to a profound truth about academic work—that it is fundamentally social and relational, despite institutional cultures that often treat it as an individual pursuit.

The Ripple Effects of Collective Care

Perhaps most significantly, this collection reveals how SUAW's impact extends far beyond individual writing sessions. The practices of care, mutual support, and collective celebration that characterise these groups create ripple effects throughout academic institutions and careers:

- **Academic mothers** find spaces to reconstruct professional identities alongside personal ones
- **Rural and remote scholars** discover they are not alone in their intellectual journeys
- **Early career researchers** develop confidence and community that sustain them through precarious career phases
- **Marginalised academics** create counter-spaces where their voices are heard and valued
- **Experienced scholars** rediscover the joy and purpose that initially drew them to academic work

Lessons for Higher Education

The success of SUAW offers crucial lessons for higher education institutions grappling with wellbeing crises, retention challenges, and cultural transformation:

Investment in Care Infrastructure: The chapters demonstrate that supporting academic wellbeing requires more than counseling services or work–life balance workshops. It requires creating ongoing opportunities for genuine connection, mutual support, and shared purpose. SUAW programs represent a low-cost, high-impact intervention that addresses systemic issues through community-building.

The Power of Horizontal Relationships: Unlike traditional mentoring or hierarchical support structures, SUAW creates horizontal relationships where academics at different career stages can learn from and support each other. This peer-to-peer model offers unique benefits, particularly for those who may feel vulnerable or inadequate in more formal support relationships.

Technology as Connection, Not Replacement: The online SUAW experiences documented here show how technology can genuinely enhance rather than replace human connection. Virtual sessions have made academic community accessible to those previously excluded by geography, caring responsibilities, or institutional constraints, while maintaining the essential elements of mutual support and shared purpose.

Small Changes, Big Impact: The chapters consistently show how relatively small interventions – a few hours per week, simple structures, basic facilitation – can have profound effects on academic wellbeing and productivity. This suggests that transformation doesn't require massive institutional overhaul but rather sustained commitment to creating conditions where academics can flourish.

Resistance and Renewal

Many chapters position SUAW as a form of resistance against the dehumanising aspects of neoliberal higher education. In a culture obsessed with metrics, rankings, and individual achievement, SUAW asserts the value of:

- **Process over product**: While publications and completions matter, SUAW emphasises the importance of sustainable writing practices and the joy of creative work
- **Community over competition**: Instead of viewing other academics as competitors, SUAW creates environments where others' success enhances rather than threatens one's own
- **Wellbeing over productivity**: Though productivity often increases, SUAW prioritises the whole person over output metrics
- **Care over carelessness**: SUAW explicitly counters what some authors call "care-less" academic cultures with practices of mutual support and concern

This resistance is not merely oppositional but generative, creating alternative models of how academic communities might function. The chapters suggest that SUAW participants don't just survive neoliberal academia – they create pockets of different possibility within it.

Toward a More Caring Academy

The vision that emerges from these pages is of an academy characterised by what several authors call "collective collegiality" – academic communities where mutual support, shared celebration, and genuine care for each other's wellbeing become central values. This is not about lowering standards or reducing rigor, but about recognising that the best scholarly work emerges from conditions of psychological safety, creative freedom, and community support.

The transformation documented here is both modest and revolutionary. Modest because it involves simple practices – showing up, writing together, sharing struggles and successes. Revolutionary because it challenges the fundamental assumption that academic work must be a solitary, competitive struggle. By gathering regularly to write in each other's company, SUAW participants have discovered that scholarship can be both excellent and joyful, both rigorous and caring.

An Ongoing Journey

As this collection goes to print, SUAW continues to evolve and spread. New groups form weekly, innovative formats emerge, and the practice adapts to changing circumstances and needs. The COVID-19 pandemic accelerated the development of online SUAW communities, creating new possibilities for inclusion and connection. Post-pandemic, hybrid models offer even greater flexibility and access.

The chapters in this volume represent snapshots of an ongoing movement – one that continues to grow and develop as more academics discover the transformative potential of writing together. Each new SUAW group adds to our understanding of how collective practices can enhance individual and community wellbeing.

A Call to Action

This collection concludes not with an ending but with an invitation. The evidence presented here demonstrates that alternatives to isolating, competitive academic cultures are not only possible but are already thriving in communities around the world. The question now is not whether SUAW works – the evidence is clear – but how widely these practices will spread and how deeply they will transform academic culture.

For readers inspired by these stories, the call to action is simple: start where you are. Whether you join an existing SUAW group, start a new one, or adapt these principles to other collaborative practices, you have the power to contribute to the transformation of academic culture. As many chapters note, SUAW works because it's simple, accessible, and immediately beneficial.

No special training, expensive resources, or institutional permission is required – just the commitment to show up and write together.

For institutional leaders, the call is to recognise and support these grass-roots initiatives. The chapters provide ample evidence that investing in collaborative writing programs generates significant returns in terms of academic wellbeing, productivity, and community-building. More importantly, they represent investments in the kind of academic culture we want to create – one that values human flourishing alongside scholarly achievement.

From Shut Up to Speak Out

The ultimate paradox of this collection is captured in one author's phrase: "Shut up and write followed by 'Don't shut up and share!'" The silence of focused writing creates space for the voices that emerge in SUAW's social moments – voices that celebrate small victories, acknowledge struggles, offer encouragement, and build the relationships that sustain scholarly work.

In a higher education landscape often characterised by isolation, competition, and burnout, SUAW offers a different model: communities where academics can be fully human, where scholarly work emerges from wellbeing rather than undermining it, and where the simple act of writing together becomes a practice of hope.

The revolution documented in these pages is quiet but profound, local but global, simple but transformative. It reminds us that even in the most challenging institutional environments, academics have the power to create communities of care, spaces of belonging, and practices that nurture both scholarly excellence and human flourishing.

The conversation continues, the writing continues, and the community grows. The question now is not whether you will shut up and write, but whether you will do so in ways that honor both your scholarly aspirations and your deepest human needs for connection, support, and shared purpose.

In the end, this collection suggests that the future of higher education may depend not on grand institutional reforms but on simple acts of academics choosing to show up for each other, to write together rather than alone, and to create the academic communities they wish to inhabit. That transformation begins with two simple words: "Come write."

Narelle Lemon
Edith Cowan University

Series Preface

As academics, scholars, staff and colleagues working in the context of universities in the contemporary climate we are often challenged with where we place our own wellbeing. It is not uncommon to hear about burnout, stress, anxiety, pressures with workload, having too many balls in the air, toxic cultures, increasing demands, isolation, and feelings of distress (Berg and Seeber, 2016; Lemon and McDonough, 2018; Mountz et al., 2015). The reality is that universities are stressful places (Beer et al., 2015; Cranton and Taylor, 2012; Kasworm and Bowles, 2012; Mountz et al., 2015; Ryan, 2013; Sullivan and Weissner, 2010; Wang and Cranton, 2012). McNaughton and Billot (2016) argue that the "deeply personal effects of changing roles, expectations and demands" (p. 646) have been downplayed and that academics and staff engage in constant reconstruction of their identities and work practices. It is important to acknowledge this, as much as it is to acknowledge the need to place wellbeing and self-care at the forefront of these lived experiences and situations.

Wellbeing can be approached at multiple levels, including micro and macro. In placing wellbeing at the heart of the higher education workplace, self-care becomes an imperative both individually and systemically (Berg and Seeber, 2016; Lemon and McDonough, 2018). Self-care is most commonly oriented towards individual action to monitor and ensure personal wellbeing; however it is also a collective act. There is a plethora of different terms that are in action to describe how one approaches their wellbeing holistically (Godfrey et al., 2011). With different terminology comes different ways self-care is understood. For this collection self-care is understood as "the actions that individuals take for themselves, on behalf of and with others in order to develop, protect, maintain and improve their health, wellbeing or wellness" (Self Care Forum, 2019, para. 1). It covers a spectrum of health-related (emotional, physical, and/or spiritual) actions including prevention, promotion, and treatment, while aiming to encourage individuals to take personal responsibility for their health and to advocate for themselves and others in accessing resources and care (Knapik and Laverty, 2018). Self-love, -compassion, -awareness, and -regulation are significant elements of self-care. But what does this look like for those working in higher education? In this book series authors respond to the questions: *What do you do for self-care? How do you position wellbeing as part of your role in academia?*

In thinking about these questions, authors are invited to critically discuss and respond to inspiration sparked by one or more of the questions of:

- How do we bring self-regulation to how we approach our work?
- How do we create a compassionate workplace in academia?
- What does it mean for our work when we are aware and enact self-compassion?
- What awareness has occurred that has disrupted the way we approach work?
- Where do mindful intentions sit?
- How do we shift the rhetoric of "this is how it has always been" in relation to over working, and indiscretions between workload and approaches to workload?
- How do we counteract the traditional narrative of over work?
- How do we create and sustain a healthier approach?
- How can we empower the "I" and "we" as we navigate self-care as a part of who we are as academics?
- How can we promote a curiosity about how we approach self-care?
- What changes do we need to make?
- How can we approach self-care with energy and promote shifts in how we work individually, collectively and systemically?

The purpose of this book series is to:

- Place academic wellbeing and self-care at the heart of discussions around working in higher education.
- Provide a diverse range of strategies for how to put in place wellbeing and self-care approaches as an academic.
- Provide a narrative connection point for readers from a variety of backgrounds in academia.
- Highlight lived experiences and honour the voice of those working in higher education.
- Provide a visual narrative that supports connection to authors' lived experience(s).
- Contribute to the conversation on ways that wellbeing and self-care can be positioned in the work that those working in higher education do.
- Highlight new ways of working in higher education that disrupt current tensions that neglect wellbeing.

References

Beer, L.E., Rodriguez, K., Taylor, C., Martinez-Jones, N., Griffin, J., Smith, T.R., Lamar, M., & Anaya, R. (2015). Awareness, integration and interconnectedness. *Journal of Transformative Education, 13(2)*, 161–185.

Berg, M., & Seeber, B.K. (2016). *The slow professor: Challenging the culture of speed in the academy.* Toronto: University of Toronto Press.

Cranton, P., & Taylor, E.W. (2012). Transformative learning theory: Seeking a more unified theory. In E.W. Taylor & P. Cranton (Eds.), *The handbook of transformative learning* (pp. 3–20). San Francisco, CA: Jossey-Bass.

Godfrey, C.M., Harrison, M.B., Lysaght, R., Lamb, M., Graham, I.D., & Oakley, P. (2011). The experience of self-care: A systematic review. *JBI Library of Systematic Reviews, 8*(34), 1351–1460. Retrieved from http://www.ncbi.nlm.nih.gov/pubmed/27819888

Kasworm, C., & Bowles, T. (2012). Fostering transformative learning in higher education settings. In E. Taylor & P. Cranton (Eds.), *The handbook of transformative learning* (pp. 388–407). Thousand Oaks, CA: Sage.

Knapik, K., & Laverty, A. (2018). Self-care Individual, relational, and political sensibilities. In M.A. Henning, C.U. Krägeloh, R. Dryer, F. Moir, D.R. Billington & A.G. Hill. (Eds.). *Wellbeing in higher education: Cultivating a healthy lifestyle among faculty and students.* Abingdon: Routledge.

Lemon, N. & McDonough, S. (Eds.). (2018). *Mindfulness in the academy: Practices and perspectives from scholars.* Singapore: Springer.

McNaughton, S.M., & Billot, J. (2016). Negotiating academic teacher identity shifts during higher education contextual change. *Teaching in Higher Education, 21*(6), 644–658.

Mountz, A., Bonds, A., Mansfield, B., Loyd, J., Hyndman, J., & Watton-Roberts, M. (2015). For slow scholarship: A feminist politics of resistance through collective action in the neoliberal university. *ACME: An International E-Journal of Critical Geographies, 14*(4), 1235–1259.

Ryan, M. (2013). The pedagogical balancing act: Teaching reflection in higher education. *Teaching in Higher Education, 18,* 144–155.

Self Care Forum. (2019). Self Care Forum: Home. Retrieved July 27, 2019, from http://www.selfcareforum.org/

Sullivan, L.G., & Weissner, C.A. (2010). Learning to be reflective leaders: A case study from the NCCHC Hispanic leadership fellows program. In D.L. Wallin. (Ed.), Special issue: *Leadership in an era of change. New directions for community colleges,* No. 149 (pp. 41–50). San Francisco: Jossey-Bass.

Wang, V.C., & Cranton, P. (2012). Promoting and implementing self-directed learning (SDL): An effective adult education model. *International Journal of Adult Vocational Education and Technology, 3,* 16–25.

Acknowledgements

Declaration of AI Use:
The authors of Chapters 3, 11, 18, 19, and 20 used various AI tools under human oversight. Specifically, Chapter 3 used mandalagaba.com (user-directed design tool), ChatGPT for word count suggestions, and Grammarly for proof-reading; Chapter 11 used ChatGPT to develop the chapter title; Chapter 18 used Microsoft Copilot and ChatGPT for editorial suggestions and word count reduction; Chapter 19 used Google and ChatGPT for sourcing, idea generation, and editorial checking; and Chapter 20 used ChatGPT for minor editorial adjustments. No data generation or core writing tasks were performed by AI.

Part I

Foundations of Community and Wellbeing

1 Shut Up & Write! A Dialogue on Community, Wellbeing, and Purpose

Narelle Lemon, Aaron Bolzle, and Malaika Santa Cruz

Introduction

Academic writing has traditionally been characterised as a solitary endeavor, conducted in isolation with minimal social connection or community support. This perspective has dominated higher education cultures globally, contributing to well-documented challenges of scholarly isolation, anxiety, and diminished wellbeing (Kinman & Johnson, 2019). Recent years, however, have witnessed growing recognition of writing as a social practice that flourishes within supportive environments. As universities grapple with increasing pressures of publication metrics and productivity demands, alternative approaches to academic writing that nurture both productivity and wellbeing have gained significant attention. Among these approaches, Shut Up and Write! (SUAW) has emerged as a particularly compelling model that transforms writing from an isolating experience into a communal practice with profound implications for scholarly wellbeing.

The current academic environment presents multiple challenges that directly impact scholarly writing and wellbeing. Research consistently demonstrates declining mental health indicators among academics, with isolation frequently cited as a significant contributor (Brown & Leigh, 2018; Lynch, 2022). This isolation is particularly pronounced in writing processes, where traditional academic cultures often reinforce competitive individualism rather than collaboration and support. While considerable research examines productivity interventions in academic writing, significantly less attention has been given to approaches that simultaneously address productivity and holistic wellbeing. As Berg and Seeber (2016) argue, conventional productivity-focused interventions can inadvertently reinforce the "culture of busy" that contributes to burnout and diminished scholarly engagement. The gap between productivity-focused approaches and wellbeing-centered practices reflects a broader tension in academia between instrumental outputs and sustainable scholarly practices. What remains underexplored is how structured, communal writing practices like SUAW can serve as interventions that bridge this gap, fostering both productive writing outcomes and enhanced wellbeing among participants.

This chapter aims to examine how Shut Up and Write! functions as a multidimensional wellbeing intervention within higher education settings. Drawing on dialogic inquiry and reflective practice methodologies, we explore the community, wellbeing, and purpose dimensions of SUAW through a structured conversation between practitioners deeply engaged in this approach. Our analysis is framed by Thomson and Coles' (2024) conceptualisation of "care-full" learning environments and Tronto's (1993) ethic of care framework, allowing us to interrogate how SUAW creates what Lynch (2022) terms "affectively egalitarian" spaces that transform traditional scholarly writing practices. By examining SUAW through these theoretical lenses, we contribute to emerging scholarship on writing as a social practice and demonstrate how intentionally structured writing communities can counter the isolating tendencies of contemporary academic cultures.

This exploration employs dialogic inquiry methodology, centred around a recorded, transcribed, and thoughtfully edited conversation between three SUAW practitioners following a writing community event in Cambridge, UK, in November 2024. This methodological approach recognises dialogue as a powerful tool for collaborative testing of ideas and exploration of concepts, allowing for fluid generation of meaning rather than producing static, definitive texts (Helin, 2016). The conversation examines multiple dimensions of SUAW practice, including its impacts on belonging, purpose, empowerment, self-compassion, and communal celebration. Key findings reveal how SUAW creates nested communities that foster belonging across institutional and geographic boundaries, provides meaningful purpose through shared intentionality, and models alternative academic cultures that prioritise both productivity and wellbeing as mutually reinforcing rather than competing priorities.

The remainder of this chapter unfolds as follows. First, we present the transcribed dialogue and reflective dialogical inquiry, which explores various dimensions of how SUAW fosters wellbeing, builds inclusive communities, rekindles passion and purpose, and boosts confidence and productivity. Following this dialogue, we provide a structured discussion that analyses key themes through theoretical frameworks related to academic wellbeing, care ethics, and "slow scholarship." We examine how SUAW represents a form of resistance to "careless" academic cultures by modelling more humane approaches to scholarly work. The chapter concludes by articulating how SUAW offers a compelling alternative to conventional writing interventions by addressing the whole person through communities characterised by belonging, purpose, and sustained engagement, demonstrating how care can become not merely an aspirational value but a lived practice within academia.

Fosters Resilience and Wellbeing

Academic writing often occurs in isolation, contributing to the well-documented mental health challenges prevalent in higher education (Kinman & Johnson, 2019). SUAW sessions directly combat this isolation by creating regular opportunities for meaningful human connection around a shared purpose. Research indicates that this collective approach to writing can significantly reduce anxiety, alleviate impostor syndrome, and enhance emotional resilience

(MacLeod et al., 2012; Johnson et al., 2017). By normalising the struggles inherent in the writing process and providing real-time peer support, SUAW creates a psychological safety net that helps scholars navigate the emotional turbulence of academic work.

The rhythmic structure of SUAW sessions – alternating between focused writing and brief social interactions – also mirrors evidence-based approaches to stress management. This deliberate oscillation helps participants develop healthier relationships with their writing, reducing burnout by transforming writing from a source of anxiety into a sustainable practice embedded within a supportive community (Cameron et al., 2009).

Builds Inclusive Academic Communities

One of SUAW's most powerful attributes is its capacity to transcend traditional institutional and disciplinary boundaries, creating third spaces where hierarchies flatten and diverse perspectives flourish. These sessions provide rare opportunities for cross-disciplinary pollination and mentoring relationships that might otherwise never form (Aitchison & Guerin, 2014). The format particularly benefits scholars from marginalised groups, who often experience heightened isolation within academia. SUAW sessions create micro-communities characterised by mutual accountability and support, fostering a sense of belonging that can otherwise be elusive in hyper-competitive academic environments (Brown & Leigh, 2018). The collective nature of these gatherings acknowledges writing as a social practice rather than purely an individual cognitive activity, challenging dominant narratives about academic production and success.

Rekindles Passion and Purpose

The relentless pressures of contemporary academia – publication quotas, grant deadlines, and performance metrics – can gradually erode scholars' intrinsic motivation and connection to the intellectual curiosity that initially drew them to academic work. SUAW sessions create deliberate spaces where scholars can reconnect with the deeper purposes underpinning their research and writing. Through informal conversations during breaks and the shared experience of struggling with difficult writing tasks, participants often rediscover joy in their scholarly pursuits. This rekindling of passion and purpose represents a crucial counterbalance to the instrumentalisation of academic writing, where publication becomes merely a means to career advancement rather than a meaningful contribution to knowledge (Sword, 2017).

Boosts Confidence and Productivity

For early-career researchers in particular, SUAW offers a structured entry point into academic writing communities. The visible progress made during sessions provides immediate evidence that writing is occurring, boosting confidence through tangible accomplishments (Murray & Newton, 2009). Moreover, the regular practice of writing in short, focused bursts helps participants develop sustainable writing habits that can be maintained alongside other academic responsibilities. The accountability inherent in SUAW sessions – showing up at designated times, articulating writing goals to peers, and sharing progress – creates positive social pressure that helps overcome procrastination and writing blocks. Research demonstrates that participants typically produce more writing during SUAW sessions than they would in isolation, not merely due to allocated time but because of the motivational effects of writing alongside others who are similarly engaged (McGrail et al., 2006).

Transforms Academic Culture

Perhaps most significantly, SUAW represents a grassroots intervention with the potential to transform broader academic culture. By prioritising both productivity and wellbeing, these sessions model a more humane approach to scholarly work that challenges the prevailing "culture of busy" and valorisation of overwork (Berg & Seeber, 2016). The democratic ethos of SUAW – where professors write alongside postgraduate students, administrators alongside faculty – creates rare opportunities for authentic connection across institutional hierarchies. This flattening effect fosters mutual recognition of shared challenges and cultivates empathy across positional differences, potentially influencing institutional cultures beyond the sessions themselves. As academia continues to grapple with wellbeing crises and questions about sustainable scholarly practices, SUAW offers a practical, evidence-informed approach that addresses multiple dimensions of academic life simultaneously. Rather than treating productivity and wellbeing as competing priorities, SUAW demonstrates how they can be mutually reinforcing when embedded within communities of practice characterised by support, accountability, and shared purpose.

Methodology

The exploration of *Dialogue on Community, Wellbeing and Purpose through and with SUAW* began as an in-person conversation in Cambridge, United Kingdom after a writing community event – recorded November 2024, transcribed, and thoughtfully edited – transforming oral exchange into written inquiry. This evolution from spoken dialogue to refined text exemplifies the fluid nature of dialogic inquiry itself, which enables the collaborative testing of ideas and exploration of concepts. Rather than producing static, definitive texts (Helin, 2016), dialogic oral reflection and then writing creates evolving narratives that facilitate the exploration of ideas and concepts, generating meaning and understanding through this process (Lemon and McDonough, 2025a, 2025b; McDonough & Brandenburg, 2019; Placier et al., 2005). As a reflective practice, this approach allows us to reflect collaboratively through conversation and language (Nehrig et al., 2010; Rashid, 2018), where engaging in dialogue enables the construction of "new meaning".

Figure 1.1 Geeking out on SUAW and the heart of its impact on wellbeing (Longarm selfie exploration series, November 2024, Cambridge).

Our Conversations: Shared Curiosity

Narelle: Shut Up and Write! as a method, process, and embodiment brings so much to individuals and collectives. It's for wellbeing and a part of wellbeing. Initial thoughts?

Malaika: We like to say that people come for the productivity but stay for the community. A lot of people just need a starting point. Maybe they're drowning in a project or they've always wanted to write a novel. They need something to grab hold of. But once they start attending, they see how easy it is to commit to that hour a week. They get a taste of it. Then it becomes about the faces they see every week and how good it feels to write with other writers.

Aaron: I love how you started that because that's exactly what gets people in the room. Writers aren't sitting around going, "Gosh, I'm starting to feel isolated and lonely. That could lead to burnout. I should mitigate that by actively finding a group of individuals where I can find a sense of belonging." No, they're like, "I need to write this thing. I'm struggling. Maybe if I go with a bunch of other people, I'll find tools or hacks to solve this problem."

And then over time, if they believe they're getting some benefit in that tangible way, they turn around and realise they've got a community. One of the things we've been excited and challenged by is how to attract the types of individuals who will truly find value in what we're providing without being explicit about the fact that this is all about wellbeing.

Malaika: Because "wellbeing" has different connotations for different people.

Aaron: And you might not get the right audience.

Malaika: Exactly. Some people associate that with things like therapy that maybe they have a conflicted relationship with, or they don't think "I'm one of those people that needs that kind of thing." I've heard from some of our academic partners that if they put the word "wellbeing" or "wellness" in their programming, people have mixed reactions. But they love that this is an opportunity for them to directly impact people's wellness in a kind of sneaky way.

Aaron: Sneaky!

Narelle: It's sneaky, stealth, but in good ways because of the intention behind it. The key aspects of Shut Up and Write! are what contributes to wellbeing because it's been consciously designed. Saying hello, welcoming people, the intentions of the method, the intentionality of how you set up a room, where you do it, how often you do it. The intentionality that it's not about feedback, it's about reporting back. These are significant contributors to the process of writing that often blocks people. Often people say "I'm so scared to share my words because I don't know if people are going to like them."

Aaron: I think there's this interesting period where we as humans have begun to connect in a completely different way than ever before. We've always connected based on intention or purpose. Recently, we've started to connect based on shared opinions or interests. And I think that's what causes some of that insecurity, because the relationships are so conditional.

What makes Shut Up and Write! create a sense of belonging is that shared intention – that's the only reason we're connecting, to support each other in the act of writing. And that is extraordinarily resilient. It's resilient through your potential for performance. It's resilient to your personal beliefs, strategies, topics, or background. I honestly think it's turning current expectations of how we connect on its head and back to something that's far more core to who we are as human beings.

Especially when it comes to Facebook groups or any platform that connects people, it always seems to be about talking about your interests. We don't do that. It's not about talking about writing. It's about supporting each other in the act of writing. And yes, some talking comes from it.

Malaika: The difference between interest and intention is something I know you talk about a lot, Aaron, especially in terms of building meaningful communities. You show up together because you all have this shared mission, even if it's somebody writing a sci-fi novel next to somebody writing a dissertation. You're still just trying to get your thoughts onto the page. It's not just "I have this interest in writing." It's that we're doing something together.

Aaron: Your interests can actually be conflicting or polar opposite, yet you can share the same intention and support each other. It's fascinating. You can have completely different beliefs about strategy or the things you're writing about. We talk so much about diversity, but we also talk about how we end up in echo chambers. When you connect on intention, you find yourself in highly diverse groups where people believe and think in completely different ways, yet you're able to find a unifying force through the shared intention of the act, not the thought.

Narelle: I'm thinking about mindfulness mechanisms here – intention, attention, attitude – and how they're a part of what Shut Up and Write! is. The intention of writing together to support each other, with the attitude of "I don't actually need to know what you're writing, but all I know is that all of us are here to write." That's pretty cool. We don't do that often with anything.

Malaika: I wish we did it with more things! There's the beneficial aspect of setting time aside in the future, saying "I'm going to do this" that gets people to do it more often. But once you're there, it also gives you permission to be totally present because you've blocked this time off, you've protected it from all the other things that would grab your time away. That mindfulness aspect, pulling people into the moment – I think many people wouldn't even realise they're doing it. It might be the only time in their life that they do.

Aaron: How many other times in your life as an adult are you told that you have this period where you must remove all distractions and focus on the one thing you've clearly stated you want to do? Bringing people out of their personal spaces and doing it on a regular cadence provides a simple pathway towards a habit that pushes them towards what they want.

We used to have more structure when we were younger. I was just thinking – it's time to play. You don't have a choice. The classroom is locked. We had this moment where we were told it's time to go do this thing. We did not have distractions from that one thing we had to do. And it was part of our daily routine.

Malaika: As soon as you said that, I had this visceral longing for those days when someone told me to go play for an hour.

Aaron: And it's only now I'm realising how valuable that is.

Malaika: How valuable that is! I might have mistaken that for something only a child could enjoy because they have a child's brain, but maybe there's an aspect of it that is just…

Aaron: That's all you have to do in that exact moment. It's literally like "go play." Just go play in your mind.

Narelle: How powerful is that? It's like that cue, reward, action cycle. We've got the cue with the invitation in the diary. I know when I go, this is what I'm going to do. There's the reward – those accomplishments. I got new words on the page or I edited or moved something forward. Those personal accomplishments. But then it's also a community accomplishment.

Everyone in that room at that time is celebrating their individual wins, and then you're collectively celebrating. We've had lots of conversations over the last couple of days about how we don't stop to celebrate because we're in this hustle culture with mega to-do lists running in our heads. We forget to actually celebrate what we've just achieved in this moment and pause to say "this is pretty cool" before moving on.

Malaika: People are craving so badly to be part of something bigger than themselves. Setting the intentionality at the beginning and going around – even if it's just "I just got 50 words done" – that's still something they celebrate, but it's no longer just their individual accomplishment. It's already a group celebration. You get to feel good about helping that person get that done. That's one of the best things about being part of the group: having a celebration that is bigger than any individual.

	And the fact that it's so accessible – even just the tiniest little piece of it can feel so powerful to people. From the very first event that Rennie started, the most consistent feedback was "Wow, that felt really good." I think that's part of it – they're already a part of something bigger.
Aaron:	I've been sharing my challenges with being able to celebrate successes, yet I'm supposed to run this organisation that's so focused on encouraging people to celebrate shared successes. I think it's a good parallel because it acknowledges how hard it can be. It's too easy to think of the enormous task of finishing the entire project or whatever major goal you've set, even when you've made tangible steps toward accomplishment.
	That leads to the vulnerability that emerges in these communities. We don't just celebrate successes – we also lament failures. When one person shares, it gives permission to others to share as well. And it doesn't feel superficial because people genuinely respond with "Oh yeah, I've been there. I'm there right now in this other way." It doesn't feel like a disconnected parent saying "It's going to be okay." This is another person on the same journey as you, who's clearly stated "I'm in it with you," who says "Yeah, that's real." And for some reason, that just makes you feel like it's going to be okay.
Malaika:	Absolutely. It's arguably just as fulfilling, if not sometimes more so, to share a failure or vulnerability. Because ultimately, we're not that much about productivity in terms of what really matters in what we're building here. It is about that connection and building meaningful quality of life.
Aaron:	It's not about productivity. It's about sustainability.
Malaika:	Sustainability.
Aaron:	One of our opportunities in the near future is to help anyone facilitating Shut Up and Write! events communicate the benefit effectively. Sometimes individuals who find Shut Up and Write! because they have a deadline misunderstand the true purpose. It's extraordinarily inefficient to leave your flat, find parking near a library, unpack your laptop, and then get interrupted every 25 minutes when you have a looming deadline. That can really tick you off if you come just once and think "I was nowhere near as productive as I would have been staying at home."
	But if you do this frequently, you're mitigating the consistent barriers that prevent sustainable writing practices. For us, it's all about building healthy, sustainable writing practices that promote wellbeing with challenging tasks.
Malaika:	And not just by removing barriers. That's a big initial part of it, but nothing becomes more sustainable than something you've fallen in love with the process of doing.

Narelle: Totally. You're attracted to the feelings generated. You rock up. You don't always know who's going to be there, but you have a general sense of "these people have been coming." You know the host, the climate, the context being created and curated in that physical space. It may be the first time someone said hello to you that day because you've left your house or office. But you're coming there thinking "I know I can geek out and have my thinking face on and I'm about to smash out some words or craft some words" and I do that every week. How fulfilling!

Aaron: I just had a thought to share – you mentioned that might be the only time somebody has said hello to you in person. I've also noticed you said you never know who's all going to show up. To say I don't have favourites at my event would be a lie – we all have favourites! There are people you really connect with, and there are times I've shown up at my event and not felt fully connected with the people there.

But what I realised is that not only are there sometimes when it might be the only time somebody says hi to you, it might be the only time you say hi to somebody else. Sometimes you get to hang out with rock stars, and sometimes you are the rock star to somebody else. There are moments where you get a lot from it, and moments where you potentially don't feel like you're getting much, but you can remind yourself that you're giving a lot.

That's the beautiful symbiotic relationship within the Shut Up and Write! ecosystem. I don't love every single social interaction at every event, but I remind myself that maybe other people really did love the social interactions that I helped create because it was the social interaction they hadn't had before.

Narelle: That's mind-blowing on so many levels because it's so true. Sometimes you facilitate gatherings where the people who turn up don't necessarily boost your cup. But the fact that they've come and say "thanks so much for creating this for me because it's boosting me so much" becomes the boost that comes to you.

Aaron: If only there was a visual cup you could watch fill up in your space!

Narelle: It almost comes back to that appreciation and celebration aspect as a host or co-host. Sometimes – I'll put my hand up – I've actually forgotten that celebration moment and thought "I just hosted that. Yes, I got some words done, but I don't know what I got out of it." When I know I've had other Shut Up and Write! experiences that have been profound where I don't feel isolated or I feel part of a community. The labelling of what you're getting and that reciprocity changes in energy levels, but it's still a massive appreciation and celebration moment. I love that so much. It shows the intricacies of all the different roles and what happens within the ecosystem of Shut Up and Write!

Malaika: And we're still just talking about the belonging aspect of wellbeing, which is only one pillar. There's still more to it.

Narelle: Totally. Relationships are part of it, but there's also communication, engagement – it's all incredibly complex. The creative outlet, the personal empowerment that we talked about last night.

Malaika: Having an external counterpart to your thoughts. It's not just a hobby. Thinking and language is part of being human, and writing is the external catharsis. Being able to take your thoughts, put them on a page and actually look at them and see how you feel about them. I've had very profound personal experiences where I've done that and actually changed what I believe. And then that goes back in and shapes my own identity.

So there are entirely other huge conversations about how it's not just creating space for people to write, but once they become more comfortable writing, they have all these aspects of empowerment. You can't necessarily tell that to the first person – you might start to sound like a cult! But once they start to feel it and ask "What is this that I'm feeling?" there's so much we have to say.

Narelle: I'm thinking about empowerment but also self-compassion—how you treat yourself as a friend, with kindness, without judgment. There are so many layers in terms of the writing process, but also the showing-up process of "I think I can write, I can't really write, I'm not sure if I can write."

It's that self-compassion aspect that comes to all the different layers of who you are as a writer – emerging as a writer, thinking of yourself as a writer, then the elements that come with being a writer. But there's also the self-compassion part about showing up and being in the space and committing to that intention of coming to Shut Up and Write, how you engage with each other. I think that pairs with empowerment – the choice, the agency that you're making on all those layers and levels. How you're showing up for yourself, but you're also showing up for each other.

Malaika: Exactly. And sometimes it's showing up for each other that gets people to show up for themselves. They feel that responsibility that other people deserve, but not everybody is yet in a place where they know that they deserve that. But even making that intention, they don't necessarily realise they're doing it, but they're also saying "I deserve this."

Aaron: I think one of the most powerful tools in wellness is feeling a sense of purpose. I genuinely believe that for some people, especially in this increasingly isolated world, you have a function but don't really feel a purpose. As society seems to have decided that the only goal is the increase of everything, people don't feel a sense of true purpose tied to the fundamental components of why we're human.

It's the simple act of knowing that you need to be there to set up a table, make sure there are enough seats for others, and ask people to start writing. That could be enough to give you a sense of purpose that pushes you through all those other moments in the week that make you feel like just a cog.

As we talk about launching additional initiatives under Writing Partners, I think about seniors. We talk about the opportunity to check on seniors, about intergenerational connections that could happen from creating writing groups that include seniors. We also talk about the cognitive benefit. But what I haven't talked about yet is: could you imagine being a grandparent, having spent your entire life with a sense of purpose – be it your family or your job – and now you're at a later stage in life and feel no sense of purpose? Like if you were to disappear, it wouldn't impact anyone? Maybe just the simplest act of "I need to be there on Wednesday" does something for somebody.

Narelle: I'm going to say yes.

Aaron: I say yes too. People need to be needed. And what's so cool is that it doesn't matter if you're the facilitator – you could just be another person in that group. You need to be there for the other people.

Narelle: Right, it's just walking through that door and showing up. The whole "I'm going to this" preparation – I've got to make sure my lovely favourite top is clean and pressed. I've got my earrings, my hat, my fashion bling. I'm getting picked up at this time. I want to arrive early because I love this seat. I really want to save a seat for someone else because I enjoy sitting next to them. I want to be up the front because I can see better. We get to share morning tea or afternoon tea together. I might bake and bring something, or I love the facilitator so much that I bake something extra for them to take home to their family. Every week you do that, let alone what's actually happening in the moment of being in that room writing.

That sense of purpose and meaning goes beyond the "what's your why" that we often talk about on social media. If no one's there for you or you're not contributing to anything – oh, my gosh, I've been this amazing person and I've done X, Y, and Z and now I'm retired and no one cares.

Malaika: You and I talked last night about the study from Stanford about "mere belonging" and the idea that the tiniest little sense of affiliation with someone in the room brings out all these wonderful qualities. The level of intervention in those studies was things like believing you shared a birthday with someone in the room – that was enough to get all these wonderful effects because we are such fundamentally social creatures.

Now think about all the little things beyond just sharing a birthday – what happens at a Shut Up and Write! event. Sharing baked goods, the shared intentionality, being part of this event with this name on this day of the week at this café. But there's also this idea of nested community, because when you're part of a Shut Up and Write! event, you're also probably part of the larger city group or the university. And then you're also a part of this global community. Think about the layers of interacting affiliation compared to just sharing a birthday with someone, and what that must do on a deep, ancestral level for people.

Aaron: I thought about how last week, before coming to Cambridge, I stopped in Cologne to meet our chapter there. I hadn't met a single person in that room, but when I walked in, there was this immediate sense of connection. I really think that to echo what Malaika is talking about, yes, you have a sense of belonging within the community you write with regularly. But it's almost like the most benevolent fraternity you can be part of, where you can walk into a room in a different country and immediately have people who want you to have a good experience.

I can only imagine what it would be like to be somebody who's truly connected to their Shut Up and Write! in Calgary, Canada, and they're flying to Athens, Greece for the first time. They reach out to the group in Athens and find out which hotel to stay at, which cafés to go to. There's something so beautiful about walking into a room and having strangers become friends very quickly, simply because we share this fundamental concept that it's possible to build community around traditionally solitary tasks, and how valuable that is.

Malaika: That's definitely a story I also hear within the academic community. Siobhan O'Dwyer and her Shut Up and Write! Tuesdays, which were hosted on Twitter, brought people together from around the world. Those people would find out they were attending the same academic conference, and suddenly it's like they had an old friend there. They had a buddy for the entire experience and would share each other's work on social media.

It's a consistent thing we've heard—in a world with so many silos, you suddenly have people you deeply trust, even if, in the case of online events, you've never been in the same room with them. The level of trust we've heard from some of these people is, "Oh, let me help you figure out where to go in this new city. I can introduce you to my friends, whatever you need." It's this level of friendship and trust that is really beautiful and perhaps unexpected.

Narelle: There's a mutual respect – it's different to saying "I play tennis and I'm part of this tennis club here and that tennis club there." The Shut Up and Write! communities and the ecosystem that exists globally has a mutual respect and a shared understanding of what the experiences are generally like. It has an underpinning of being human, of being kind, of compassion, of gratitude, of genuine curiosity for and with each other that is quite unique.

Just experiencing this room in Cambridge, you've got people from all over coming into one place. And there was a shared understanding, a shared passion, but a shared connection where you're sharing a cup of tea and the conversations went immediately from "Hi, how are you? Where are you from?" right into deep conversations that would generally take quite a few months to get into.

Malaika: And there's something to be said for the kind of people it draws. Tyler (Shore) said those were the nicest people he'd ever been in a room with.

Aaron: I agree with that, but I also think that the ecosystem we're cultivating encourages that kindness. I don't want to think it's contingent on the individuals. The individuals make the community, and the community makes the ecosystem.

I don't think it's happenstance that this symposium we put together this week had the friendliest, most energetic dinner with everybody the other night. I don't hear that kind of chatter among people who have only met each other that day. I've never seen anything like it. I walked around to make sure nobody was feeling left out, and there wasn't a single person who wasn't engaged in wonderful conversation – and I'd say half the room identifies as introverts! They were there the entire day engaging at a level that's kind of unbelievable.

Even people from our team who we know are extraordinarily introverted and have very small social batteries these days – it seemed like somebody had plugged in a power booster for them. There's something magical about it. The people are wonderful, yes, and it's something that encourages those wonderful people to be even more wonderful.

Malaika: Absolutely. The sense of the whole being greater than the sum of the parts was one of the most consistent things everybody was feeling. The kind of feedback I got from people, the wide-eyed sense of wonder when they came up to me: "I've never experienced anything like this. This is so wonderful. I've made so many friends, so many deep, meaningful connections in the spirit of collaboration." I'm still processing it. I knew everybody who got invited and had a sense of what to expect – I knew it would be an incredibly wholesome experience – and I'm still blown away.

Aaron: So the challenge becomes: I think the people who need this the most are the ones we can't directly target. Because you lose what makes Shut Up and Write! really accessible and simple. The productivity gets them in the door.

Malaika: The community is what gets them to stay.

Aaron: And I don't think there are so many individuals who don't even realise they're lacking the community they could have. Who feel like they don't need any kind of productivity help. I can't tell you the number of times I've met with people who are very productive, who say "I've been published so many times. I don't need help writing." And I think, "Oh, but you do."

The challenge is figuring out how to communicate this process correctly to the people who need it most. Writing Partners is a non-profit, and Shut Up and Write! as an initiative is focused on solving problems. We measure our success on how efficiently we're able to take the resources we're given and translate that into impact. For us, that impact is that person who didn't realise they needed this, and then suddenly wakes up one day and realises they couldn't do without it.

Malaika: Yeah.

Aaron: I don't identify as a writer. I have written, but I didn't start my Shut Up and Write! group because I needed to get my writing done. I started it because if I'm going to be making major decisions about how this organisation supports organisers and facilitators, I should know what it's like to be one. So to create a chapter in a city that didn't have one and then run the first event and grow with it has created many opportunities for me to learn.

But what came as a surprise was – I don't think I could stop now. I don't even really want to write that much! But I love it. Because it's the dedicated time I have with these individuals where I see them accomplishing things. That's addictive. My background's in music – I'd say I am a musician. But now I'm like, "I'm a musician who likes to run Shut Up and Writes." So the challenge is: how do you get the skeptic, the person who doesn't think they need it, to a place where they suddenly realise this is the missing link they didn't know they needed? And not do it in a forceful way, but in a "you'll thank us" way.

Narelle: Totally. And how do you convince leaders who are all about productivity? "Give me the stats of what this is going to contribute. How much money is this going to save me?" That's important in higher education and many other places. How do we educate up, sideways, all around? How do we translate and communicate this for those who haven't found it yet or don't know what it is?

Aaron: You're asking a few different questions. So much of the conversation is about how to ensure universities understand they should provide resources to facilitators to keep this going. The answer is – universities, if they haven't seen it yet, are about to see a major shift in how students interact with campus. If universities were proactive in thinking about resources they're using to provide tools to students, they'd realise the vast majority of communication they're providing to those students is going unseen and unheard.

Universities will start spending significant resources on getting students back on campus and engaged because it's far easier for them to communicate available resources en masse than individually when students are locked in their dorms or flats. Universities shouldn't hesitate to spend resources on providing spaces for students to come back on campus. Any university that isn't super excited about an incredibly efficient program that brings students back on campus – I don't know what they're focusing on. They should start selling their real estate.

Narelle: I have many thoughts on this. I've spent time at many universities across different countries, and there's a strong through-line at the moment about why people aren't coming back to campus, both staff and students. Generally, the ruling is "you must come back to campus." Recently I heard someone say, "Why are we putting heating and air conditioning on for bookshelves?"

Aaron: But why don't people want to come back? Because before the pandemic, so much effort was made to sterilise the environment that community had to be founded outside the campus, for both students and faculty. So what you're asking them to do is leave the community they love to go to your campus. Why not instead focus on building the community they love where they are?

From a marketing background, having worked at Apple for an extended period, you have to understand consumer behaviour. These are all consumers of the product you have. If they don't want your product, the answer isn't forcing them to have it – it's evolving what your product is. If what they want is the ability to control aspects of their environment, find out what aspects of your environment are causing problems. If they hurry back to where they feel safe, where their community is, find out why. And build that, remove the barriers that prevent it from happening on campus.

I would be on campus in a heartbeat if that's where I saw all my favourite people and had the opportunity to collaborate and connect in meaningful ways without unrealistic obstacles. I think if you ask most faculty and students, they would say university administration tends to get in the way more often than not. Maybe it's time for universities to look at that and see how they might provide a pathway for cultivating an ecosystem that allows people to organically want to be there.

Narelle: So many thoughts!

Aaron: I just honestly think we see this in companies too. As a remote consultant, companies talk about bringing people back so often, and it frustrates me to no end because I want to be in an office. I work from home right now and I so want to be in an office. Malaika knows because I call her way too often saying "I've been staring at a screen too long. I just need human contact." I would love to be in an office. So if people are saying they don't want to be in your office…

Narelle: Then let's change that up. I used to love writing in cafés. The moment I discovered that many moons ago – I don't even necessarily need to talk to anyone beyond the person I order my green tea from. If it's a regular café, they know as soon as I walk through the door that I need a green tea. We don't even have a conversation anymore, but that space and what's being cultivated there – I could go and do that in the office.

Aaron: Ray Oldenburg, right? "The Great Good Place," 1989. The third place is a space outside of work and home that you're not directly responsible for, but you actively contribute to. And just by showing up and being in that space, you're contributing to what makes that café wonderful.

Narelle: Last question. Joy.

Aaron: It's my favourite character from *Inside Out*.

Malaika: That's my middle name.

Narelle: It's so important. A lot of people have been talking about the joy that comes from facilitation, creating the opportunity, watching the joy in others, the joy they get themselves, the joy from the wider community. It's a positive emotion that's often talked about a lot. I want to know what other positive emotions emerge around Shut Up and Write! – what pops into your head in terms of positive emotions that are critical as part of the method or an outcome of the experience?

Malaika: Well, the method is a set of broad principles that helps us cultivate based on what we've learned, but they're flexible to each community. I think what they really help us do is cultivate the unexpected, the emergent. Rennie, in his talk at this event, asked people to keep an open space for serendipity. The joy felt at these events is the unpredictable – you get humans in a room together and surprising things happen.

When I think of the joy I experience at Shut Up and Write! events, it's in these unexpected, surprising moments that are, in a way, almost predictable to me at this point. Because I'm so familiar with how common it is when you put yourself in this open mindset around other people like that. There's this sense of wonder when you discover things in a unique moment with a unique person – there's never been that exact moment before. So for me, the joy is tightly wound with the serendipitous and the surprise. What do you think, Aaron?

Aaron: There's so much I could say. I had a friend who's fairly religious who said recently that he can't help but be reminded of creation when it comes to the experience of working within a Shut Up and Write! and being at the genesis of new ideas. Seeing that spark of creativity in the eyes of the people surrounding us at the table.

Pride is something that we often hear as a negative, but there's a pride that's very valuable. The pride of accomplishing what you set out to accomplish. There's no greater feeling. There are memes all the time like "decided to be healthy, ate a salad" with a picture of the person who just ate their first salad being like "I am super healthy!" Or the moment you finally decide to start going to the gym and you go twice in that same week. How incredible is it to be part of a group that's a mechanism for so many people who have always said they wanted to start on that one writing project? To be the thing that keeps them going when nothing else did. I'm proud to be a part of that.

And I love the democratic aspect – the fact that decisions aren't made by a leader but by the group. There's not a lot of dictating what happens. There's true ownership in the community being built.

My group is pretty vulnerable. We talk about a lot of stuff. We're really honest about our shortcomings, failures, and difficulties. There are times where I sit down to write and don't get much down at all because my head was too busy. What I would say is valuable – and it's overused – but it's "safe." There's nothing more safe than knowing you're within a group of people who don't really care what your opinions are but care that you share the same intentions. It doesn't matter how good your work is, how much you do, or your thoughts on the latest happening everyone's talking about. None of that matters. Safe for everyone.

Malaika: …Safe for everyone. And just to build a little bit on what you said about ownership, there was something that we learned from the youngest members of our symposium. Freya, Charlotta, and Cornelia, who are recent graduates. They hosted for their undergraduate population, but they – and maybe it's something about the openness of a young mind – they've taken this methodology and applied it in so many aspects of their life. And they feel truly empowered by it. They will apply it to like, "Oh, let's get some art done" or "Let's cook together" or whatever. They'll take principles and, to them, it still feels like the same methodology that helped them build community at university, but it's also empowering them to get things done, to create, or to just be present and conscious in the moment with something. They still think of it as the same principles. And they feel empowered by it. So that was so inspiring to everyone in the room.

Aaron: You know, I would ask you as a global expert on wellbeing, as someone who has seen so many different programs and initiatives and mindsets about how to create wellbeing in academic research and PhD and all these things – why do you care about Shut Up and Write!? What is it that makes this worth your time?

Narelle: I think it's legacy. For everybody involved, at all the different levels. And it doesn't matter about titles. It doesn't matter about hierarchy.

Shut Up & Write! A Dialogue on Community, Wellbeing, and Purpose

It doesn't matter about where you are. It actually comes back down to the core of who you are as a person and being human. And I think that's what, that's why it works.

Because we get rid of all of the crap that actually makes us hate each other and take each other out and do all those things that we go home and cry about and can't process – and none of that is in the room. In any of the rooms I've ever been into, whether it's something I've curated or I've come in.

I think about the first time I went to a Shut Up and Write! I was feeling so isolated, questioning so many things, and there was an invite, and I was like, "I'm so introverted, I'm so scared right now, but I'm going to go in, and be brave and rock up on this Friday morning in a cafe on a different campus."

And I sat at a shared table and that was the beginning of my love affair. But it's the legacy of what came with that and what continues to come with that. And you watch those little "aha!" moments land for people as being humans, let alone what happens about writing and where those words go out. It doesn't matter what you write, but those words go out and impact others.

So it's that legacy ripple effect for me. And I think that that's just huge. Absolutely huge.

Malaika: That's the word that I've been feeling all week. And so the fact that you just said it, I'm a little emotional.

Aaron: That's why I do this. You know, I feel lucky that I've had so many different experiences in my life, both personally and professionally.

And why I continue to work on this project and choose to dedicate my life and my time to it is for exactly what you're talking about. I think we've become complicit in a dynamic that is forced down us every single day that does not have to be reality. And, you know, we joke that Shut Up and Write! is the most wholesome corner of the internet, but I think it's kind of real.

I think it's true. And I think that it's based off of the things that you're talking about and what we're able to undo about the expectations of hierarchy and focusing on a truly sustainable way that we can cultivate an ecosystem that's safe.

Malaika: Yeah.
Aaron: People need community. People need to belong. Every person, even if they don't—
Malaika: Know it. That's—
Narelle: Pretty powerful.

Discussion

In this chapter we have illuminated how SUAW functions as more than merely a productivity tool; it constitutes a multidimensional wellbeing intervention addressing several critical dimensions of academic flourishing. Drawing on Thomson and Coles' (2024) framework for care-full teacher learning, SUAW exemplifies how particularity, politics, and purpose can be integrated to create transformative experiences for participants. SUAW's strength lies in its capacity to establish what Tronto (1993) describes as an "ethic of care" within academic writing spaces. This manifests through attentiveness to participants' diverse needs, responsibility in creating supportive environments, competence in facilitating meaningful interactions, and responsiveness to the challenges writers face. The model creates what Lynch (2022) terms an "affectively egalitarian" space where care, rather than competition, becomes the organising principle.

The wellbeing benefits of SUAW operate across multiple dimensions. First, it directly addresses isolation – a significant contributor to mental health challenges in academia (Kinman & Johnson, 2019) – by transforming writing from a solitary activity into a communal practice. The alternating rhythm between focused work and social connection mirrors evidence-based approaches to stress management, creating what Berg and Seeber (2016) call a "slow scholarship" that sustains rather than depletes participants. Second, SUAW fosters belonging through what Malaika describes as "nested community" – concentric circles of affiliation from immediate writing groups to global networks. This structure provides what Oldenburg (1989) terms a "third place" between work and home, where participants experience what Stanford researchers call "mere belonging" – the profound psychological benefits that emerge from even minimal social connection (Walton et al., 2012). Additionally, SUAW cultivates purpose by positioning participants as contributors to a collective endeavour rather than isolated competitors. As Aaron articulates, "People need to be needed," highlighting how the simple act of showing up regularly for others creates meaning that extends beyond instrumental writing goals. This aligns with research showing that purpose and meaning significantly contribute to wellbeing and resilience (Ryff, 2014).

Perhaps most significantly, SUAW represents a form of resistance to careless academic cultures (Lynch, 2022) by modelling a more humane approach to scholarly work. By prioritising sustained engagement over frantic productivity, it challenges what Berg and Seeber (2016) call the "culture of busy" that pervades contemporary academia. SUAW creates spaces where vulnerability is normalised, failure acknowledged, and success collectively celebrated – practices that directly counter the competitive and isolating individualism often embedded in academic structures.

Conclusion

This chapter has articulated how SUAW represents a care-full approach to academic writing that integrates productivity with wellbeing. Unlike conventional writing interventions focused narrowly on output, SUAW addresses the whole person through creating communities characterised by belonging, purpose, and sustained engagement. In a higher education landscape increasingly marked by isolation, competition, and measurement, SUAW offers a compelling alternative – what Aaron calls "the most wholesome corner of the internet." Its power lies not in complex interventions but in creating spaces where, as Narelle observes, "we get rid of all of the crap that actually makes us hate each other." By fostering communities where people write together rather than against each other, SUAW demonstrates how care can become not merely an aspirational value but a lived practice within academia that embraces the integration of wellbeing in the acts of scholarly writing.

References

Aitchison, C., & Guerin, C. (2014). *Writing groups for doctoral education and beyond: Innovations in practice and theory.* Routledge.

Berg, M., & Seeber, B. K. (2016). *The slow professor: Challenging the culture of speed in the academy.* University of Toronto Press.

Brown, N., & Leigh, J. (2018). Ableism in academia: Where are the disabled and ill academics? *Disability & Society, 33*(6), 985–989. https://doi.org/10.1080/09687599.2018.1455627

Cameron, J., Nairn, K., & Higgins, J. (2009). Demystifying academic writing: Reflections on emotions, know-how and academic identity. *Journal of Geography in Higher Education, 33*(2), 269–284. https://doi.org/10.1080/03098260902734943

Helin, J. (2016). Dialogical writing: Co-inquiring between the written and the spoken word. *Culture and Organization, 25*(1), 1–15.

Johnson, S., Willis, S., & Evans, J. (2017). An examination of stressors, strain, and resilience in academic and non-academic U.K. university job roles. *International Journal of Stress Management, 25*(3), 235–253. https://doi.org/10.1037/str0000060

Kinman, G., & Johnson, S. (2019). Special section on well-being in academic employees. *International Journal of Stress Management, 26*(2), 159–161. https://doi.org/10.1037/str0000131

Lemon, N., & McDonough, S. (2025a). Dialogic reflective writing as a method for exploring collaborative practices in higher education. *Journal of Academic Development, 30*(2), 145–162.

Lemon, N., & McDonough, S. (2025b). Interstate dialogues: Chronicles of rhythms of time and the art of self-care of a mobile academic. In S. McDonough & N. Lemon, (Eds.), *Exploring time as a resource for wellness in higher education: Identity, self-care, and wellbeing at work* (pp. 102–113). Routledge.

Lynch, K. (2022). Care, love and solidarity: Creating affectively egalitarian societies in a world of inequality. *International Journal of Care and Caring, 6*(1–2), 3–22.

MacLeod, I., Steckley, L., & Murray, R. (2012). Time is not enough: Promoting strategic engagement with writing for publication. *Studies in Higher Education, 37*(6), 641–654. https://doi.org/10.1080/03075079.2010.527934

McDonough, S. & Brandenburg, R. (2019). Who owns this data? Using dialogic reflection to examine an ethically important moment. *Reflective Practice, 20*(3), 355–366. https://doi.org/10.1080/14623943.2019.1611553

McGrail, M. R., Rickard, C. M., & Jones, R. (2006). Publish or perish: A systematic review of interventions to increase academic publication rates. *Higher Education Research & Development, 25*(1), 19–35. https://doi.org/10.1080/07294360500453053

Murray, R., & Newton, M. (2009). Writing retreat as structured intervention: Margin or mainstream? *Higher Education Research & Development, 28*(5), 541–553. https://doi.org/10.1080/07294360903154126

Nehrig, J., Laboy, W. T., & Catarius, L. (2010). Connecting reflective practice, dialogic protocols, and professional learning. *Professional Development in Education, 36*(3), 399–420. https://doi.org/10.1080/19415250903102432

Oldenburg, R. (1989). *The great good place: Cafés, coffee shops, community centers, beauty parlors, general stores, bars, hangouts, and how they get you through the day.* Paragon House.

Placier, P., Pinnegar, S., Hamilton, M. L., & Guilfoyle, K. (2005). Exploring the concept of dialogue in the self-study of teaching practices. In C. Kosnik, C. Beck, A. R. Freese & A. P. Samaras (Eds.), *Making a difference in teacher education through self-study: Studies of personal, professional and program renewal* (pp. 51–64). Springer.

Rashid, R. A. (2018). Dialogic reflection for professional development through conversations on a social networking site. *Reflective Practice, 19*(1), 105–117. https://doi.org/10.1080/14623943.2017.1379385

Ryff, C. D. (2014). Psychological well-being revisited: Advances in the science and practice of eudaimonia. *Psychotherapy and Psychosomatics, 83*(1), 10–28. https://doi.org/10.1159/000353263

Sword, H. (2017). *Air & light & time & space: How successful academics write.* Harvard University Press.

Thomson, P., & Coles, R. (2024). Towards a framework for care-full teacher learning: Stories from the British art show professional development programme. *Professional Development in Education.* https://doi.org/10.1080/19415257.2024.2433069

Tronto, J. C. (1993). *Moral boundaries: A political argument for an ethic of care.* Routledge.

Walton, G. M., Cohen, G. L., Cwir, D., & Spencer, S. J. (2012). Mere belonging: The power of social connections. *Journal of Personality and Social Psychology, 102*(3), 513–532. https://doi.org/10.1037/a0025731

2 From Isolation to Connection
How Online Shut Up & Write! Fosters Wellbeing for Remote Scholars

Stephanie Milford

Introduction

Broome, Western Australia, is a small coastal town in the Kimberley region, known for its red cliffs, turquoise waters, and endless skies. However, it is also one of the most remote places in the world. With a population of around 14,000, it is geographically closer to Indonesia than to the state capital Perth, situated 1299 miles away. This remoteness is more than physical; Broome is a place where distance is measured not only in miles but also in the absence of opportunities left behind.

I moved to Broome with my partner for his career pursuits. While I fully supported this decision, it meant, for a time, leaving behind the professional opportunities that aligned with my aspirations. Campos-Zamora et al. (2022) found that health professionals in rural settings face a wide range of challenges in accessing professional development activities, even when highly motivated. I hadn't fully grasped how the geographical and professional distance from my goals would affect me. The disconnect I felt wasn't merely physical – being removed from the academic, social, and professional circles I had envisioned was profoundly isolating. The social and intellectual exchanges I associated with university campuses and professional development were replaced with long stretches of solitude, punctuated by the occasional social interaction in the workplace.

Although I found part-time work that provided structure to my days, the role, while valuable, was not stimulating in the way that I sought. It fell outside the field I had spent years training in. I yearned for environments that stretched my skills and fostered academic growth. In Broome, such professional development opportunities were scarce. Research indicates that professionals working in remote or rural areas frequently encounter barriers to career-enhancing opportunities and report higher levels of dissatisfaction (Dymmott et al., 2022; Couch et al., 2021; Holloway et al., 2020). Despite my best efforts, I felt increasingly detached from the academic and professional trajectory I had once envisioned for myself.

A Shift in Direction: Online Learning and a PhD

In an attempt to satiate my intellectual curiosity, I turned to online learning, enrolling in a Master by Coursework program. For two years, this program provided the academic and social stimulation I had been craving. I became part of a community of fellow scholars who shared not only the same content but also the same challenges. Online tutorials and group work offered connection and fulfillment.

After completing my Master's program, a mentor encouraged me to consider pursuing a PhD. Although I wrestled with self-doubt, I saw a PhD as the next logical step in continuing my academic journey. What I didn't anticipate, however, was that this decision would exacerbate the loneliness that I previously felt.

The Solitude of PhD Writing

Unlike the collaborative atmosphere of my Master's program, my PhD journey was marked by solitude. Living in Broome intensified this, as the geographical distance from academic peers and professional networks amplified the emotional toll. As Cantor (2019) observed, isolation is a common challenge for PhD students, stemming from physical separation and the solitary nature of doctoral work. While I had three incredibly supportive supervisors, they were spread across different states in Australia, and our interactions were limited to fortnightly meetings and frequent email correspondence. Cacioppo & Cacioppo (2014) suggest that loneliness can impair executive functioning and harm overall wellbeing, and I began to feel the effects on my work.

The mental health challenges facing PhD students are well documented with research pointing to heightened rates of anxiety, depression, and burnout, even among those in well-resourced institutions (Levecque et al., 2017). For remote students, these challenges are often compounded by distance from peers, services, and academic supports. Kozar and Lum (2015) observe that isolation can erode connection and stall academic progress.

Seeking Connection: From Disconnection to Engagement

Skakni (2018) notes, intellect alone is not enough for a student to complete a PhD. To counterbalance the seclusion of academic work, I actively sought engagement through various activities. Research shows that PhD students often adopt coping mechanisms such as increased social interactions, professional development, and non-academic pursuits to manage loneliness (Janta et al., 2014). In this spirit, I joined local soccer, volleyball, and netball teams, and enrolled in a Spanish-language class. These offered social engagement, but didn't fill the academic void, and my writing remained slow.

Seeking more meaningful connection, I volunteered for my university's young alumni committee, mentored through the alumni program and joined the university student mental health advisory board. These were enriching experiences, offering growth and interaction, but they didn't bridge the academic gap or accelerate my writing.

In my continued efforts to find a solution, I also tried online writing groups offered by my university. These groups, however, were hybrid in nature, designed primarily for in-person students with online participants included as an afterthought. Technical issues such as poor audio and video quality were common, and sessions often ended prematurely. Engagement opportunities were limited, with online participants frequently feeling like spectators rather than active contributors. These challenges highlighted the difficulty of accessing meaningful academic support and connection in a remote setting.

It was during this time that COVID-19 struck, creating a paradigm shift in the landscape of higher education. Traditional academic spaces, once buzzing with in-person interactions, suddenly moved online (Garcia-Morales et al., 2021). For many on-campus PhD students, these shifts distanced them from established social networks (Pyhältö et al., 2023). For me, however, it was a turning point. Among the new virtual opportunities that emerged, Shut Up & Write! (SUAW), became the lifeline I needed. Unlike hybrid formats, where online participants often felt peripheral due to poor sound and video quality, this SUAW was fully online, removing geographical barriers. For the first time, I could participate equally from my remote location in Broome.

Shut Up & Write!

Initially conceived as an on-campus initiative, SUAW's virtual transition opened new possibilities for remote students like me. The premise was simple yet effective: structured, writing sessions with timed blocks where participants would gather (online), with brief check-ins, and silent work periods. While I initially joined for the practical benefit of dedicated writing time, SUAW quickly became more than that – it was the source of connection and encouragement I had been missing. As Lorenz and Patrie (2024) reflect, regular participation in virtual writing communities offer both accountability and emotional support, demonstrating that meaningful connection is possible even when participants are geographically dispersed.

SUAW followed a simple structure: brief check-ins to articulate writing goals, timed Pomodoro writing blocks (Cirrilo, 2018), and short reflection breaks. A grid of strangers, each quietly pursuing their goals, reminded me that I wasn't alone in my struggles. Using the Pomodoro technique has been shown to improve efficiency and mood during study sessions (Biwer et al., 2023) and this structure brought discipline to my writing process.

One of the most significant benefits of SUAW was the external structure it provided, which helped me cultivate internal discipline. Before SUAW, my thesis often felt paralysing. Without a clear routine, I found it difficult to start, frequently delaying my writing until deadlines loomed uncomfortably close.

Figure 2.1 Writing from the Edge – The Kimberley Coastline as a Backdrop to Shut Up & Write!

SUAW reframed my approach, by breaking down the daunting task of thesis writing into manageable chunks. Regular sessions helped me build a sustainable writing habit.

Beyond the sessions, I adopted SUAW's structured approach for my independent writing. I began setting specific goals, incorporating regular breaks, and reflecting on my progress. Research demonstrates that writing groups increase productivity by fostering self-efficacy and self-regulation (Proulx et al., 2023). These habits became ingrained, helping me focus on the writing process rather than the overwhelming scope of my thesis.

Power of Community and Accountability

Beyond the productivity boost, SUAW offered something more valuable: a sense of community. In higher education "belonging" is often linked to student retention (Burke, 2019; Pedler et al., 2022). This newfound community revitalised my enthusiasm for my studies whilst alleviating some of the ever-present self-doubt. Crawford et al. (2022) found that students' sense of belonging is shaped by relationships, and familiarity with systems. Though silent, the blocks were bookended by meaningful check-ins.

Many participants, like me, were navigating their own PhD journeys from various corners of Australia. The shared experience of academic writing created a powerful sense of solidarity. We bonded over common gripes about confirmation of candidature protocols, ethics applications, and the misunderstandings of those "non-PhD" people around us. Research by Alisic et al. (2024) found the importance of perceived social support in mitigating the feelings of isolation that many PhD students experience, highlighting the role that structured, communal activities like SUAW play in promoting emotional resilience.

Through SUAW, I developed relationships with fellow researchers who shared similar struggles, forming an academic community that felt deeply relational. In one SUAW session, I unexpectedly reconnected with someone I had known in primary school. This encounter highlighted the surprising ways that SUAW fosters connection, bridging both academic and personal networks.

Normalising Struggles, Building Resilience

The emotional demands of writing a PhD are considerable, often marked by frustration, self-doubt and fatigue. Living in Broome amplified these challenges. However, SUAW provided a space where these emotions could be normalised. Writing alongside others who faced similar struggles made me feel less alone. The brief check-ins and debriefs helped me reframe setbacks as part of the academic journey rather than signs of failure.

The reflective nature of SUAW also played a key role in reshaping my relationship with my writing. At the start of each session, participants articulated their writing goals, and, at the end, we would reflect on what we had accomplished. Even on days when progress felt minimal, these reflective moments encouraged me to focus on what I had accomplished rather than what I hadn't. This shift fostered a more compassionate and constructive perspective on my work.

Over time, my participation in SUAW began to reshape how I saw myself, not just as a student writing a thesis, but as a scholar with something meaningful to contribute. The shift reflected a deepening sense of academic identity. As Subedi et al. (2022) note, academic writing groups can be pivotal in forming scholarly identity by providing spaces for reflection, validation, and shared knowledge construction.

In addition to participating in SUAW, I made a conscious effort to maintain a healthy balance between my academic and personal life. I set clear boundaries and scheduled breaks, walking on the beach or going to the gym, to reset and avoid burnout during intense writing periods. Together, these strategies not only sustained my progress but also bolstered my emotional and physical wellbeing.

Unexpected Opportunities, Professional Growth

As a remote PhD student, networking was a challenge. SUAW created space to connect with other higher degree research (HDR) students and early career researchers (ECRs). These interactions introduced me to unfamiliar but valuable methodologies and theories. Conversations during breaks offered fresh perspectives, helping me to expand my methodological toolkit and strengthen theoretical frameworks.

In one break, a participant shared a data analysis technique I had not previously considered. This inspired a new approach that enriched my analysis. These informal yet insightful exchanges fostered mutual academic growth, offering opportunities to learn about HDR-specific training in research design, data analysis, and time management – opportunities I might not have found otherwise.

We frequently shared research interests and post-PhD aspirations, creating a supportive environment to discuss professional development. Writing groups like SUAW have been shown to build relationships and dismantle competitive barriers, fostering a collective commitment to the research community (Tyndall et al., 2019). As I approached the final stages of my PhD, these connections proved invaluable. One member, recalling my research, referred me to a project aligned with my interests and recommended me for a position. This referral helped me secure further academic opportunities, demonstrating the lasting professional impact of these connections.

Reflections on my PhD Journey

Reflecting on my PhD journey, I can confidently say that SUAW was far more than a writing tool. I often wonder what my PhD trajectory might have looked like without SUAW. Would I have persisted? Most likely – but at a cost to my wellbeing. The early stages, marked by isolation and lack of momentum, were draining. SUAW offered the connection, and encouragement, I needed to remain grounded and emotionally resilient. The habits I developed through SUAW not only advanced my research but also strengthened my capacity to manage the demands of the doctoral journey.

Living in Broome, I learned that while physical remoteness is challenging, connection is never out of reach. Through shared screens, muted mics and silent support, SUAW bridged the gap between isolation and community. For remote PhD students, the importance of connection and support cannot be overstated. Contrary to assumptions, SUAW demonstrated that online groups can foster genuine academic connection and care. The virtual format didn't dilute the sense of belonging; it deepened it by removing barriers.

It transformed my experience from one of disconnection and stagnation into one of belonging, progress, and professional growth. For those navigating similar challenges, I encourage incorporating SUAW into your routine. It not only improves productivity but also fosters a thriving, connected, and supportive academic environment.

Strategies

1 **Join a structured writing group**: This can be in-person or online. Groups like SUAW provide accountability, structure, and community. Consistent participation can improve writing productivity and reduce isolation.
2 **Use the Pomodoro technique**: Breaking writing into manageable sessions improves focus and efficiency.

3 **Engage in online academic networks**: Actively participate in virtual seminars, workshops, and mentorship programs to expand your academic connections.
4 **Set boundaries for work–life balance**: Establish clear writing schedules and incorporate regular self-care activities to prevent burnout.
5 **Seek out peer support**: Connecting with fellow researchers fosters motivation and provides valuable academic insights.

References

Alisic, A., Noppeney, R., & Wiese, B.S. (2024). When doubts take over: A longitudinal study on emerging disengagement in the PhD process. *Higher Education, 88*, 1165–1182. https://doi.org/10.1007/s10734-023-01164-z

Biwer, F., Wiradhany, W., Oude Egbrink, M.G.A., & de Bruin, A.B.H. (2023). Understanding effort regulation: Comparing 'Pomodoro' breaks and self-regulated breaks. *British Journal of Educational Psychology, 93*, 353–367. https://doi.org/10.1111/bjep.12593

Burke, A. (2019). Student retention models in higher education: A literature review. *College and University, 94*(2), 12–21.

Cacioppo, J.T., & Cacioppo, S. (2014). Social relationships and health: The toxic effects of perceived social isolation. *Social and Personality Psychology Compass, 8*(2), 45–89. https://doi.org/10.1111/spc3.12087

Campos-Zamora, M., Gilbert, H., Esparza-Perez, R.I., Sanchez-Mediola, M., Gardner, R., Richards, J.B., Lumbreras-Marquez, M.I., & Dobiesz, V.A. (2022). Continuing professional development challenges in a rural setting: A mixed-methods study. *Perspectives on Medical Education, 11*(5), 273–280. https://doi.org/10.1007/s40037-022-00718-8

Cantor, G. (2019). The loneliness of the long-distance (PhD) researcher. *Psychodynamic Practice, 26*(1), 56–67. https://doi.org/10.1080/14753634.2019.1645805

Cirrilo, F. (2018). *The Pomodoro technique: The acclaimed time-management system that has transformed how we work.* (Currency edition). Currency.

Couch, A., Menz, H.B., Coker, F., White, J., Haines, T., & Williams, C. (2021). Factors that influence workplace location choices in the different allied health professions: A systematic review. *Australian Journal of Rural Health, 29*(6), 823–834. https://doi.org/10.1111/ajr.12768

Crawford, N.L., Emery, S.G., Allen, P., & Baird, A. (2022). I probably have a closer relationship with my internet provider: Experiences of belonging (or not) among mature-aged regional and remote university students. *Journal of University Teaching & Learning Practice, 19*(4).

Dymmott, A., George, S., Campbell, N., & Brebner, C. (2022). Experiences of working as early career allied health professionals and doctors in rural and remote environments: A qualitative systematic review. *BMC Health Services Research, 22*(1), 951.

Garcia-Morales, V.J., Garrido-Moreno, A., & Martin-Rojas, R. (2021). The transformation of higher education after the COVID disruption: Emerging challenges in an online scenario. *Frontiers in Psychology, 12*, 616059. https://doi.org/10.3389/fpsyg.2021.616059

Holloway, P., Bain-Donohue, S., Moore, M. (2020). Why do doctors work in rural areas in high-income countries? A qualitative systematic review of recruitment and retention. *Australian Journal of Rural Health, 28*(6), 543–554. https://doi.org/10.1111/ajr.12675

Janta, H., Lugosi, P., & Brown, L. (2014). Coping with loneliness: A netnographic study of doctoral students. *Journal of Further and Higher Education, 38*(4), 553–571. https://dx.doi.org/10.1080/0309877X.2012.726972

Kozar, O., & Lum, J.F. (2015). Online doctoral writing groups: Do facilitators or communication modes make a difference? *Quality in Higher Education*, *21*(1), 38–51. https://doi.org/10.1080/13538322.2015.1032003

Levecque, K., Anseel, F., De Beuckelaer, A., Van der Heyden, J., & Gisle, L. (2017). Work organization and mental health problems in PhD students. *Research Policy*, *46*(4), 868–879. https://doi.org/10.1016/j.respol.2017.02.008

Lorenz, D.E., & Patrie, N. (2024). The importance of showing up (virtually): A reflection on practice of an online doctoral writing community of practice. *The Open/Technology in Education, Society, and Scholarship Association Conference*, *4*(1), 1–11. https://doi.org/10.18357/otessac.2024.4.1.292

Pedler, M.L., Willis, R., & Nieuwoudt, J.E. (2022). A sense of belonging at university: Student retention, motivation and enjoyment. *Journal of Further and Higher Education*, *46*(3), 397–408. https://doi.org/10.1080/0309877X.2021.1955844

Proulx, C.N., Rubio, D.M., Norman, M.K., & Mayowski, C.A. (2023). Shut Up & Write!® builds writing self-efficacy and self-regulation in early-career researchers. *Journal of Clinical and Translational Science*, *7*: e141, 1–7. https://doi.org/10.1017/cts.2023.568

Pyhältö, K., Tikkanen, L., & Anttila, H. (2023). The influence of COVID-19 pandemic on PhD candidates' study progress and study wellbeing. *Higher Education Research & Development*, *42*(2), 413–426. https://doi.org/10.1080/07294360.2022.2063816

Skakni, I. (2018). Doctoral studies as an initiatory trial: Expected and taken-for-granted practices that impede PhD students' progress. *Teaching in Higher Education*, *23*(8), 927–944. https://doi.org/10.1080/13562517.2018.1449742

Subedi, K.R., Shrma, S., & Bista, K. (2022). Academic identity development of doctoral scholars in an online writing group. *International Journal of Doctoral Studies*, *17*, 279–300. https://doi.org/10.28945/5004

Tyndall, D.E., Forbess III, T.H., Avery, J.J., & Powell, S.B. (2019). Fostering scholarship in doctoral education: Using a social capital framework to support PhD student writing groups. *Journal of Professional Nursing*, *35*(4), 300–304. https://doi.org/10.1016/j.profnurs.2019.02.002

3 Moreton Bay Fridays

Creating Community in a Regional University Campus through Convivial Co-located Quiet Writing

Deanna Grant-Smith, Katie McIntyre, Karen Hands, David Schmidtke, Rory Mulcahy, and Margarietha de Villiers Scheepers

Introduction

Regional universities experience unique challenges in building community (Christensen and Nislen, 2021; Eddy & Hart, 2012). The academics who work there, even when located on the outskirts of major conurbations (Ellis et al., 2002), can experience marginalisation and fewer opportunities for research collaborations due to the distance from larger academic hubs (Goriss-Hunter & White, 2024) and teaching-oriented focus (Anderson et al., 2020). In multi-campus regional universities, distance hinders the equitable provision and coordination of developmental activities and "personal encounters" across campuses (Pinheiro & Berg, 2017, p. 7). These challenges are often more pronounced at satellite campuses where staff, resources, and research activities are limited compared to the flagship campus, reducing access to research development activities (Pinheiro et al. 2016). Staff and higher degree research students at these sites may feel isolated, disconnected, and fearful of missing opportunities to develop research skills and enhance performance (Ağlargöz, 2017). More limited interaction with the broader university can foster feelings of mistrust and marginalisation (Madikizela-Madiya, 2018), while not being co-located to lead to fewer opportunities to engage in spontaneous informal information sharing and support (Goriss-Hunter and White, 2021). Combined these factors can undermine the wellbeing and research productivity of academic staff at the satellite campuses.

To address their "geographically and institutionally peripheral position in a metrocentric higher education system" staff at regional universities must mobilise "scarce resources to create unique solutions to local issues" (Schmidt et al., 2024, p. 1). An example can be found in the growing popularity of Shut Up and Write! (SUAW!) to improve researcher self-efficacy and research productivity (Proulx et al., 2023). Providing a regular, quiet space for independently writing alongside peers offers collegial interaction that positively supports scholarly identity and academic resilience (Fegan, 2016). These "spaces of wellbeing" (Beasy et al., 2020, p. 1093) benefit higher degree research students, early career academics and established faculty alike (DeFeo et al., 2016; Johnson et al., 2017).

This chapter explores our experiences as a group of research-active staff at a geographically dispersed multi-campus regional university who meet weekly to engage in co-located quiet writing. We propose our SUAW! group functions as a tool of conviviality (Illich, 2021) that supports belonging and wellbeing through community-making. Our collective reflections are interrogated through communicative democracy (Young 2000) to advance six practical strategies for creating a vibrant and supportive writing community.

Moreton Bay Fridays

Moreton Bay Fridays (MBF), as we became known, was initiated by the school's research leadership team to increase research productivity. However, it quickly became owned by the members who, rather than approaching it as an extractive process, were motivated to create community and authentic relationships based on collegiality and joy.

> The work we do is so atomised across time and locations…Writing can be isolating and slow…the rejections can feel degrading! I wanted to work in a supportive and collegial environment and share this experience with others. I also wanted the routine, structure and sense of accountability that comes from sharing goals and ideas with others.

Fostering the conviviality described here by a member relies on inclusive social practices and spaces that build community, generate resources, and create a sense of belonging through meaningful, authentic connections (Guercini & Ranfagni, 2021). In contrast to academic systems that commodify research and reduce relationships to output metrics, conviviality prioritises relationships and communal wellbeing, enabling creative and autonomous self-expression through work (Illich, 2021). A quiet co-located writing group, like MBF, can be a tool of conviviality if it functions as a space for interacting with others in generous solidarity. MBF invoked principles of mutual aid through active participation and sharing knowledge and skills as equals in the writing endeavour. Resisting hierarchy and competitive dynamics, its open membership and voluntary nature align with Illich's (2021) advocacy for informal, reciprocal approaches to learning.

Convivial spaces help us to "relearn to depend on each other" (Illich 2021, p. 30). Through MBF, rather than a solitary pursuit, writing together became a shared practice and eudaemonic space fostering wellbeing, self-determination, and collective flourishing (Mikus et al., 2022). To reflect on MBF as convivial practice we responded to a series of prompts and the visual metaphor of a mandala. Following Cressey (2006), this collective reflection was a shared, dialogic process through which we critically examined our experiences and assumptions to foster learning, mutual understanding, and social transformation.

Figure 3.1 The mandala as visual metaphor for Moreton Bay Fridays.

The nucleus of the mandala represents our coming together at a scheduled day, place, and time while the intricate radiating spokes symbolise our distinctive writing and career trajectories. Each layer reinforces our interconnected, yet individual contributions and their role in enriching our collective experience, while the outer border reflects the close-knit community we formed. The mandala's repeating symmetry echoes the social and professional bonds that saw us return each week, while its organic shape conveys the messiness of both writing and community.

Strategies for Creating Convivial Spaces of Writing, Research and Connection

Communicative democracy (Young, 2000) emphasises the importance of diverse voices, respectful engagement and ongoing dialogue in building caring communities.

In advancing communicative democracy, Iris Marion Young (2000) identifies three elements for creating an inclusive space – greeting, narrative, and rhetoric. *Greeting* involves recognising and respecting others through respect and welcoming gestures to build mutual recognition and trust. *Narrative* emphasises the importance of sharing stories and personal experiences to enrich understanding of each other's lived reality, bridge difference, and foster empathy and identity.

Rhetoric concerns how information is conveyed, the value placed on different communication styles, and the legitimacy granted to different perspectives.

Using this analytical frame to analyse our reflections, we identified six strategies for creating convivial collective writing spaces based on our practices.

Strategy 1: Create Everyday Spaces for Regular Convivial Interaction

The rhythms and routines of academic life can challenge our opportunities to find space for writing. MBF generated an "everydayness" (Atasay, 2013, p. 67) of convivial interaction. The regularity of weekly extended meetings (9 a.m.–12 p.m.) with a consistent process supported the weaving of new practices into local routines, "bringing a regularity of environment that constitutes the basis of trust relations" (Wise & Noble, 2016, p. 427). The mix of quiet writing time and social interaction offered *"focused writing time with no distraction"* while *"chatting in between writing helped me feel connected to the broader university conversations"*. Maintaining a consistent schedule allowed the writing sessions to be embedded in members' calendars:

> MBF became an anchor to my week. I really valued the supportive and friendly atmosphere forged on these days, and if I had a hectic Mon–Thur without writing at all, I knew I would prioritise attending on the Friday and that the time would be productive. The benefits were twofold: productive in terms of writing, and personally/professionally as I met colleagues I hadn't known before and came to know other colleagues better.

Strategy 2: Invoke Greeting and Narrative through Shared Rituals

Each MBF writing session had a dedicated check-in and close-out and time for informal conversation so we could discuss writing plans and progress, and topics of shared interest. A consistent agenda provides a familiar atmosphere that "animates social relations, generates individual immersion and encourages self-narratives" (Guercini and Ranfagni, 2021, p. 366). It also set a collegial and welcoming tone while providing reassurances of productivity: *"Each week I felt welcomed by the group and that they were genuinely pleased that I came. I enjoyed being able to share what I was working on and hearing what others were working on too."* Beyond feelings of belonging and connection, it was *"motivating to share our goals at the start of each MBF and then recap our progress at the end."* This ritualised sharing also performed a regulatory function by creating shared accountability for participating well: *"People made an effort to come which made me make an effort to use the time wisely."*

Strategy 3: Accelerate Empathy and Identity Through Storytelling

Storytelling can bring "community (understood as shared commons) and conviviality (as empathetic difference) into dialogue" (Neal et al., 2018, p. 71) by validating struggles and aspirations. Recognising the diversity of members' disciplines, lived experience, and writing styles, we established group norms that ensured all voices were heard and valued. This encouraged members to share their expertise and perspectives fostering collective learning, and our shared commitment to writing together created a deeply supportive environment. MBF also embodied Young's concept of a transformative politics of difference which seeks to recognise, value, and embed difference rather than seeking to eliminate it (Cameron & Grant-Smith, 2005; Young 1990).

> Those who attended were there because they also wanted to connect with colleagues, they wanted to listen and support others, possibly more than they wanted to share about their own work and/or receive support. People wanted to be there, and they wanted others to be there.

Strategy 4: Create a Physical Space for Self-care and Care of Others

Our reflections confirm that a writing community grounded in conviviality fosters care for both individual writing and the wellbeing of others (Beasy et al., 2020). Valuing the collective while honouring individual contributions created a writing community where we felt emotionally supported to engage communally while meeting personal needs. Consistent attendance helped counteract isolation by building a sense of shared purpose and mutual respect. This support extended naturally through the informal, serendipitous exchanges that emerged from sharing physical space, further entrenching *"the sense of community that comes from knowing we are all in this together"*. This sense of connection extended beyond the writing sessions with the benefit that *"feeling [more] connected can lead to less feelings of isolation and loneliness even when you are not in the room anymore"*.

Strategy 5: Celebrate Progress, not Perfection

Conviviality centres relationships, mutual care, and being together in community, while productivity emphasises efficiency and outputs. In MBF, we sought to balance the need for writing performance with the need for care-full interaction and support. A SUAW! group grounded in conviviality must navigate the tension between fostering deep relationships and supporting both individual and collective aspirations. The challenge is to hold space for both. When well-balanced, convivial writing spaces can enhance productivity by creating trust, inspiring creativity, and reducing the fear of failure, allowing members to produce work that feels authentic and meaningful. Linking conviviality and care also affirms that writing is not merely an intellectual activity but a holistic one, involving emotional resilience and personal growth. Prior research shows that goal setting and sharing progress in SUAW! groups enhance motivation and build self-esteem (Proulx et al., 2023). We also found that acknowledging and celebrating milestones—whether completing a draft, submitting a paper, or simply meeting a session target of writing a few hundred words—was affirming and contributed meaningfully to our collective and individual confidence and motivation.

Strategy 6: Build Connections Beyond Writing through Sharing Food

Sharing food can be a powerful practice in fostering conviviality and embodies the principles of inclusion, connection, and mutual care. In a writing group or any communicative space, sharing food reinforces the communal aspect of dialogue, connecting people emotionally and symbolically by communicating care and belonging. MBF included a coffee break where we shared snacks brought from home. Sharing food in this way signals hospitality and strengthens relationships by creating a warm and welcoming atmosphere and a sense of shared connection beyond the writing itself. The neutral, egalitarian space of the coffee line became an unintimidating space for asking questions and sharing ideas. These included the *"many incidental and accidental exchanges that led to deeper personal and professional engagement… collective dismay about the discomfort of the chairs, the Scotch Finger's position as the Queen of all biscuits, bright overcoats that were accidental late-night online purchases"*.

Time spent reheating lunches brought from home after the session shifted the focus from transactional exchanges to relational ones, evoking the more conventionally applied definition of conviviality as embodying qualities of the Aristotelian concept of eutrapelia such as geniality, amiability and sociability (Illich, 2021). The connective and convivial power of sharing food and space is described in this final reflection:

> MBF gave me a reason to come to campus…I liked the lunch after as more informal chats could occur while people were already on campus. There is a real benefit to hearing and seeing everyone typing. Online you could get distracted doing something else but in the room, you sit and you are there typing away like everyone else! I think being in the room creates a buzz of activity about research and simple things like a smile, or eye contact make you feel positive about the experience. You feel connected being in the space.

Conclusion

Our version of SUAW!, grounded in the principles of conviviality and communicative democracy, fostered connectedness and a sense of belonging. By embedding the practical strategies outlined in this chapter, SUAW! becomes more than time for writing; it becomes a living expression of conviviality, where connection and care are as central as creativity and productivity. Our experience shows that inclusive, respectful, and supportive social and professional interactions, transform isolation into connection, creating a vibrant academic community where members feels valued and supported. Our approach supported individual wellbeing, collective growth and collaboration, ultimately strengthening both productivity and local research culture.

References

Ağlargöz, O. (2017). 'We are at this campus, there is nothing in this campus…': Socio-spatial analysis of a university campus. *Tertiary Education & Management*, 23, 69–83. https://doi.org/10.1080/13583883.2016.1207798

Anderson, L., Gatwiri, K., & Townsend-Cross, M. (2020). Battling the 'headwinds': The experiences of minoritised academics in the neoliberal Australian university. *International Journal of Qualitative Studies in Education*, 33(9), 939–953. https://doi.org/10.1080/09518398.2019.1693068

Atasay, E. (2013). Ivan Illich and the study of everyday life. *The International Journal of Illich Studies*, 3(1), 56–77. https://journals.psu.edu/illichstudies/article/view/59300/59024

Beasy, K., Emery, S., Dyer, L., Coleman, B., Bywaters, D., Garrad, T., Crawford, J., Swarts, K., & Jahangiri, S. (2020). Writing together to foster wellbeing: Doctoral writing groups as spaces of wellbeing. *Higher Education Research & Development*, 39(6), 1091–1105. https://doi.org/10.1080/07294360.2020.1713732

Cameron, J., & Grant-Smith, D. (2005). Building citizens: Participatory planning practice and a transformative politics of difference. *Urban Policy and Research*, 23(1), 21–36. https://doi.org/10.1080/0811114042000335296

Christensen, L.S., & Nislen, N.E. (2021). Deconstructing quality at multi-campus universities: What moderates staff and student satisfaction? *Quality Assurance in Education*, 29(2/3), 198–208. https://doi.org/10.1108/qae-03-2021-0034

Cressey, P. (2006). Collective reflection and learning: From formal to reflective participation. In D. Boud, P. Cressey, & P. Docherty (Eds.), *Productive reflection at work: Learning for changing organizations* (pp. 55–65). Routledge.

DeFeo, D.J., Kilic, Z., & Maseda, R. (2016). From productivity to process: Flipping the writing group. *Academic Journal of Interdisciplinary Studies*, 5(3), 544–550. https://www.richtmann.org/journal/index.php/ajis/article/view/9838

Eddy, P.L., & Hart, J. (2012). Faculty in the hinterlands: Cultural anticipation and cultural reality. *Higher Education*, 63, 751–769. https://doi.org/10.1007/s10734-011-9475-2

Ellis, B., Sawyer, J., Dollard, M., & Boxall, D. (2002). Working as rural academics. *Australian & International Journal of Rural Education*, 12(1), 43–50. https://doi.org/10.47381/aijre.v12i1.482

Fegan, S. (2016). When shutting up brings us together: Several affordances of a scholarly writing group. *Journal of Academic Language & Learning*, 10(2), A20–A31. https://journal.aall.org.au/index.php/jall/article/view/404

Goriss-Hunter, A., & White, K. (2021). Teamwork and regional universities: The benefits for women of a third space. *Australian Universities' Review*, 63(2), 11–21. https://files.eric.ed.gov/fulltext/EJ1324621.pdf

Goriss-Hunter, A., & White, K. (2024). Using email interviews to reflect on women's careers at a regional university. *Australian Educational Researcher*, 51, 651–665. https://doi.org/10.1007/s13384-023-00617-9

Guercini, S., & Ranfagni, S. (2021). Conviviality as social practice in business relationships: Concepts and insights from a case of expatriates. *Journal of Business & Industrial Marketing*, 36(3), 357–371. https://doi.org/10.1108/JBIM-12-2018-0380

Illich, I. (2021). *Tools for conviviality*. Marion Boyars.

Johnson, L., Roitman, S., Morgan, A., & MacLeod, J. (2017). Challenging the productivity mantra: Academic writing with spirit in place. *Higher Education Research & Development*, 36(6), 1181–1193. https://doi.org/10.1080/07294360.2017.1300140

Madikizela-Madiya, N. (2018). Mistrust in a multi-campus institutional context: A socio-spatial analysis. *Journal of Higher Education Policy & Management*, 40(5), 415–429. https://doi.org/10.1080/1360080X.2018.1478609

Mikus, J., Rieger, J., & Grant-Smith, D. (2022). Eudaemonic design to achieve well-being at work, wherever that may be. In M. Montoya-Reyes, I. Mendoza-Muñoz, G. Jacobo-Galicia, & S.E. Cruz-Sotelo (Eds.), *Ergonomics and business policies for the promotion of well-being in the workplace* (pp. 1–32). IGI Global.

Neal, S., Bennett, K., Cochrane, A., & Mohan, G. (2018). Community and conviviality? Informal social life in multicultural places. *Sociology*, *53*(1), 69–86. https://doi.org/10.1177/0038038518763518

Pinheiro, R., & Berg, L.N. (2017). Categorizing and assessing multi-campus universities in contemporary higher education. *Tertiary Education & Management*, *23*, 5–22. https://doi.org/10.1080/13583883.2016.1205124

Pinheiro, R., Charles, D., & Jones, G. (2016). Translating strategy, values and identities in higher education: The case of multi-campus systems. *Tertiary Education & Management*, *23*(1), 1–4. https://doi.org/10.1080/13583883.2016.1248858

Proulx, C.N., Rubio, D.M., Norman, M.K., & Mayowski, C.A. (2023). Shut Up & Write!® builds writing self-efficacy and self-regulation in early-career researchers. *Journal of Clinical & Translational Science*, *7*(1), e141. https://doi.org/10.1017/cts.2023.568

Schmidt, M., Aberdeen, L., Carlon, C., & Eversole, R. (2024). Invisible innovation: Intellectual labour on regional university campuses in Australia. *Journal of Sociology*. https://doi.org/10.1177/14407833241252711

Wise, A., & Noble, G. (2016). Convivialities: An orientation. *Journal of Intercultural Studies*, *37*(95), 423–431. https://doi.org/10.1080/07256868.2016.1213786

Young, I.M. (1990). The ideal of community and the politics of difference. In L.J. Nicholson (Ed.), *Feminism/Postmodernism* (pp. 300–323). Routledge.

Young, I.M. (2000). *Inclusion and democracy*. Oxford University Press.

4 Shut Up and Write! Online

Affective Atmospheres and Postdigital Pedagogies of Care

Miriam Reynoldson and Anna Farago

Introduction

> I can hear the sound of my cat's tongue lapping at the little cup of water by the window. Yesterday's empty mug of finished tea sits on the bench beside my desk, and a fallen picture frame is resting against the side of the bookshelf, waiting to be re-hung. I could attend to these things, but not just now. My camera's off, my microphone's off, but I'm on Zoom and my time is committed to Anna, the person on the other side. We haven't spoken in twenty minutes, but our last words were a promise: 'Eight fifty.' That's how long we'll work, before reporting back.
>
> Miriam, session 1

Being a doctoral candidate is tough. We are developing our academic identities through immersion in many intricate layers of research practice, while trying (and not always succeeding) to balance our adult life commitments and obligations. We struggle with feelings of isolation, overwhelm, guilt, imposter syndrome. Mental health risks, including burnout, are very real. It's especially complicated for those of us who are older, studying part-time or fully online. Numerous studies report that Higher Degree by Research (HDR) students benefit from peer and community support, social interaction, and supervisors who care – but that institutional support for these can be patchy (Brownlow et al., 2023; Melián & Meneses, 2024).

We are graduate educational researchers who participate in Shut Up And Write! (SUAW) online via Zoom video conferencing. In the faculty where we met, the graduate research committee coordinates a group session each week, but the beauty of SUAW online is that once you're connected to other SUAWers, you can run your own session anytime, anywhere. Typically, SUAW has been a face-to-face practice, where writers meet at a café or other common space to chat a little, then write in silence. For us, it's always been online. We have families, jobs, homes outside the city, even interstate. Commuting to campus to sit in silence is hard to justify – and, frequently, it's not an option at all. It's too easy to push the seedlings of your academic

42 *Fostering Wellbeing through Collective Writing Practices*

Figure 4.1 SUAW Zoom patchwork 2025 (Artist: Anna Farago. Included with permission.)

identity aside when it there are so many other demands to attend to. So if it wasn't online, it wouldn't happen for us. But we think SUAW online has value beyond its convenience.

We offer the proposition that SUAW online exemplifies a postdigital pedagogy of care, requiring a collective choice to engage in reciprocal sharing and silence with others who, like us, are whole people with academic ambitions, affective needs, and complex adult lives. We are together but apart, in our own spaces and also in each other's. We slowly build connection, understanding, and empathy whilst chatting between the focused writing time. We talk about the journeys we are on, about writing, about getting flow and focus, about neurodiversity, juggling work and study, family life, and relationships. By participating in online SUAW, we create learning communities that foreground affect and relationships, regardless of geographical distance, to create decentralised atmospheres of solidarity and support.

Peering through the (Zoom) Window

After sharing various SUAW online sessions throughout the first year of our doctoral studies, Anna and Miriam dedicated three sessions specifically to reflecting on SUAW online and the affects it enables us to co-create with and for each other as we grow our academic identities.

That these Zoom sessions occur whilst I sit at my desk at home (which used to be Adrian's) is important. Firstly, it's where I have my/our stuff all around me and I feel comfortable writing. Stacked and sprawled around me are piles of printed handouts, journal articles, handwritten and scribbled notes, dog-eared books, empty and half-finished tea in cups, stationery, and all manner of random stuff.

The bookshelf behind me houses novels, art books, family photos, overdue and partially completed tax returns, souvenirs, and boxes of still-to-be-sorted documents. All these materials hold memory, knowledge, agency, residue of being touched, and quite a bit of dust.

The most affecting object sits on my windowsill, a collection of feathers I've found during my early morning neighbourhood walks arranged in a tiny glass vase. I started this feather collecting habit since Adrian died, carrying on a tradition of his, to display them on the sill. Some of the birds represented in my current feather collection include magpie, tawny frogmouth, rosella and galah. When we visit his grave, I take along the collection, often with a few cut pieces of native grasses from our garden, or my favourite yellow paper daisies. I arrange them in a little posy and put them in the spot above the plaque where fresh flowers are meant to go.

I have developed a much more free-flowing process of writing since he died. I like to think this is because this desk and its surrounding atmosphere holds him and his memory in all the bits and pieces and objects surrounding me. But it also recalls his process of writing whilst sitting here – his version of a Pomodoro writing technique. He would place a stack of colourful Lego blocks on the windowsill that measured how many 25-minute writing block sessions he had completed. He would have two stacks, one for how many writing sessions he'd completed, and another for how many he had to go.

Anna, session 1

After our first experimental session, we swapped our writing, our thinking, and photographs of our spaces. This is something we had never done before. In keeping with the simple tenets of SUAW, we don't swap or critique work, and we try to be disciplined about periods of silent writing time. Anna prefers shorter blocks of 20 or so minutes, so it's especially important to stay present and focused. We had only caught glimpses of each other's worlds.

Anna's desk is so filled with stories and lives, it's almost overwhelming to read. It strikes me, reading her words, how much her writing space brings into mine when we shut up and write together. We share the knick-knacks and artefacts of unfinished life admin – the tax documents and dirty dishes and dusty shelves. We both have family things around us, behind us, permitted in frame of our webcams. But I hadn't known about Anna's feathers – about the tradition they extend or the journey they'll make.

> A glimpse like this into the writing space of an online SUAW partner gives me a new sense of where I am and where I've been each time we write together. This is a part of the atmosphere that surrounds me when our cameras go off. I don't spend much time imagining the spaces of my silent interlocutors. It only matters that they are there, and that we've made a promise to each other. But whether I know it or not, this is what the promise brings with it: a whole life, a personal world, a set of commitments extending far beyond me.
>
> Miriam, session 2

The Affective Atmospheres of SUAW Online

A SUAW session is a conscious act of contributing to a collective affect: an atmosphere. We choose a space, we come together, we commit to work, and then, in silence, we do it. Affective atmospheres, in Anderson's (2009) sense of the term, are singular things which arise out of a multiplicity of bodies (human and non-human) affecting one other. Atmospheres emanate from every time and space we inhabit: they are our 'ongoing sensory and affective engagement with our lives' (Sumartojo & Pink, 2018, p. 30). When we sit at home and write, atmosphere emanates from the assembled furniture, the clutter and desktop hardware, the sounds of traffic and birds, and our own bodies. But when, instead of travelling to an in-person SUAW session, we dial in via Zoom, that atmosphere becomes another body in the assemblage. So too does Zoom itself.

> When Miriam invited me to write about our SUAW online sessions, one of the first things I thought about was how I would be able to write about an imaginative game I play with myself. I decided to fess up and ask about the view that I had imagined she was looking out to.
>
> I asked her to send me photos of what she can see around her as she works. She sent me photos of a neat desk, with an empty cup, a few shots of the bookshelf I'd been trying to see in more detail, and a view of a window with a blind pulled down. In many ways, it was way more interesting to chat to her about life and imagine her world than trying to write to the photos she had sent me.
>
> Anna, session 3

This is a postdigital view, which acknowledges not only that digital technologies have become ubiquitous in our lives, but that their existence and functionings play undeniable roles in shaping those lives (Fawns et al., 2023). The postdigital is sociological, ontological, and political; it also urges awareness of the material properties of things we dismiss as 'virtual' (Knox, 2019). Hardware and software, like all other bodies, actively contribute to the production of affective atmospheres through their ability to perturb other physical objects and human behaviour (Ash, 2013).

During a SUAW online, Zoom is actively generating space and time through its involvement in the meeting. Zoom creates an envelope in which to locate the meeting (a 'Zoom room') which manifests temporally as a time-boxed meeting invitation and spatially as a window on a computer desktop. It is also itself enveloped in the spaces and times of each person who attends it. Each of us exists simultaneously in the Zoom room and in our own writing environment. Additional layers of spatio-temporality are added as the Zoom room envelops us in each other's worlds – for instance, different members of our group are in different Australian time zones, and so we are inhabiting Zoom time as well as each other's clocks and calendars.

> With SUAW online, there's every possibility you might switch off the input devices and go for a walk. Or, more realistically, answer your emails. Of course I have done this. Once during a longer 'write', I went out for milk. But although I couldn't hear or see my SUAW peers – although they, behind their black Zoom thumbnails and muted microphones, might have been doing the same – it wasn't the right thing to do, and I could feel it in the silent presence of the meeting window, which I returned to once the milk was in the fridge, to find out how the others' writing had gone.
>
> Miriam, session 3

A great deal of affective labour goes into meeting through Zoom – no wonder we complained during the pandemic of 'Zoom fatigue'. We feel those layers of atmosphere and the presence of the bodies from which they emanate. We feel them emotionally and ethically. To accommodate another person's spatio-temporalities is effortful, an act of generosity. So is sharing our own.

SUAW Online as a Postdigital Pedagogy of Care

The notion of a pedagogy of care emerged from Nel Noddings' (1984) framework of moral education. As a teaching philosophy, pedagogies of care centre the importance of caring, reciprocal relationships in learning contexts. This matters for doctoral candidates because although we occupy (many) learning contexts and are ourselves in the ongoing process of becoming educators, much of our learning is undertaken alone, during long hours of reading and database-wrangling.

While the importance of candidate–supervisor relationships cannot be understated, a good supervision team is simply not enough to support the winding, many-layered doctoral journey. Doing a doctorate, like any educational act, is a process of becoming (Irwin, 2017) whereby we are assembling objects, ideas, structures in dynamic waves of intensities to create new understandings (p. 199). It's not just academic skills we're developing, but an academic self, who for the time being must share a body with our already-formed adult self and assume the status of scholarly apprentice (Harrison &

Grant, 2015). Supervisor pedagogies vary widely; while some supervisors maintain strict emotional distance from their charges, many others (particularly women) provide considerable pastoral care (Guerin et al., 2015). This can itself be deeply unsustainable and carry risks of its own. It is essential for becoming-academics to build communities of support beyond the supervisory dyad.

To connect with becoming-academic peers through SUAW is a powerful way to build such a community. Moreover, to connect online enables us to address a great many of our needs together. Early career academics (ECAs) experience a range of negative affects associated with task overwhelm, time pressure, bureaucracy, and complexity of university systems (Willson & Given, 2020), and this is no different, in our experience, for doctoral candidates. As ECAs, we are undergoing profound transitions in our professional identities, and can gain feelings of belonging and stability through building relationships with peers where we are able to seek and share not only information and advice but also solidarity and support. Like many ECAs, we are time-poor and struggle to manage our competing needs for teaching, writing, information seeking, peer connection, and the endless minutiae of coordinating research. SUAW online enables us to be together, yet invisible and silent, allowing for periods of focus and periods of help-seeking.

> These online SUAW sessions are very nourishing for talking through our graduate research journey, the teaching and education-focused conversations we have, sharing journal articles and talking about academic language and culture, and all kinds of other personal and life admin topics. These are the details that nurture.
>
> Anna, session 3

We understand social space as both physical and relational. The distance between two points is a matter not of metres but of connections, of categories, of flows (Castells, 2020; Mol & Law, 1994). In SUAW online, we are proximate because we are co-connected (via a Zoom link), we are co-categorised (as graduate researchers), and we share a present flow (a shared orientation to shut up and write). Each time we dial in, we choose what to 'bring' to the collective. Conscious choices about what audiovisual settings are configured, what is visible onscreen, and what to say, all shape the space we share.

Although each of us is working on some separate aspect of our different doctoral projects, we all have something valuable to bring. Like members of any community of practice, newcomers are able to gain technical insight from the experience of others further into their candidature, and in time are able to put these insights to use and share their own (Lave & Wenger, 1991). But far more important are the affects we bring: shared frustrations and struggles, expressed admiration, questions acknowledging one other as knowledgeable becoming-academics.

Conclusions: On Caring in the Cloud

The notion of an online pedagogy of care was introduced at a timely moment during the stresses and struggles of emergency remote teaching during the COVID-19 pandemic (Burke & Larmar, 2021), and continues to have vital relevance across contexts of remote learning. Burke and Larmar (2021) drew on decades of experience teaching online to suggest that caring should be modelled, discussed, practiced, and reinforced in online learning contexts. We add to that the importance of a critical, postdigital view of the technological mediation of caring online. Online isn't just a place where we are, but a thing that shapes *what we can be to each other*.

We suggest that, through mindful engagement in activities like SUAW online, graduate researchers can develop both a postdigital awareness and a pedagogy of care to support one another through candidature and beyond.

References

Anderson, B. (2009). Affective atmospheres. *Emotion, Space and Society, 2*(2), 77–81. https://doi.org/10.1016/j.emospa.2009.08.005

Ash, J. (2013). Rethinking affective atmospheres: Technology, perturbation and space times of the non-human. *Geoforum, 49,* 20–28. https://doi.org/10.1016/j.geoforum.2013.05.006

Brownlow, C., Eacersall, D. C., Martin, N., & Parsons-Smith, R. (2023). The higher degree research student experience in Australian universities: A systematic literature review. *Higher Education Research & Development, 42*(7), 1608–1623. https://doi.org/10.1080/07294360.2023.2183939

Burke, K., & Larmar, S. (2021). Acknowledging another face in the virtual crowd: Reimagining the online experience in higher education through an online pedagogy of care. *Journal of Further and Higher Education, 45*(5), 601–615. https://doi.org/10.1080/0309877X.2020.1804536

Castells, M. (2020). Space of flows, space of places: Materials for a theory of urbanism in the information age. In *The City Reader* (7th ed., pp. 240–251). Routledge.

Fawns, T., Ross, J., Carbonel, H., Noteboom, J., Finnegan-Dehn, S., & Raver, M. (2023). Mapping and tracing the postdigital: Approaches and parameters of postdigital research. *Postdigital Science and Education, 5*(3), 623–642. https://doi.org/10.1007/s42438-023-00391-y

Guerin, C., Kerr, H., & Green, I. (2015). Supervision pedagogies: Narratives from the field. *Teaching in Higher Education, 20*(1), 107–118. https://doi.org/10.1080/13562517.2014.957271

Harrison, S., & Grant, C. (2015). Exploring of new models of research pedagogy: Time to let go of master-apprentice style supervision? *Teaching in Higher Education, 20*(5), 556–566. https://doi.org/10.1080/13562517.2015.1036732

Irwin, R. L. (2017). Becoming a/r/tography. In M. R. Carter & V. Triggs (Eds.), *Arts education and curriculum studies: The contributions of Rita L. Irwin* (pp. 193–210). Routledge, an imprint of the Taylor & Francis Group.

Knox, J. (2019). What does the 'postdigital' mean for education? Three critical perspectives on the digital, with implications for educational research and practice. *Postdigital Science and Education, 1*(2), 357–370. https://doi.org/10.1007/s42438-019-00045-y

Lave, J., & Wenger, E. (1991). *Situated learning: Legitimate peripheral participation* (1st ed.). Cambridge University Press. https://doi.org/10.1017/CBO9780511815355

Melián, E., & Meneses, J. (2024). Alone in the academic ultraperiphery: Online doctoral candidates' quest to belong, thrive, and succeed. *The International Review of Research in Open and Distributed Learning*, 25(2), 114–131. https://doi.org/10.19173/irrodl.v25i2.7702

Mol, A., & Law, J. (1994). Regions, networks and fluids: Anaemia and social topology. *Social Studies of Science*, 24(4), 641–671. https://doi.org/10.1177/030631279402400402

Noddings, N. (1984). *Caring: A Feminine Approach to Ethics and Moral Education*. University of California Press.

Sumartojo, S., & Pink, S. (2018). *Atmospheres and the experiential world: Theory and methods*. Routledge.

Willson, R., & Given, L. M. (2020). "I'm in sheer survival mode": Information behaviour and affective experiences of early career academics. *Library & Information Science Research*, 42(2), 101014. https://doi.org/10.1016/j.lisr.2020.101014

Part II
Doctoral and Graduate Student Experiences

5 Everyday Tales of an Online 'Shut Up & Write! (SU&W) PhD Research Community'

Margaret (Meg) Davis, Sandra Croaker, Natalie Lindsay, and Bronwyn Charles

Introduction

> I mostly want to remind her of the recipes of healing, and give her my own made-on-the-spot remedy for the easing of her pain. I tell her, "Get a pen. Stop crying so you can write this down and start working on it tonight."
>
> (hooks, 2015, pp. 113-114)

We are four white Australian women, descendants of different generations of settlers studying on the unceded lands of the Gurambilbarra people at James Cook University (JCU) of North Queensland. The evolution of our Shut Up & Write! group with feminist insights, influences our wellbeing and persistence with graduate research studies. The diversity of our life experiences and our challenges as women PhD students include juggling employment, relationships, caring of children at different developmental stages, negotiating school holidays, messy homes, menopause, aging, and caring for friends and extended family. Our shared professional social work career experiences include academia, government and community service delivery, management, and private practice. One member has completed her study. Three are close to completion. Our ages range from the 40s to the 70s. Our lifestyles diverge through active parenting, grand parenting, dual and single independent family households, and hours of paid work. All members engage as local advocates for human rights and women's needs that are influenced by global political, environmental, and economic influences. We volunteer with service agencies and serve on boards of governance of community services. Our individual research studies reflect our personal and professional social work practice, including topics such as deaths in hospital emergency departments, mothering experiences of parenting anxious children, social work education that responds to the effects of climate change on communities, and the resettlement experiences of former refugee women in North Queensland. The group is not closed. We welcome other women according to their individual schedules.

52 *Fostering Wellbeing through Collective Writing Practices*

Figure 5.1 Early days of SU&W, Kuranda North Queensland: October 2021. (Left to Right: Sandra, Natalie, Bronwyn, Margaret (Meg).)

Group Evolution

> Just as women know in many different ways, we must be known in many different ways.
>
> (Reinharz, 1992, p. 106)

Dealing with our fears of failure, family expectations, and academic challenges, we regularly grapple with symptoms of the ever-resurfacing imposter syndrome (Patzak et al., 2017). The isolating nature of undertaking a postgraduate research degree can be particularly challenging for women. Institutional supports, mental health resources, and interventions such as online writing groups can improve students' mindset and self-efficacy (Nori and Vanttaja, 2023; Craddock et al., 2011). Postgraduate researchers are encouraged through the JCU's Graduate Research School to host online student writing groups. A Social Work Departmental staff member of JCU, who reflected on the transformative influence of feminism in personal and social work roles, co-ordinated an online network of social work postgraduate research students across the two university campuses of Cairns and Townsville (Carrington, 2016). Notably, only female students responded and met through a conference hosted by the University College of Arts Society and Education in Cairns and a writing retreat supported by the university. Drawing on the energy of like-minded people to share wins and to support each other through self-doubt, guilt, and the labour of navigating studies, negotiating relationships and caring responsibilities, we decided to form an online Shut Up & Write! group. The Pomodoro technique, which promotes the value of 25 minutes of writing with 5-minute breaks, was agreed on as an appropriate method (Cirillo, n.d.). Bronwyn nominated a set time and offered to host a Zoom room. The information was shared amongst social work Higher Degree Research (HDR) students and their supervisors. As trust and enthusiasm of group members accelerated, Bronwyn's Zoom room was available 24 hours a day, 7 days a week.

Bronwyn's recollections of the evolution of the group speak to an organic process:

> Although we four are the core members, Fridays are a popular day when other JCU women from across Australia are available to join us. I recall the energy and focus of an emergency department nurse from remote Northern Territory as she completed her Masters of Philosophy study of the Remote Area Safety Project (Wright, 2021). Laura was very studious and consistent. Whenever I needed a buddy student, I would join the Zoom room and find Laura there! We shared the excitement of her success and her interview with a renowned Australian journalist on national radio. Once Laura left, we found ourselves to have a little less structure. At times we would be consistent. At other times we would drop away, appreciating the flexibility to join when it suited our individual living circumstances.

Mutual support in the early phases of the group motivated us to arrange other writing retreats, aided by local members providing accommodation and hospitality for those outside of Townsville.

Feminist Influences

Feminist writer Denise Thompson posits that the primary influence on women's lives is patriarchy, whereby women are consigned to a lesser status by men (affected also by race and class oppression) engaging in power struggles (2001). Through reflection and discussion, we recognised that feminism underscores the organic processes and support as they evolved in the Shut Up & Write! group. Rowland and Klein (1996) argued that radical feminists get to the "root" of concerns to ensure that "women's experiences and interests are at the centre of our theory and practice" (p. 10). For women in academia, the principle offers strength, insight, and guidance in a domain where men have traditionally dominated. We consider the group's organic nature and level of support throughout our PhD studies, as a feminist and a political action (Thompson, 2001). Just as radical feminists challenge the structure and systems that protect male supremacy and power across society's structures and systems, feminism stakes out our rights to the academy (De Beauvoir, 1989; Firestone, 1970; MacKinnon, 1989; McLellan, 2010). Global structures of power that protect the beliefs and advantages of men at every turn, do so at the expense of women's agency, health, and safety (De Beauvoir, 1989; Firestone, 1970; MacKinnon, 1989; McLellan, 2010).

Linda Smith (2021) pointed out that "Theory enables us to deal with contradictions and uncertainties. Perhaps more significantly, it gives us space to plan, to strategize, to take greater control over our resistances" (p. 42). Sharing the academic space with other women in a collaborative and supportive way stands against the internal voice that would have us believe our peers are our competitors and that says to all of us at one time or another that we don't belong. Shared values of feminism and rights-based Social Work practice underscore our online 'Shut Up & Write!' sessions. The critical lens of radical feminism and our research topics that centre human rights and critical social work have facilitated insight and caring to our Shut up & Write! session, offering relief from life's demands and motivation to shut up, focus, and write! The feminist functioning of the group has strengthened individual motivation and resilience of the skills required for research studies.

Group Benefits

Our group demonstrates passion and mutual support for "women's commonalities and women's distinctive ways of being for each other" (Raymond, 2001, p. 38). Our sessions provide focused time to support our research experiences and support each other holistically as we write, listen, counsel, and give and receive feedback. We are flexible and inclusive in how we structure our time online. We come together as our whole selves, providing a rich range of experiences from which to draw inspiration and encouragement. Our group demonstrates an understanding of each other's individual caring responsibilities for family or friends. When online, laughter and groans of frustration interweave through individuals' task focus and discussions. Breaks may feature musical favourites, the sharing of anecdotes of our lives, exercises to relieve muscles and to stimulate our brains, and discussions. Sometimes, individuals bounce ideas off others. We offer support to anyone experiencing frustration and a mind block on a section of her writing.

The informality and flexibility of the online space complements the ebb and flow of women's lives, understanding the challenges of getting to, and staying at, the desk to write. An informal text invite to study by one member to others, outside of agreed regular times, is a powerful motivator to a member who may be procrastinating. The flexible ease of access enhances online connection and an open, supportive atmosphere. Thus, one woman can text specific members or all group members, announcing her intent to study. Sandra reflects on the motivating 'pull effect' of the informal process:

> My phone makes a noise. I ignore it. It makes a noise again. I look. A message from Bronwyn. 'Hi Hon, we are on zoom. Are you coming in?' I struggle with myself. I just want to be left alone, no talking, no thinking, no writing. Don't they know I have to do more important things

today? Clean up the breakfast mess, respond to work emails, write that overdue evaluation. I pause in my rant. Your PhD work is important too, I hear my supervisors' voices: 'You need to set that work as your priority, or else it will get swallowed up by everything else'. They are correct, but why do I find it then so difficult to set my PhD as my priority? Why does everything else come first? I know why. I just can't muster the energy to fight against the establishment today or quieten my inner critic. Or can I? I need to get back to Bron, I don't want to be rude to her just because I am angry with myself and the world.

I open my laptop, making sure my camera does not go below my chest line and my background is blurred to cover the mess behind me. I see Bronwyn's and Meg's faces on the screen, both busy doing something. Meg quickly sends a chat message when she sees me coming in. 'Hi Sandra, we have a break in 5min'. I smile and wave to the camera. I somehow feel encouraged by their deep focus on whatever they are doing. I open my data file, get myself a cuppa and wait for the 5 minutes to pass. I am looking forward to chatting with them. By midday, I have accomplished some solid writing. I had a good laugh with Bronwyn and Meg. I feel still exhausted, but it's different to this morning. I have achieved something for myself. I am feeling okay. I know I can do this, one persistent step after another on this journey we are walking together.

Similarly, Natalie shared her experience of receiving a spontaneous text:

Okay, children at school, I'm showered, suitably dressed, with coffee at hand ready to sit down and log on to my computer and the SU&W zoom. Feeling exhausted from just getting to this point of the morning I wonder if I should just go it alone as really, what have I got to contribute to the group anyway? But I haven't been on in a while and it's a morning when I have no other commitments happening, which seem to be always scheduled for the morning. By the time they're done it's almost school pick up time.

I open my laptop. Damn! It's not charging. It's okay I'll use my partner's laptop that now lives on my desk. I plug my headset in. Nope. It doesn't want to work with his computer. Right. I love technology I say like a mantra to myself. I quickly go hang the load of washing out that I put on earlier. I take some deep breaths and do a bit of self-talk to remind myself that people are there waiting. Waiting to support and encourage me.

I sign in to the Shut Up & Write! link on my phone and breathe a sigh of relief when I see the smiling faces welcome me to the session. After a quick catch up it's time to get to work. Yes! It's easier to keep on track and have less of a wandering mind when I can see others diligently working. I really do need to get on here more often than I do.

Knowing that someone is online has acted as a motivator to each of us at our various study low points. The passion for women friends kicks in and contributes to a zealous approach for others, above self (Raymond, 2001). Dorothy Smith (1999) addressed the difficulties of writing "that speaks in and of the world as it is in women's, in people's, actual experience" (p. 25). She suggested that women's knowledge making be inclusive of the power dynamics (macro and micro) that affects the standpoint of women's "everyday/every night knowledge" (1999, p. 68). Smith's thesis emphasised that our intellectual and research experiences do not exist in a social vacuum. Thus, within the community of this group, we have moved through the initial experience of feeling invisible and inept in academia. The group acceptance and dynamics of support make us visible and feel stronger and capable of knowledge production. We have supported each other at candidature milestones and have delivered a joint presentation sharing our experience at two conferences.

Meg writes:

> Squeezing in a PhD requires giving and receiving kindness with companion students. Being understanding of each other's caring roles is encouraging. As someone who has procrastination down to a fine art, when I know that others are online 'doing' it helps me to prioritise the PhD and feel motivated. And it's worth it! The companionship across a diverse group of clever, witty and dedicated women through the lens of a range of disciplines and research inspires me. The discussions range from parenting, household, garden and camping trips through to academic discussions of theory and methodology.
>
> Encouragement and motivation flow as each member embraces different stages of the PhD. Flexibility influences a bonus of mutual support at any time, including weekends or evenings when we can 'grab a moment'. Respecting an individual's conflicting roles and demands is paramount... there is no pressure to join or to stay on for the whole time. Indeed, there have been occasions when I have chosen not to join in...simply due to being 'on a roll' with a particular task or choosing the pull of solitude and quiet contemplation...OR being aware that I may be a distraction to others. We sometimes make each other accountable to a deadline either by direct request to one another online or by individual email. We celebrate each other's milestones and take heart to face our next hurdle. We support each other to attain the rigour of research that reflects the power, ingenuity, insights and collective strengths that women bring to research.

Conclusions

Grounded in feminist theory, the women in this Shut Up & Write! group have crafted an online postgraduate study group that supports women's wellbeing and their valuable contribution to academia. A network of social workers has generated an open group atmosphere that is readily accessible and empathetic to women's navigation of competing demands and responsibilities. The online Shut Up & Write! group benefits from flexible availability, core elements of respect, and a passionate awareness of our strengths and belief in the importance of the knowledge we strive to produce.

Bronwyn's recollection reflects the sentiment of the four of us:

> I have created life-long friendships and support through this regular contact. I am not sure how I would have continued on with my studies without the support of my Shut Up & Write! friends.

References

Carrington, A. (2016). Feminism under siege: Critical reflections on the impact of neoliberalism. In B. Pease, S. Goldengay, N. Hosken, & S. Nipperess (Eds.), *Doing critical social work: Transformative practices for social justice* (pp. 226–240). Allen & Unwin.

Cirillo, F. (n.d.) The Pomodoro Technique https://francescocirillo.com/pages/francesco-cirillo

Craddock, S., Birnbaum, M., Rodriguez, K.L., Cobb, C., & Zeeh, S.P. (2011). Doctoral students and the impostor phenomenon: Am I smart enough to be here? *Journal of Student Affairs Research and Practice*, 48, 429–442.

De Beauvoir, S. (1989). *Le deuxième sexe*. Vintage.

Firestone, S. (1970). *The dialectic of sex: The case for feminist revolution*. Bantam Books.

hooks, b. (2015). *Sisters of the yam: Black women and self-recovery* (3rd ed.). Routledge.

MacKinnon, C.A. (1989). *Toward a feminist theory of the state*. Harvard University Press.

McLellan, B. (2010). *Unspeakable: A feminist ethic of speech*. Otherwise Publications.

Nori, H. & Vanttaja, M. (2023) Too stupid for PhD? Doctoral impostor syndrome among Finnish PhD students. *Higher Education* 86: 675–691 https://doi.org/10.1007/s10734-022-00921-w

Patzak, A., Kollmayer, M., & Schober, B. (2017). Buffering impostor feelings with kindness: The mediating role of self-compassion between gender-role orientation and the impostor phenomenon. *Frontiers in Psychology*, 8.

Raymond, J.G. (2001). *A passion for friends: Toward a philosophy of female affection*. Spinifex.

Reinharz, S. (1992). *Feminist methods in social research*. Oxford University Press.

Rowland, R., & Klein, R. (1996). Radical feminism: History, politics, action. In D. Bell & D. R. Klein (Eds.), *Radically speaking: Feminism reclaimed* (pp. 9–36). Spinifex Press.

Smith, D.E. (1999). *Writing the social: Critique, theory and investigations*. University of Toronto Press.

Smith, L.T. (2021). *Decolonizing methodologies: Research and Indigenous peoples*. Bloomsbury Publishing.

Thompson, D. (2001). *Radical feminism today*. SAGE Publications.

Wright, Laura (2021) *The remote area safety project (RASP): Analysing workplace health and safety for remote area nurses in Australia*. Masters (Research) thesis, James Cook University. ResearchOnline@JCU.

6 From Procrastination to Productivity

Developing Collegial Interconnectedness through Belonging, Being and Becoming

Jacqui Peters, Rachel Finneran, Pennie White, and Katrina MacDonald

Being, Belonging, and Becoming Together in the Academy

Like many academics, the authors have engaged in numerous Shut up and Write! (SUAW) sessions. We often turn up to SUAWs with many administrative tasks more pressing than the intended writing priorities. So why has this SUAW series, established and co-led by early career researchers (ECRs), been so successful? Why do we look forward to these weekly sessions more than others? How has this group helped us progress towards the completion of a paper or chapter that we might have given up on? How has this group enabled us to ameliorate the isolation so often felt in academia?

Through this chapter, we share our experiences navigating the liminal space of becoming academics and writers, in embracing a collective enduring SUAW that has led to productive and measurable outcomes and developed trusting collegial friendships and supported our wellbeing. We use the work of Lave and Wenger (1991), alongside the Early Years Learning Framework (EYLF) for Australia (DET, 2009), which help us unpack this phenomenon in terms of belonging, being, and becoming. The EYLF outlines a holistic framework for learning and development, expressing the importance of connection, learning in the present moment, alongside the development of identity. Using co-authored autoethnography, we reflect through text and creative media on our SUAW experiences as being interdependent rather than solo; of sharing the highs, lows, and complexities of the writing process safely and with joy, contributing to our wellbeing; and of our individual growth as writers and colleagues amongst the many pressures that exist in the neoliberal university environment (e.g., Burton & Bowman, 2022). Cutting through the noise and spending time immersed in writing individually with collegial interconnectedness has carved a space to acknowledge and embrace our writer identities. We share these experiences as a means of expounding the value of this SUAW to belonging, being and becoming.

Context

Knowledge work in the modern university is complex, influenced by marketisation, competition, and new managerialism (Connell, 2019; Smyth, 2017). Professional autonomy and collaborative intellectual relationships shape professional identity, growth, and productive work in this space (MacDonald et al., 2022). ECRs are novices in navigating the structures, operations, and expectations of their workplaces and the transition from 'apprentice' to independence occurs during a time of vulnerability (McAlpine et al., 2018), requiring support for developing academic identity through socialisation and acculturation (Willson & Given, 2020). The professional growth for ECRs during this transition can be thought of as being "stirred into" academic practices and "learning how to go on" in these (Kemmis, et al., 2014, pp. 58–60). Mahon et al. (2019) argue that often this learning is informal and enabled by enough time and space for: creativity; participating in critical dialogue and engaging reflexively in conversations; flexibility and autonomy; developing relationships that are positive, productive, and build trust; and immersion in higher education community scholarly activities. While formal learning such as through mentoring is important, these informal networks are critical in developing ECRs' sense of agency and success (Matthews et al., 2014; McAlpine et al., 2018), and supporting their wellbeing.

SUAW sessions are an effective informal learning approach to support academic writing. These sessions transform writing from a solitary practice into a social one by bringing researchers together in a shared space to write simultaneously (Mewburn et al., 2014). The writing sessions are broken up by short social breaks to discuss progress, making SUAW opportunities for building writing skills, self-efficacy, self-regulation, and productivity (Mayowski et al., 2023). SUAW sessions are valuable when there is a lack of institutional support in fostering a sense of community and are a sustainable way to develop scholarly identity and collegiality (Fegan, 2016; Mewburn et al., 2014).

Situated Learning Fostering Belonging, Being, Becoming

The themes of belonging, being, and becoming in the Australian EYLF (DET, 2009) are relevant to lifelong learning (Formenti & West, 2018). These themes embrace the formal and informal connections with others and their interplay with identity development. A premise at the heart of lifelong learning is the social nature of learning with others in context. This resonates with the notion of situated learning theorised by Lave and Wenger (1991). A juxtaposition of the themes of the EYLF, along with theorisations from situated learning (as per White, 2022), provides a rich theoretical framework for understanding the way academics connect, learn together, and develop their identity over the trajectory of their academic life. This is useful in understanding the voluntary, informal learning of our sustained SUAW group.

Autoethnography – Permission to Share Our Practice

In deciding how to share this phenomenon, we settled on a co-authored autoethnography that permitted us to document our experiences in the SUAW as worthy of examining (Edwards, 2021) and aligned well with the notion of a community of practice (Wenger, 1998). Personal vignettes seemed an ideal means of reflexively and explicitly interrogating our experiences (Humphreys, 2005) and distilling them into a short, but coherent summary of our SUAW sessions. We wrote independently, reading each other's vignettes in a Zoom meeting, immediately prior to developing our collegial artwork. The intention was to use the reveal of the vignettes to 'move' us artistically. We now share the vignettes that demonstrate the early stages of the reflexive process.

Sharing our stories

Vignette 1 (V1): I was appointed just as Covid hit, so missed forming connections at a crucial time for an ECR. Our ECR network gave me the opportunity to connect with colleagues at a similar career stage, becoming a core group of four participating in SUAW sessions. These sessions have allowed me to carve out space in my week to work towards performative expectations of my role, such as publications. Our diverse research interests and discussions have fuelled shifts in my thinking, but more than anything, this group has given me a place to belong: a joyful place in what can sometimes be a frustrating, infuriating, and care-less institution; a place to ask questions about aspects of academic work that are mystifying and opaque; a place to celebrate small (and big) wins and milestones with each other; a source of support, care, and affection; a place to rehearse and discuss big ideas – to be a critical friend. These relationships give meaning to my work and provide critical support to my wellbeing and development of my academic identity.

Vignette 2 (V2): Being an ECR has been a journey saddled with imposter syndrome. However, joining this ECR SUAW soon revealed that I didn't need to be anything but me in that space, and these people were ECRs with similar stories, trying to find ourselves as academics and writers amongst workload models, teaching, research, and service. From this network emerged a small, lingering group who hung tight to the SUAW timeslots, turning up regularly, listening to each other share their writing, their snags, their personal ups and downs and, most importantly, their achievements. We problem-solved for each other, getting our heads inside other's papers and chapters. I looked forward to this virtual time and place, where I knew I would not be judged, where the imposter syndrome quickly dissipated, and where I found my tribe. I have other tribes, but this one is special. The isolation of writing has given way to a regular one or two hours of joyful productivity, sandwiched by sharing and caring to start and finish, which has been critical to maintaining this practice weekly for over 12 months.

Vignette 3 (V3): For me, maintaining regular writing momentum and feeling part of a workplace community can be challenging. The SUAW sessions have provided me with a consistent structure and a sense of belonging within a community of ECRs. These weekly meetings are invaluable, as they ensure I carve out time to focus on preparing manuscripts from my PhD for publication, a task that might otherwise take a back seat to more immediate work-related demands. The network fostered through these sessions has led to supportive discussions and sharing advice on the challenges and successes we all face at one time or another along the writing journey. I keep attending the SUAW sessions as working within those timeslots has created a safe and supportive space in which we can all be accountable for achieving our goals individually and collectively. This consistent support is integral to my progress, not only for the immediate task of manuscript writing but also in building long-term habits for productive, reflective scholarly work.

Vignette 4 (V4): I quickly became one of the mainstays of the inner circle of the SUAW group. Recently, the term 'awesome foursome' was bantered about. I feel I belong in the SUAW group and look forward to coming because of the connections with others that have been fostered over time. I feel safe to be my most vulnerable self. I appreciate the sharing and support between insiders to navigate academic life. I like to admire, encourage, and celebrate the success of my 'colleague friends'. This is not a term I attribute to everyone I work with. It takes time to become colleague friends. I enjoy my engagement in the group as our relationships have deepened over time and we are able to appreciate insider shared humour off the back of the challenges we face. It is the relationships and connections that are formed through the regular engagement that are the real drivers for me.

Inserting our vignettes into a word cloud generator, we used the output as inspiration for our shared artwork. Collaborative artmaking is a valid and useful form of autoethnography (Hannigan et al., 2023). As is a familiar practice in our SUAW sessions, we shared, bounced off each other, and made mistakes, nourished by the well-understood-but-never-actually-spoken 'no judgement' rules that have been a large part of the success of our SUAW group.

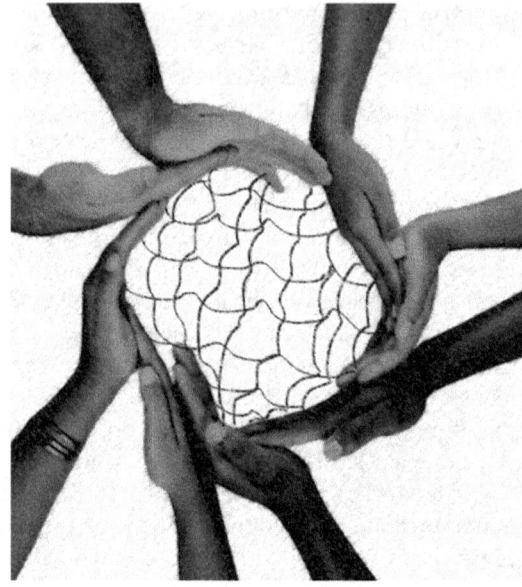

Figure 6.1 Being, belonging, and becoming. (Adapted from Accurs, n.d.)

Eventually narrowing down a means that worked for all of us, together-but-apart, we brought to the shared screen free digital images that most resonated with us when reflecting on our experiences as ECRs in SUAW. We collectively chose an image of hands in a circle (Accurs, n.d.), which resoundingly represented the way our togetherness supported our wellbeing. Using the collaborative platform Miro, we adapted the work to symbolise our shared experiences as academics, writers and colleague-friends.

Feeling the Tensions

The vignettes offered a small insight into our personal narratives working in the liminal space of ECR, and the tensions that exist in developing a professional identity in a neoliberal university. The image above further illustrated our feelings that this shared commitment to writing has been transformational. Combined, we expressed the joy, compassion, care, safety, collegiality, and significance of others in this endeavour. As a way of understanding our vignettes and further exemplifying the work of the SUAWs, we lean on the EYLF (DET, 2009) and Lave and Wenger (1991).

Belonging

A strong sense of belonging has resonated for us all from this experience. The vignettes speak of the interdependence developed between members. This is consistent with DET's (2009) definition of belonging, which alludes to relationships being central to defining one's identity. Our collective wellbeing was fostered through "forming connections", "a place to belong", "a source of support, care, and affection" (V1); and "a sense of belonging within a community of ECRs" (V3) to "admire, encourage, and celebrate the success of my colleague friends" (V4). This reinforces the importance of feeling safe and welcome, and creating space to do important identity (and writing) work. Belonging enables sharing, learning and risk-taking – each of which characterises legitimate participation (Lave & Wenger, 1991). With the safety net of feeling a legitimate participant, we described the space as "a place to ask questions", "to rehearse and discuss big ideas" (V1); where "imposter syndrome quickly dissipated, and where I found my tribe" (V2); but also where we "shared advice on the challenges and successes" (V3) and "insider shared humour" (V4). What this meant for us is reflected in the artwork – hands together (albeit in a virtual space), forming a safety net of sorts, connected, and feeling positive sentiments that helped to balance the performative discourse outside the space.

Being

As ECRs developing our academic identity, our SUAW group created a supportive place where we could be ourselves in all our vulnerability. This is emphasised, for example, where we noted, "that I didn't need to be anything but me" (V2) and "I feel safe to be my most vulnerable self" (V4). These feelings are exemplified in our artwork where the diverse hands come together, and, without judgment (V2), and as "colleague friends" (V4), form a safe space to be who we are. Further, our regular SUAW space gave us a "joyful place" in which to forge caring and supportive relationships (V1) and a "consistent structure" (V3) to collaboratively work through challenges in our writing, teaching, and research. In our artwork, this is represented in the hands working alongside each other, together. The notion of *being*, of coming to know ourselves, is illustrated in the vignette snippets, being in the present and "building and maintaining relationships with others, engaging with life's joys and complexities, and meeting challenges in everyday life" (DET, 2009, p. 7). Through inhabiting our SUAW space, we created a "space which has meaning for its users" (Temple 2018, p. 136), giving us "an opening, a way of gaining access to sources for understanding through growing involvement" (Lave & Wenger, 1991, p. 37).

Becoming

In working side-by-side and learning in this social context, we experienced the development and shaping of our personal identities and professional practices (Lave & Wenger, 1991) through shared aspirations around achievement in publishing and academic life. Our publishing progress was developed by "a regular one or two hours of joyful productivity, sandwiched by sharing and caring to start and finish" (V2) and this supported "working towards performative expectations of my role, such as publications" (V1). The impact of SUAW was evident in consideration of present and future benefits: "This consistent support is integral to my progress, not only for the immediate task of manuscript writing but also in building long-term habits for productive, reflective scholarly work" (V3) and "I appreciate the sharing and support between insiders to navigate academic life" (V4). The vignette snippets represent the notion of becoming; "this process of rapid and significant change that occurs...learning to participate fully and actively..." (DET, 2009, p. 7) around our shared aspirations and increased confidence around publishing that became more secure as a part of our academic identity.

Conclusion

Our SUAW sessions on Zoom brought geographically dispersed academics together and, over time, transformed from simply a space for writing into an important place of being, belonging, and becoming for us as ECRs. We each pursued our own writing journeys in these sessions, while offering and receiving support from each other in ways that supported our wellbeing. This chapter represents a special milestone in that journey; the transition from writing alongside each other to writing together as a collective. It is a testament to the transformative power of SUAW sessions in fostering individual and collaborative growth in tertiary settings.

References

Accurs, Y. (n.d.) Diversity teamwork and creative hands in synergy of employee workers together in collaboration [Photograph] *Freepik*. https://www.freepik.com/premium-photo/diversity-teamwork-creative-hands-synergy-employee-workers-together-collaboration-work-table-group-people-hand-circle-unity-agreement-help-team-community_35889353.htm

Burton, S., & Bowman, B. (2022). The academic precariat: understanding life and labour in the neoliberal academy. *British Journal of Sociology of Education, 43*(4), 497–512. https://doi.org/10.1080/01425692.2022.2076387

Connell, R. (2019). *The good university: What universities actually do and why it's time for radical change*. Zed Books Ltd.

DET (Department of Education and Training). (2009). *Belonging, being & becoming: The early years learning framework for Australia*. https://www.acecqa.gov.au/sites/default/files/2018-02/belonging_being_and_becoming_the_early_years_learning_framework_for_australia.pdf

Edwards, J. (2021). Ethical autoethnography: Is it possible? *International Journal of Qualitative Methods, 20*. https://doi.org/10.1177/1609406921995306

Fegan, S. (2016). When shutting up brings us together: Several affordances of a scholarly writing group. *Journal of Academic Language and Learning, 10*(2), A20–A31. https://journal.aall.org.au/index.php/jall/article/view/404

Formenti, L., & West, L. (2018). *Transforming perspectives in lifelong learning and adult education: A dialogue*. Springer. https://doi.org/10.1007/978-3-319-96388-4

Hannigan, S., Raphael, J., & White, P. (2023). Evolving teacher education practice through collaborative arts-based autoethnography. In E. Anteliz, D.L. Mulligan, &

P.A. Danaher (pp. 48–61), *Routledge international handbook of autoethnography in educational research*. Taylor & Francis.

Humphreys, M. (2005). Getting personal: Reflexivity and autoethnographic vignettes. *Qualitative Inquiry*, 11(6), 840–860. https://doi.org/10.1177/1077800404269425

Kemmis, S., Wilkinson, J., Edwards-Groves, C., Hardy, I., Grootenboer, P., & Bristol, L. (2014). *Changing practices, changing education*. Springer.

Lave, J., & Wenger, E. (1991). *Situated learning: Legitimate peripheral participation*. Cambridge University Press.

MacDonald, K., Diamond, F., Wilkinson, J., Sum, N., Longmuir, F., & Kaukko, M. (2022). Creating spaces of learning in academia: Fostering niches for professional learning practice. *Studies in Continuing Education*, 44(2), 266–283. https://doi.org/10.1080/0158037X.2021.1956890

Mahon, K., Heikkinen, H., & Huttunen, R. (2019). Critical educational praxis in university ecosystems: Enablers and constraints. *Pedagogy, Culture and Society*, 27(3), 463–480. https://doi.org/10.1080/14681366.2018.1522663

Matthews, K. E., Lodge, J. M., & Bosanquet, A. (2014). Early career academic perceptions, attitudes and professional development activities: Questioning the teaching and research gap to further academic development. *International Journal for Academic Development*, 19(2), 112–124. https://doi.org/10.1080/1360144X.2012.724421

Mayowski, C. A., Proulx, C. N., & Rubio, D. M. (2023). 113 Shut Up & Write! builds writing self-efficacy and self-regulation in early-career researchers. *Journal of Clinical and Translational Science*, 7(1), 33. https://doi.org/10.1017/cts.2023.196

McAlpine, L., Pyhältö, K., & Castelló, M. (2018). Building a more robust conception of early career researcher experience: What might we be overlooking? *Studies in Continuing Education*, 40(2), 149–165. https://doi.org/10.1080/0158037X.2017.1408582

Mewburn, I., Osborne, L., & Caldwell, G. (2014). Shut Up & Write! Some surprising uses of cafés and crowds in doctoral writing. In *Writing groups for doctoral education and beyond* (pp. 218–232). Routledge.

Smyth, J. (2017). *The toxic university: Zombie leadership, Academic Rock Stars and Neoliberal Ideology*. Springer.

Temple, P. (2018). Space, place and institutional effectiveness in higher education. *Policy Reviews in Higher Education*, 2(2), 133–150. https://doi.org/10.1080/23322969.2018.1442243

Wenger, E. (1998). *Communities of practice: Learning, meaning and identity*. Cambridge University Press.

White, P. (2022). Reflections on developing academic identity during the pandemic. In B. Cahusac De Caux, L. Pretorius, & L. Macaulay (Eds.), *Research and teaching in a pandemic world* (pp. 527–544). Springer Nature. https://doi.org/10.1007/978-981-19-7757-2_35

Willson, R., & Given, L.M. (2020). "I'm in sheer survival mode": Information behaviour and affective experiences of early career academics. *Library & Information Science Research*, 42(2), 1–8.

7 And See What Comes to You in the Silence

Reflecting on the Restorative Potential of "Shut Up and Write!"

Haidee Hicks

Introduction

> Do not be afraid to disappear. From it, from us, for a while. And see what comes to you in the silence.
>
> (Michaela Coel, 2021)

In this chapter, I present a series of personal narratives where I reflect on my experience of "Shut Up and Write!" (SUAW) and the ways in which it has offered a uniquely restorative space across the different domains of my academic life. The catalyst for this reflection is a quote from Michaela Coel in her 2021 Emmy Award acceptance speech where she invites writers to consider the possibilities of silence, silent writing, and its creative potential. I remember the moment I heard this quote – it caught my breath and affected me on a deep, visceral level. This chapter therefore responds to Coel's invitation and I consider the ways in which silent writing practices have enriched and sustained my academic life and that of those around me. I begin to consider this in relation to writing and the connections that form when we write together in silence. In his poem "Ash Wednesday", T.S. Eliot (1963) describes being "enfolded in silence" (p. 102), which is an apt description of the silence that is at the heart of SUAW practices. It is this intersection of silence, wellbeing, and restorative practices that is the starting point for my narrative. In these narratives, I am exploring academic wellbeing through a restorative lens, where SUAW is impactful across social, emotional, and psychological dimensions of wellness.

The three short narratives in this chapter rest on the idea that SUAW offers a restorative space that enhances its value beyond productivity metrics. This perspective challenges us to think about how this writing practice may sustain the writer and has us thinking more holistically about academic wellbeing. Silent writing practices offer us the opportunity to slow down, to pause, to intentionally turn inwards in the creative process. In working actively with silence, we are open to its possibilities. We are more able to respond to new insights that come forward. Anderson (2023) poses questions about the importance of silence:

DOI: 10.4324/9781003633327-9

But why is it that we crave silence? Or what is it in us that needs silence? Silence certainly enhances our powers of attention, and it is a break and rest from the stimuli of the external world…By learning to appreciate silence and its benefits, one also learns to truly listen. (p. 11)

In this chapter, I propose that SUAW is more than just learning to 'shut up'; rather it is an active space of silent creativity and an embodied practice that nurtures the writer through the sitting and listening, and a deeper engagement with a creative process. The silence of SUAW has always provided me with a space for intentional listening: to my own thoughts, the ideas that come forward, and the emotions that accompany the writing process and often inform it.

Beyond the value of silent writing as an individual self-care strategy for writers, I remain intrigued by the paradoxical notion of 'silent collegiality' as a restorative practice. While SUAW practices help us to resist noisy, distracting, and frenetic academic contexts, it is equally valuable in creating a space for solidarity *and* calm. In their research, Su et al. (2022) explore the "possibilities for academics to find silence, quietude, and respite from the 'hurley-burley', allowing them to 'stand back' from this for a time" (p. 277). I have continued to reflect on the inherent paradox of SUAW – creating community, solidarity, and a wellbeing space *in silence*. Our personal challenges are somehow less potent when shared with our fellow writers, who are undoubtedly experiencing similar dilemmas with their own writing.

Restorative Silence for the Writer

During my PhD, being part of a SUAW community anchored my writing practice. Every Saturday I would "disappear" and attend the writing group: a temporary reprieve from my personal responsibilities. Soon after arriving, I began my writing rituals – lining up my flasks of tea and untangling laptop cords while attempting to arrange the scribbled notes that hinted at possible directions for my writing that day. I started to move into silence, anticipating that the words would flow, and that the ideas would arrive. The predictability and rhythm of this routine seemed to work. The familiar, rhythmic, pomodoro structure was almost soothing. Writing for ten Pomodoros (pomodori) gave me hope that my research would progress. And it did. This space offered reassurance: week after week. Looking back, I suspect that it enhanced both my writing and my wellbeing much more than I realised at the time.

Doctoral writing groups have attracted attention in empirical research in recent years, including the ways in which these groups become spaces of wellbeing (Beasy et al., 2020; Cannell et al., 2023). Despite this, concerns about doctoral students' mental health and wellbeing persist and are well documented in the higher education literature (Butler-Rees & Robinson, 2020; Casey et al., 2023). While institutional priorities focus on candidates' timely completion of key milestones and submission dates, writing collectives such as SUAW have not been fully examined in relation to their impact on doctoral student wellbeing

Figure 7.1 "Disappearing" every Saturday to attend the SUAW group. Image includes ten Pomodoro timers, each set to 25 minutes.

and self-care. In my experience, writing groups have provided heartfelt offerings of encouragement as well as the quiet solidarity of silence. Beyond writing companionship, these relationships continued to restore my energy and optimism, and enriched my wellbeing. I am therefore curious to know how the SUAW experience might enrich diverse academic communities while revealing the value and potential of silent writing practices.

Restorative Silence in Writing Retreats

> Our academic writing retreats have offered a new space for quiet collegiality, providing a space where we can write together, create, and listen to what is being elevated in the silence. In the first retreat we found ourselves talking about our writing and our "writerly" identities and the challenges we encounter in the academic writing process. It was also a space for self-compassion where we could be kind to ourselves and our writing. Undoubtedly, the retreat marked a space for collegial solidarity. Working in a companionable silence, we had a moment to breathe and to think. One colleague provided feedback that the retreat "held the space", describing acts of care and collegiality that were important to them throughout the retreat.

There is an emerging interest in the higher education literature in relation to academic wellbeing and restorative spaces (Rhew et al., 2021). This includes an examination of structured writing retreats where colleagues write together for 2 or 3 days at a time, often away from their university (Eardley et al., 2021; Grant, 2006; Hammond, 2021; Kornhaber et al., 2016; Murray & Newton, 2009). The retreat in my work team was intentionally designed as an opportunity to progress writing projects and engage with our writing in a deeper way, amidst the frenetic pace of our academic work. Such retreats have provided a welcome opportunity for us to write in a collegial silence: a pause between two semesters. While the design of the retreat was informed by the work of academics such as Murray (2014) and Grant (2008), my colleagues valued it as a wellbeing space, to think and dedicate time to their writing. Grant (2006) argues that writing retreats create increased feelings of collegiality while responding to the complexity of academic lives (p. 717). In the busy-ness of academia, our writing practices are often compressed between other demands; therefore, our silent writing practices become even more important for both the *writer* and the *writing*. Equally significant is the act of nurturing wellbeing spaces highlighted by Hurd and Singh (2021), including those situated in shared spaces like writing retreats. Reflecting on this writing retreat, some questions emerged: How can a writing retreat become also a "restorative space"? Where are our collective spaces for wellbeing located in the neoliberal academy and how can we disappear into them?

In thinking about wellbeing spaces and geographies of health, Fleuret and Atkinson (2007) describe wellbeing geography in relation to their 'Spaces of Wellbeing' model. Beginning with 'spaces of capability' (p. 113), they argue the importance of wellbeing through participant self-fulfilment. Alongside this, the 'Spaces of Wellbeing' model also incorporates 'space of security' (p. 113) which focuses on intersections of social, spatial, and individual support. In relation to SUAW, 'spaces of wellbeing' comprise the physical space that is conducive to the development of interconnections between participants and the sharing of support or information to other individuals. The physical space itself is important in relation to it being quiet, enabling focused, silent work, while allowing connections to form and develop "therapeutic spaces" (p. 113). This encompasses the quiet, almost meditative, silent writing space that is centred in the SUAW practice. Fleuret and Atkinson (2007) argue that the focus on healthful relationships at the point where 'spaces of capability', 'therapeutic spaces', and 'spaces of security' intersect can create geographies of wellbeing. Therefore, the potential of writing retreats cannot be overlooked, as moving away from campus for a dedicated period can consolidate these wellbeing spaces more easily than the more concentrated SUAW sessions. During writing retreats, academics have a unique opportunity to experience a deeper, sustained, silent writing practice and a more creative, reflective, engagement with their work. Such retreats build on the SUAW practice and points to the need to embed these spaces into the academy, while acknowledging their unrealised restorative potential.

Restorative Silence for the Student

> In my undergraduate research methods class, I asked my students to engage in silent writing, pomodoro style. My instructions: please draft or write up some aspect of your thesis for 25 minutes. Your writing does not have to be perfect – it is a draft. I explained that SUAW had been a critical part of my academic life and

continued to support my own writing practice, particularly in those challenging moments when I felt anxious about my writing. While I felt like the SUAW practice was a gift to the students as researchers and writers, they were uncertain and even anxious. I could see them wondering: how can we possibly fill 25 minutes of silent writing? Once engaged in the task, they became quiet and calm, settling into their writing. The quietness almost seemed to have a soothing effect and hinted at moments of self-compassion and reassurance. The focused, dedicated writing experience interrupted cycles of anxiety. For a moment, the students experienced confidence in their writing and could see possibilities in the quiet writing space. After the first pomodoro, students acknowledged – and even celebrated – the small steps they had taken in their writing. Connections were formed between students. They were keen to share what they had written. A small group of students in the class later told me that they had started meeting for their own pomodoro writing sessions. One student wrote in their thesis acknowledgement: thank you for showing me the value of a pomodoro!

I intentionally designed a restorative writing practice that would embed self-compassion and appreciative inquiry, while seeking to disrupt anxiety and self-doubt. The SUAW process was embedded into an appreciative inquiry – where the students themselves were able to observe the value of their own work and their peers' writing. Engaging students in SUAW offered pedagogies of care and created space for solidarity and self-compassion (Neff et al., 2007). Students enrolled in this class were understandably anxious about the uncertainty of the academic writing process. Many of my students were at the start of their research projects and had not yet developed a writing practice. As such, silent writing alongside their peers was initially uncomfortable, given that these students had not experienced quiet, reflective writing until their final year of study. Instead, their experience in higher education had been marked by pressure and performativity. For these students, SUAW created a restorative space: care for the *writer* and the *writing*, a space that validated self-compassion and centred an ethic of care. Silent writing practices were embedded into each class during the semester and soon became a community of writer wellbeing, a pivotal learning experience for final year students as they prepared to graduate and commence full time employment.

We rarely 'gift' students with a practice that is restorative: calming anxiety while elevating self-compassion. Drawing on a SUAW practice in class offered a holistic pedagogy while engaging students in a community of silent writing as they observed their emerging writing skills. More importantly, however, it offered students a moment of self-compassion, encountering their writer-self in a moment that was quiet, calm, and yet creative and appreciative. This promotion of relationships and learning communities highlighted the restorative impact of SUAW, adapted to the needs of research students. My students experienced SUAW in a way that was empowering and enabling – to write and communicate their important ideas and then share it with peers, bringing their writing into their community. This approach to academic writing was informed by Neff et al.'s (2007) concept of self-compassion that encompasses "warmth and non-judgmental understanding rather than belittling their own pain or berating themselves with self-criticism" (p. 140). They also provide a salient reminder to writers: the mindful, calm, observation of writing practices can offer much-needed reassurance. Gaard and Ergüner-Tekinalp (2022) similarly describe the importance of contemplative writing opportunities and their work offers a challenge to all of us who write in silent spaces: how can we collectively support a more intentional approach to our writing while being kind to ourselves in the process?

Conclusion

In this chapter, I have reflected on my experience in different SUAW communities and the restorative potential that silent writing offers to participants. The silence invites us into a space that nurtures both the writer and the writing in often-unexpected ways. Silent writing practices allow us to listen to our thoughts, our reflections, and our own scholarly wisdom. We are afforded a space to reconnect with our passion and our curiosity while being nurtured in our academic work. Writing together in the silence builds community and empathy: we develop empathy for our fellow writers in the silence as each of us experiences both challenges and the joys of writing. In our SUAW space, we disappear into our own silence and together hope for whatever the silence may bring to us and our writing. Responding to Michaela Coel's invitation then, to "see what comes to you in silence", we are open to the transformative possibilities that come from creating, crafting, and listening in the silence. The practice of SUAW offers a uniquely restorative space for academic writing as we, too, find ourselves disappearing into the silence.

References

Anderson, S. (2023). *The lost art of silence: Reconnecting to the power and beauty of quiet*. Shambhala. http://ebookcentral.proquest.com/lib/rmit/detail.action?docID=30787757

Beasy, K., Emery, S., Dyer, L., Coleman, B., Bywaters, D., Garrad, T., Crawford, J., Swarts, K., & Jahangiri, S. (2020). Writing together to foster wellbeing: Doctoral writing groups as spaces of wellbeing. *Higher Education Research & Development*, 39(6), 1091–1105. https://doi.org/10.1080/07294360.2020.1713732

Butler-Rees, A., & Robinson, N. (2020). Encountering precarity, uncertainty and everyday anxiety as part of the postgraduate research journey. *Emotion, Space and Society*, 37, Article 100743. https://doi.org/10.1016/j.emospa.2020.100743

Cannell, C., Silvia, A., McLachlan, K., Othman, S., Morphett, A., Maheepala, V., McCosh, C., Simic, N., & Behrend, M. B. (2023). Developing research-writer identity and wellbeing in a doctoral writing group. *Journal of Further and Higher Education*, 47(8), 1106–1123. https://doi.org/10.1080/0309877X.2023.2217411

Casey, C., Taylor, J., Knight, F., & Trenoweth, S. (2023). Understanding the mental health of doctoral students. *Encyclopedia*, 3(4), 1523–1536. https://www.mdpi.com/2673-8392/3/4/109

Coel, Michaela (2021, September 19) *Writing for a Limited or Anthology Series or Movie: 73rd Emmys* [Video]. Youtube. https://youtu.be/7FI6kwRFRtU?si=xw793K5hKLeSqrTb

Eardley, A. F., Banister, E., & Fletcher, M. (2021). Can academic writing retreats function as wellbeing interventions? *Journal of Further and Higher Education*, 45(2), 183–196. https://doi.org/10.1080/0309877X.2020.1744542

Eliot, T. S. (1963). *T.S. Eliot collected poems*. Faber & Faber.

Fleuret, S., & Atkinson, S. (2007). Wellbeing, health and geography: A critical review and research agenda. *New Zealand Geographer*, 63(2), 106–118. https://doi.org/10.1111/j.1745-7939.2007.00093.x

Gaard, G. C., & Ergüner-Tekinalp, B. (2022). *Contemplative practices and anti-oppressive pedagogies for higher education: Bridging the disciplines*. Routledge.

Grant, B. M. (2006). Writing in the company of other women: Exceeding the boundaries. *Studies in Higher Education*, 314, 483–495. https://doi.org/10.1080/0307507060080

Grant, B. M. (2008). *Academic writing retreats: A facilitator's guide*. HERDSA.

Hammond, K. (2021). Threat, drive, and soothe: Learning self-compassion in an academic writing retreat. *Higher Education Research & Development*, 40(7), 1437–1451. https://doi.org/10.1080/07294360.2020.1830037

Hurd, F., & Singh, S. (2021). 'Something has to change': A collaborative journey towards academic well-being through critical reflexive practice. *Management Learning*, 52(3), 347–363. https://doi.org/10.1177/1350507620970723

Kornhaber, R., Cross, M., Betihavas, V., & Bridgman, H. (2016). The benefits and challenges of academic writing retreats: An integrative review. *Higher Education Research & Development*, 35(6), 1210–1227. https://doi.org/10.1080/07294360.2016.1144572

Murray, R. (2014). *Writing in social spaces: A social processes approach to academic writing* (1st ed.). Routledge. https://doi.org/10.4324/9781315755427

Murray, R., & Newton, M. (2009). Writing retreat as structured intervention: Margin or mainstream? *Higher Education Research & Development*, 28(5), 541–553. https://doi.org/10.1080/07294360903154126

Neff, K. D., Kirkpatrick, K. L., & Rude, S. S. (2007). Self-compassion and adaptive psychological functioning. *Journal of Research in Personality*, 41(1), 139–154. https://doi.org/10.1016/j.jrp.2006.03.004

Rhew, N. D., Jones, D. R., Sama, L. M., Robinson, S., Friedman, V. J., & Egan, M. (2021). Shedding light on restorative spaces and faculty well-being. *Journal of Management Education*, 45(1), 43–64. https://doi.org/10.1177/1052562920953456

Su, F., Wood, M., Alerby, E., Da Re, L., & Felisatti, E. (2022). 'When the hurley-burley's done, when the battle's lost and won': Exploring the value and appropriation of silence and quietude in academia. *European Journal of Higher Education*, 12(3), 277–292. https://doi.org/10.1080/21568235.2021.1930566

8 Beyond the Individual
Reflections on Writing, Identity, and Wellbeing in Academia

Gillian Kimundi

Introduction

As I write this, I am in the last stretch of my third year as a full-time PhD candidate in Finance, based in Melbourne. As an international student, I am facing questions about my future, including whether I should pursue an academic or a non-academic career path and whether I should stay in Australia or return home. While the future remains unclear for now, reflecting on the professional and personal strides I have made over the past few years has been insightful, especially as I think about the motivations that led me to start this journey.

I began this PhD with a passion for finance, excited at the prospect of knowledge creation and contributing to conversations in financial sector policy. For me, earning this PhD would not only signify having a sense of mastery and expertise – it had also become the end goal in itself. I remember when I was starting out, all I could do was envision myself in cap and gown holding my testamur. That image still appears from time to time but fades as the demands of graduate research take over.

While that initial clarity anchored me in the early stages, the everyday experiences of doctoral life gradually opened up new dimensions of the journey, ones I had not fully anticipated. I recall that during my induction seminar, one of the speakers emphasised the likelihood of imposter syndrome hitting us at some point of candidature. *Imposter phenomenon* was first defined over 40 years ago as a conviction that your competence, intellect, and success are fraudulent and ready to be exposed any given moment, conveying an inability to internalise your esteem (Clance & Imes 1978; Clance (1985)). The prevalence of imposter syndrome in academic life is well explored (Burford et al. 2022; Cristea & Babajide 2022) and is often attributed to competition, outcome orientation, and audit culture. Breeze (2018) reframes it as a public feeling, one that calls for a critique of the structural standards of success as opposed to reflecting individual deficiency. Towards the end of my first year, I found myself grappling with this – on the one hand, I got validation from doing my research and figuring things out, and on the other hand I occasionally felt like I did not know what I was doing while everybody else did.

DOI: 10.4324/9781003633327-10

74 Fostering Wellbeing through Collective Writing Practices

Figure 8.1 Like glimpses through a canopy, my sense of purpose is slowly emerging.

In working through this tension, I have had to engage in deeper reflection about what progress and success mean for me as a researcher. Over time, I have come to understand my PhD journey as less about reaching a single moment of achievement – and more concerned with consistent, often quiet growth. Ultimately, it is in days spent writing, rethinking, discussing, and repositioning my research in existing scholarship that I have seen meaningful development. This shift happened along the way, and I found that engaging in communal writing spaces were an important catalyst for a process-oriented mindset. In this chapter, I describe how participating in Shut Up and Write! helped me redefine my sense of purpose for my PhD journey by focusing more on process than outcome, and, most importantly, to viewing my contributions as a part of broader pursuit of knowledge creation. Much like peering through a canopy of trees, clarity on my purpose has begun to emerge in steady glimpses, reminding me why I am doing this (see Figure 8.1).

Text Work, Identity Work, and Wellbeing

Kamler and Thomson (2007) highlight a tension in doctoral research of navigating between text work and identity work. The authors elaborate that "research is a practice of writing" (p. 167), a social practice with protocols shaped by the disciplines and the scholars who embody that discipline. A fundamental part of text work is in the organisation and structuring of ideas and mapping those within the context of other scholars' contributions. Related to this, is an equally fundamental aspect linked to the identity of the scholar: what they are trying to say and how to express it critically and authoritatively within the frameworks and protocols of the discipline they are writing in. I resonate with the occasional lack of confidence in your writing and your ideas – erasing entire paragraphs because the words feel inauthentic and/or like an imposition to the field. Kamler & Thomson (2007) describe this particular experience as a graduate researcher entering "occupied territory" (p. 170).

The significant intellectual undertaking of research and of positioning oneself within scholarly conversations has the potential to shape how academics view themselves. The complexity of academic identity in higher education spaces has been well documented. Henkel (2005) suggests that the core dimensions of academic identities are their discipline and academic freedom, portraying that scholars define themselves within fixed boundaries. On the other hand, Clegg (2008) suggests that there is a fluidity and distinctiveness to academic identities that makes them complex dimensions shaped by personhood and the external environment. In this latter sense, identity construction within academia is increasingly multifaceted. From the perspective of doctoral study, while identity is very much centred on knowledge production (Cotterall 2013; Xu & Grant 2020), it is also layered with personal, cultural, and institutional factors that interact to create unique academic experiences for candidates (Douglas 2021; Xu 2022).

I found myself confronting these ideas at the end of my first year. Although I had successfully completed my confirmation of candidature and had the guidance of a great supervisory team, writing and contextualising my empirical analysis had become an overwhelming task. While I had previously thrived in my routine and structure, I found it difficult to get things done. The quiet of working from home once familiar and appreciated was not cutting it anymore. I decided to start studying regularly from campus, hoping the change in environment would help me regain momentum. That's when I first heard about the on-campus Shut Up and Write! sessions. Coincidentally, I had just started tutoring that semester, and my classes were scheduled right after writing sessions, The timing could not have been better – it gave me a focused mid-week boost on my research before heading to class.

I expected to feel some pressure from seeing other people work, especially given I was coming out of this unexplainable slump in my research. To my surprise, however, the sessions offered a sense of camaraderie. The communal writing reminded me that text work is central to any researcher and is an activity that cuts across disciplines. It is through writing and re-writing that I am better able to contextualise, refine, and share my contributions to academic research. Maher et al. (2008) describe this most adequately – viewing writing as "the activity and practice of scholarly work itself" (p. 266). In this new routine and in this communal space with researchers from different disciplines, I began to reframe my perspective of my PhD journey and got back on track with my work.

I did come to realise that much of what I was writing and learning had become so internalised that I found it difficult to explain my research without lapsing into jargon and the technical aspects. Perhaps because of imposter syndrome, I did not want it too sound too simplistic. Attending Shut Up and Write! highlighted the importance of clarity in how I articulated my research, particularly to those outside my field. The more I spoke about my research, the more certain ideas began to crystallise, helping me further clarify where my work fit into the broader scholarly conversation. It felt like having a lighthouse, a script that illuminated the bigger picture of my research, beyond the technical execution. With that clarity, the task of writing also became less overwhelming, and I found myself reconnecting with the core questions that initially drove me to start the research project in the first place. It offered more than just structure and momentum, but it also became a form of identity work.

This growing awareness that my research contribution did not exist in a vacuum, but rather within a wider academic ecosystem, brought to focus a deeper psychological dimension of my research journey. It echoed the importance of connection within my academic community, aligning with a well-known psychological construct of human wellbeing known as the self-determination theory (Deci & Ryan 1985, 2000). According to this theory, wellbeing is characterised by three psychological needs: autonomy (the agency to influence), competence (sense of mastery and efficacy), and relatedness (connectedness and a sense of belonging).

Among these, it is the concept of relatedness that I found particularly resonant. Relatedness goes beyond the visible structures of shared knowledge, peer review, or collaborative research and reflects how we locate ourselves in the scholarly community. Douglas (2021) notes that graduate researchers' learning identities as approached from a sociocultural perspective are shaped by the networks and contexts they participate in. For me, participating in these communal writing spaces became such a context.

This concept has continued to shape how I think about my sense of purpose in this PhD journey and beyond. Firstly, my view of research has become less about proving myself in isolation, becoming more concerned with seeing my contribution as a part of a greater scholarly effort and shared activities that cuts across disciplines. This does not diminish my individual accomplishments as a researcher, but in fact reinforces them by recognising that I exist in an ecosystem of knowledge pursuit. Secondly, and perhaps most importantly, it has become clear that my growth throughout this process – through the wins, and despite the doubts and discomfort, is a key part of my purpose.

Strategies for Wellbeing

These reflections that follow highlight some of the practical takeaways that have supported and sustained how I think about purpose, identity, and progress as a graduate researcher:

1. Write and Talk
   A significant part of my progress has come from talking about my research and improving how I communicate my ideas. Shut up and Write! has been a great space to interact with scholars from different disciplines. In doing so, I not only gain an appreciation of how they frame their research, but also learn to present my research in a simpler way that articulates its broader significance.

2. Reframing writing as a shared scholarly practice, and, most importantly, as part of knowledge creation
   Writing is not just a means to an end – not just a step towards getting a paper or thesis out. For me, it is central to how I create and comprehend existing and new ideas. I acknowledge that the body of academic research I come across has had scholars who like me invested time, effort, and intellect refining their ideas and writing to ensure they contribute meaningfully to a broader scholarly conversation. Reframing writing in this way has allowed me to see it as not just a task, but, as Maher et al. (2008) put it: "the activity and practice of scholarly work itself" (p. 266).

3. Cultivating an academic identity that evolves with me
   Many graduate researchers will be familiar with the phrase, "A PhD is a marathon, not a sprint." Eliud Kipchoge, one of the most celebrated marathoners, once said: *"When I'm on the starting line, my mind starts reviewing what I have been doing the last five months."* His confidence comes from knowing he has trained well and that he has earned his winning titles. This perspective has reshaped how I think about success in this PhD journey and beyond – regarding it not as a single point in time achievement but as the accumulation of intellectual and personal growth over time. Through this, I have come to see my academic identity as something that evolves with me and that is shaped by my experiences and consistency.

4. For the most part, go where you feel inspired
   It is easy to get caught up in the day-to-day demands of a PhD and to lose sight of how deeply my research is influenced by the environments I work in. Taking time to reflect on where I feel inspired has been meaningful. It could be my dedicated workspace at home, my local coffee shop, the focused atmosphere on campus, or a combination of all these places on different days. I have learnt that I respond to the rhythms around me and that often shapes the clarity I have in my work and more importantly, how I deal with moments where clarity is absent.

Conclusion

In this chapter, I reflect on my individual experiences as a graduate researcher through the lens of communal writing sessions. I describe how participating in these shared writing spaces has shaped my approach to scholarly text work and academic identity, and also contributed to the broadening of my sense of purpose as a graduate researcher. What began as an individual pursuit and professional milestone defined by intellectual rigor and disciplinary mastery has evolved into a much deeper appreciation of my scholarship. Participating in Shut Up and Write! not only offered structure, momentum, and collegiality in my doctoral journey, but also revealed writing to be a shared scholarly practice. Drawing on self-determination theory and the importance of relatedness for human wellbeing, I explore how this space served a reminder that my research and professional contributions are stronger in an ecosystem, with other researchers pursuing knowledge creation. Through these reflections I am sustaining a sense of purpose in my graduate research journey – one rooted in growth, process and community.

References

Breeze, M. (2018). Imposter syndrome as a public feeling. In Y. Taylor, & K. Lahad (Eds) *Feeling academic in the neoliberal university* (pp. 191–219). Palgrave Studies in Gender and Education. Palgrave Macmillan, Cham. https://doi.org/10.1007/978-3-319-64224-6_9

Burford, J., Fyffe, J., & Khoo, T. (2022). Working with/against imposter syndrome: Research educators' reflections. In M. Addison, M. Breeze, & Y. Taylor (Eds) *The Palgrave handbook of imposter syndrome in higher education* (pp. 377–394). Palgrave Macmillan. https://doi.org/10.1007/978-3-030-86570-2_23

Clance, P. R. (1985). *The impostor phenomenon: Overcoming the fear that haunts your success*. Atlanta: Peachtree Publishers Ltd.

Clance, P. R., & Imes, S. A. (1978). The imposter phenomenon in high achieving women: Dynamics and therapeutic intervention. *Psychotherapy: Theory, Research & Practice, 15(3)*, 241–247, https://doi.org/10.1037/h0086006

Clegg, S. (2008). Academic identities under threat? *British Educational Research Journal, 34(3)*, 329–345, https://doi.org/10.1080/01411920701532269

Cotterall, S. (2013). The rich get richer: International doctoral candidates and scholarly identity. *Innovations in Education and Teaching International, 52(4)*, 360–370.

Cristea, M., & Babajide, O. A. (2022). Impostor phenomenon: Its prevalence among academics and the need for a diverse and inclusive working environment in British higher education. In M. Addison, M. Breeze, & Y. Taylor (Eds) *The Palgrave handbook of imposter syndrome in higher education.* (pp. 55–73). Palgrave Macmillan, Cham. https://doi.org/10.1007/978-3-030-86570-2_4

Deci, E. L., & Ryan, R. M. (1985). *Intrinsic motivation and self-determination in human behavior*. New York: Plenum Press.

Deci, E. L., & Ryan, R. M. (2000). The "what" and "why" of goal pursuits: Human needs and the self-determination of behavior. *Psychological Inquiry, 11(4)*, 227–268, https://doi.org/10.1207/S15327965PLI1104_01

Douglas, A. S. (2021). Dimensions of fit for doctoral candidates: Supporting an academic identity. *Research Papers in Education, 37(6)*, 954–974

Henkel, M. (2005). Academic identity and autonomy in a changing policy environment. *Higher Education, 49(1/2)*, Universities and the Production of Knowledge, 155–176, https://doi.org/10.1007/s10734-004-2919-1

Kamler, B., & Thomson, P. (2007). Rethinking doctoral writing as text work and identity work. In B. Somekh, T. A. Schwandt (Eds) *Knowledge production: Research work in interesting times* (pp. 166–179). Routledge.

Maher, D., Seaton, L., McMullen, C., Fitzgerald, T., Otsuji, E., & Lee, A. (2008). 'Becoming and being writers': The experiences of doctoral students in writing groups. *Studies in Continuing Education*, *30(3)*, 263–275.

Xu, L., & Grant, B. (2020). Doctoral publishing and academic identity work: Two cases. *Higher Education Research & Development*, *39*(7), 1502–1515, https://doi.org/10.1080/07294360.2020.1728522

Xu, X. (2022). An autoethnography of an international doctoral student's multidimensional identity construction. *The Australian Educational Researcher*, *50*, 1423–1437, https://doi.org/10.1007/s13384-022-00557-w

Part III
Creative and Collaborative Approaches

9 Changing the Script
Collective and Creative Possibilities

Timothy Clark

Prologue

On a rainy day at a university somewhere in the west of England, colleagues are reflecting on a successful 'Shut Up and Write!' session, where progress has been made with chapters for a collaborative edited collection:

Colleague 1: 'I didn't expect to make that much progress, it just happened…'
Colleague 2: 'I don't know what it is about these sessions, but it's just different to writing at home.'
Colleague 1: 'Is it because we're more accountable to each other? I can't just wander off and load the dishwasher!'
Colleague 2: 'Maybe, but I also wonder if I ever would have solved my introduction problem without talking about it here first.'

Introduction

Whilst this collection is framed by the title 'Shut Up and Write!' (SUAW), the purpose of this chapter is to reflect on the transformative potential of what may sit in between these headline periods of purposeful, silent, focused writing time in a group writing session or retreat. Perhaps somewhat ironically, it may be argued that a significant part of the value of *'shutting up'* and *writing* actually comes from appreciating and carefully considering the nature of the *talking* and *thinking* which sits alongside it.

The chapter draws on examples of creative non-fiction writing in the form of play scripts (Dobson & Clark, 2024). The purpose of these is twofold: firstly, through these I aim to capture and explore illustrative experiences and reflections, opening by representing consideration of the value of writing collectively and later illustrating the potential of SUAW to foster space for different types of writing. Secondly, through these examples I also aim to embody the role of SUAW in my own narrative, in harnessing space, and confidence, for entangling dialogue with creative and academic writing to create new possibilities and understandings. In doing so, I propose that SUAW has the potential to 'change the script', both metaphorically and literally.

A Personal Perspective: Playing the Role

Based in a large teaching intensive university in the UK, my current role involves leading and developing the research portfolio of its school of education and childhood. Within this role I have been involved in, and at times facilitated, numerous sessions at my institution in line with the SUAW model. Introduced by a colleague, these sessions are informed by Rowena Murray's writing retreat methodology (Murray & Newton 2009), which embeds set writing periods (in our case usually 60–90 minutes) alongside regular opportunities for collaborative target-setting, updates and reflections. Whilst the concept of these is simple, it is clear from personal experience, as well as from conversations with colleagues and research students, that their potential in terms of supporting both writing and thinking is significant.

Over recent years I have embarked on a relatively rapid transition in my career, which has seen writing, particularly writing for publication, come to the forefront. Having navigated the wellbeing challenges of progressing into a role in academia via a professional doctorate in education (see Clark, 2024), my previous professional leadership experience quickly enabled a new transition as I progressed from a role as a lecturer and early career researcher into my current research leadership role. Yet, I was initially very conscious of the potential misalignment between this new identity and, what I perceived at the time as, my relatively limited publication profile. Whilst predominantly internally driven, my previously very positive relationship with academic writing was at risk of being compromised by a growing 'publish or perish' mindset (Lee, 2014, p. 1) as I simultaneously sought to demonstrate my academic and leadership credentials in this new space. The significance of SUAW sessions here is that they ultimately offered opportunities to support with both of these challenges – helping to develop my own writing whilst contributing to collective research leadership through building a research community, enhancing research collegiality, and supporting researcher development. Engaging with, and prioritising, monthly SUAW sessions organised by a colleague, provided opportunities to increase my writing productivity, communicate more regularly with research colleagues (including postgraduate students) and to look forward to protected writing time.

My visual contribution is a photograph I took on a lunchtime 'wellbeing walk' at a recent SUAW session on the university campus. The black-and-white image (Figure 9.1) is a landscape photograph of a large pond, with reeds in the foreground and trees in the background. Fortunate to be located on a large campus with significant green space, the wellbeing walks encompass and represent many of the most valuable features of the SUAW sessions. An informal pause in our writing days, yet often a primary space for a different form of talking and thinking (Keinänen, 2016), this space can act as a prime problem-solving opportunity in a writing session. Seemingly serendipitous breakthroughs, coming in the 'gaps in between' the writing. For me the image also represents possibilities, entanglements and uncertainty – rarely do our walks

Figure 9.1 A space for thinking and talking on a SUAW wellbeing walk.

have a defined plan, destination, or even leader. On this particular walk a postgraduate student suggests we navigate the campus' numerous ponds, I reflect:

> *It is a cold winter's afternoon, and the sun is low in the sky. We wander out of the warm and busy writing room, with laptops, books and notepaper strewn across the table, collect our coats, meet at the door and head out across the car park. Despite having worked at the university for 5 years, I find myself following others along a path I had not actually noticed before. I quickly forget some of my earlier frustration with a writing section I just could not get to flow and begin talking to a postgraduate student about their research. We discuss authorial voice, although the conversation is interspersed with questions and observations about the pond in front of us ('What kind of bird is that?'). I am interested to learn about their work and pleased to be able to offer some reflections from mine. When I return to the room, taking a moment to tidy my particularly messy spot prior to the next writing block, some phrasing for that section just comes into my head – as if by magic.*

Whilst the wellbeing walk is typically positioned as the 'break' from the writing, providing a moment out from the quest to produce something tangible, it often acts as much more than this. The entanglement of pondering, reflecting, and talking, alongside the change in mood and focus, playing a key role in enabling these creative and collective possibilities.

Collective and Creative Possibilities: Embracing the Journey

The short opening script in this chapter represents an example of what is, in my experience, a relatively common exchange between colleagues and/or postgraduate research students following a SUAW session – often highlighting surprise at their value and grasping for an understanding about exactly what contributes to this. Many authors have highlighted the potential of group writing sessions to support academics with developing a sense of community, some conceptualising regular writing groups as developing a form of community of practice (Wiebe et al., 2023) and noting particular value in terms of supporting confidence, motivation, and belonging for early career academics (Maheux-Pelletier et al., 2019). In addition, as many of the other chapters in this collection attest, SUAW sessions can have a wide range of benefits in terms of writing and wellbeing, including supporting with organisation, protecting writing time, and creating a sense of shared accountability. However, as Colleague 2 alludes in the final sentence in the opening script (*'I...wonder if I ever would have solved my introduction problem without talking about it here first'*), beyond these aspects, through their collaborative format, these sessions also offer something more in terms of influencing decisions in, and about, the writing we are doing. The collective nature of a SUAW session means that through dialogue about our writing, new possibilities become open to consideration as we are navigating our writing journey. In terms of interactions this may be most obvious in the direct exchange of ideas or as a product of the opportunity to articulate our writing and plans in a different way, to a different audience. For example, we may reflect on whether Colleague 2's 'introduction problem' was solved by a more experienced colleague's suggestions or support during a facilitated discussion period or whether the requirement to re-frame and explain their challenge as part of their plan for the day helped to focus their thinking and move the writing forward. Either way, this collective space frequently seems to offer something more in terms of getting 'unstuck' and feeling positive about writing.

Moving beyond these practical understandings, Grant and Knowles (2000, p. 6) refer to collective writing sessions as having the potential to become more complex 'imaginative spaces'. They position writing in these spaces as a socially constructed process which may include 'playing' with texts and ideas and suggest that this has implications for identity, supporting the process of being, and becoming, a writer in academia. Elements of this understanding also represent a shift from a pragmatic focus on the value of writing sessions through the lens of individual interactions as tangible exchanges, to the poststructuralist notion of 'intra-action', understood as the 'movement generated in an encounter...in a process of becoming different' (Davies & Gannon, 2012, p. 361). From this perspective, a SUAW session offers us increased potential for an 'entanglement' of ideas, identities, purpose, and possibilities. Where writing may have typically been experienced as a solitary process, potentially framed by notions of imposter syndrome and unrealistic comparisons to others – particularly for early career academics or those experiencing transitions (Wilson & Cutri, 2019) – here it has the potential to become a social process creating possibilities to think, and feel, differently about our work. In this 'entanglement' we may question whether being part of the group presents different possibilities and contexts for this problem-solving than we would have accessed independently but also speculate on the difference highlighted by Colleague 1 (*'Is it because we're more accountable to each other?'*). Is this just about accountability and a practical exchange of advice, or does it also extend to the significance of the social (writing) environment on our sense of confidence, identity, and purpose?

Thinking beyond a solely task- or product-driven understanding of the value of these collective spaces, we can also consider their potential to instil permission to be creative and to approach writing differently. Whilst acknowledging the role of SUAW sessions in directly helping us to meet goals and deadlines, if we embrace the idea that they hold the potential for additional affective benefits relating to notions of wellbeing, identity, and purpose, then writing facilitated here can be reframed as also having purpose as a tool for 'thinking' (Menary, 2007, p. 621) and perhaps for 'becoming' and 'being' (Grant & Knowles, 2000, p.11) as academics. This can include offering opportunities for embracing different forms of writing exercises, with the potential to provide a new lens, develop understanding of an idea or research data, and overcome blocks. Within this space there is potential to legitimise and support different forms of writing – for example, short periods of freewriting may help to encourage a sense of fluency and develop ideas outside of the constraints of writing a product for an audience (Murray and Newton, 2009). Alternatively, handwriting may act as a powerful and physical opportunity for 'visual thinking' (Saner, 2014, p.118), which allows us to move beyond an interaction which is increasingly hosted via a relationship with a laptop screen. Another alternative form of writing, and one which I have chosen to represent within this chapter, is the use of creative writing as a tool to represent, reflect on, and analyse ideas and understandings. The examples here embrace a form of creative non-fiction, a tool I was introduced to as part of an arts-based research (ABR) approach, where the value of writing as a provocation and a tool for making ideas more engaging and thinking about audiences 'outside of the academy' are embraced (Leavy, 2018,p.192).

Writing Differently

In a small-group SUAW session for a collaborative research project exploring creativity in doctoral research, there is a focus on writing for an emerging literature review.

Group Facilitator: 'I'd like to propose a 30-minute period where we use a creative writing approach to revisit our understanding of the literature review. There is no need to refer to the literature directly in this and we'll use the examples for discussion at the end of this period.'

Colleague 1: 'I'm not sure how confident I feel about creative writing, but I'll give it a try...'

Colleague 2: 'OK, what do you think about an ivory tower Professor character to represent the academy's dismissal of creative methodologies in doctoral research?'

Colleague 1: 'If the Professor represents the academy, maybe the students can evoke the ideas of creativity and resistance, advocacy, audience, compliance...'
Colleague 2: 'Hang on, perhaps those are actually our key themes? Could we go back to the structure?'
Colleague 1: 'Wow, where did that come from? We just brought the literature review to life, didn't we?'

The significance of SUAW sessions in introducing these possibilities for engagement in alternative forms of writing is that in these collective spaces, perhaps typically facilitated by more experienced and influential colleagues, there is the potential to legitimise and introduce techniques for writing which do not always need to be product-focused. In doing so, there is an opportunity for impacts on our relationships with writing, as a potentially joyful and transformative experience, rather than an item on our 'to do' list and a product we must create.

The second script (above) seeks to illustrate a 'lightbulb' moment provoked by engaging with a different form of writing. It is inspired by my introduction to, and experimentation with ABR, as a tool to re-frame and understand the ideas in my writing differently, but perhaps also to 'oppose' pressures and expectations and better understand and distil my identity as a writer (Yoo, 2017). In the context of ever-increasing demands and expectations, engaging with creative writing as part of our academic identities can play an important role in supporting ongoing wellbeing through the generation of an important sense of presence and 'timelessness' (Yoo 2019, p.148). For me, utilising SUAW as an opportunity for entangling my writing with walking, talking, and experimentation has played a key role in navigating a positive relationship with writing, as something purposeful, creative, and collaborative, rather than solely a product-focused pressure.

SUAW Tips

Having considered the significance of writing collectively and creatively in my own experience of SUAW, below are some 'top tips' based on my experience of engaging with SUAW:

Embrace and create opportunities for dialogue. It is, of course, important that in planning SUAW sessions we privilege protected space for focused writing; however, we should not underestimate the value and significance of the conversation which sits alongside this. In our SUAW sessions, we typically plan 15 to 20 minutes of discussion for every 90 minutes of writing. This usually begins with an opportunity for each person to say something about their plans, progress, and challenges.

Take a wellbeing walk. As highlighted above, walking and talking can play an active role in thinking and problem-solving. In my experience I rarely solve a writing problem when sat in front of a screen. Again, whilst there can be a pressure to fit as much writing time as possible into a SUAW session, a short break for a local wellbeing walk – particularly taking in green spaces – can often enhance productivity, further support with building community, and provide problem-solving moments.

Experiment with different forms of writing. As illustrated in this chapter, sometimes there can be personal value in experimenting with different approaches to writing. Whether this is a five-minute free-writing period, as suggested by Murray and Newton (2009), or re-imagining a literature review, as a play script, sometimes approaching a writing task in a different way can support thinking and help to re-frame ideas and purpose. This can be the case even if there is no intention that this specific format will form part of whatever final 'product' we are aiming for.

Conclusion

In the context of aspects of my own narrative, this chapter has provided an illustration and reflection on the value of SUAW as a potentially transformative space – focusing on the potential for it to be about more than just 'shutting up' and 'writing'. The collective nature of SUAW sessions and their potential to facilitate engagement with different forms of writing creates possibilities for developing our identities as writers, our relationships with writing and for becoming 'unstuck' and making progress in our writing. In this respect it aims to illustrate the potential for it to 'change the script' both on paper and in relation to our own journeys as academics.

References

Clark, T. (2024). From researching professional to professional researcher: Learning the rules of the game. In *Navigating tensions and transitions in higher education* (pp. 112–123). Routledge.

Davies, B., & Gannon, S. (2012). Collective Biography and the Entangled Enlivening of Being. *International Review of Qualitative Research*, 5(4), 357–376. https://doi.org/10.1525/irqr.2012.5.4.357

Dobson, T., & Clark, T. (2024). Embracing hybridity: The affordances of arts-based research for the professional doctorate in education. *Teaching in Higher Education*, 29(7), 1862–1878.

Grant, B., & Knowles, S. (2000). Flights of imagination: Academic women be(com)ing writers. *International Journal for Academic Development*, 5(1), 6–19.

Keinänen, M. (2016). Taking your mind for a walk: A qualitative investigation of walking and thinking among nine Norwegian academics. *Higher Education*, 71, 593–605.

Leavy, P. (Ed.). (2018). *Handbook of arts-based research*. Guilford Publications.

Lee, I. (2014). Publish or perish: The myth and reality of academic publishing. *Language teaching*, 47(2), 250–261.

Maheux-Pelletier, G., Marsh, H., & Frake-Mistak, M. (2019). The benefits of writing retreats revisited. In N. Simmons & A. Singh (Eds.), *Critical collaborative communities* (pp. 92–105). Brill.

Menary, R. (2007). Writing as thinking. *Language sciences*, 29(5), 621–632.

Murray, R., & Newton, M. (2009). Writing retreat as structured intervention: Margin or mainstream? *Higher Education Research & Development*, 28(5), 541–553.

Saner, B. (2014). Handwriting is xphysicalx visual thinking. *Visual Arts Research*, *40*(1), 118–120.

Wiebe, N. G., Pratt, H. L., & Noël, N. (2023). Writing retreats: Creating a community of practice for academics across disciplines. *Journal of Research Administration*, *54*(1), 37–65.

Wilson, S., & Cutri, J. (2019) Negating isolation and imposter syndrome through writing as product and as process: The impact of collegiate writing networks during a doctoral program. In: L. Pretorius, L. Macaulay, & B. Cahusac de Caux (Eds.), *Wellbeing in doctoral education: Insights and guidance from the student experience* (pp 59–76). Singapore: Springer. https://doi.org/10.1007/978-981-13-9302-0_7

Yoo, J. (2017). Writing out on a limb: Integrating the creative and academic writing identity. *New Writing*, *14*(3), 444–454.

Yoo, J. (2019). Creative writing and academic timelessness. *New Writing*, *16*(2), 148–157.

10 Shut Up and Write!, Connect, and Support

Bridging the Gap to Support Rural Postgraduate Students

Daniel P Wadsworth, David Duncan, Stacey Whitelaw, Kate McCubbery, Rebecca Terlich, Alexandra Potter, Michelle Gossner, Ishwar Koirala, Erin Harcourt, Jolene A Cox, and Dylan Poulus

Introduction

Background

Almost one-in-three Australians live rurally (outside major cities), with ~13 percent of Australian postgraduate students from rural communities (AIHW, 2024; Napthine et al., 2019). Postgraduate-qualified individuals living in rural areas are uniquely placed to answer calls for locally-led rural research (Alston et al., 2023). Rural postgraduate students, however, face challenges, including geographical distance, potential isolation, and limited access to resources, services, and support networks (Brownlow et al., 2023; Drury et al., 2006). Four-year postgraduate completion rates subsequently decrease with rurality, leading to calls for improved access, participation, and integration of higher education in rural communities, and to boost research training capacity (O'Kane et al., 2024; Department of Education, 2019). Improving educational opportunities for rural communities supports a more skilled rural population better equipped to respond to the unique challenges facing their communities (Napthine et al., 2019).

Postgraduate studies are a lonely pursuit and often solo practice, exposing students to an increased risk of poor mental health (Mills et al., 2024; Micsinszki & Yeung, 2021; Wilson & Cutri, 2021). The rural postgraduate experience can feel even more isolating, being likened to traversing a void, feeling alone, and set adrift as geographic isolation limits the sense of community and support (Brownlow et al., 2023; DeSouza et al., 2020; Drury et al., 2006). Communities of practice (CoP) present ideal learning environments (Brown and Duguid, 2000), with a psychological sense of community identified as the single-largest contributing factor for thriving in postgraduate studies (Petridis, 2015).

Writing groups are common activities within CoPs, offering communal writing experiences with shared goals to develop better writing habits (Kumar and Aitchison, 2018). This collaborative environment enhances individual knowledge and skills and the collective knowledge of the group, increasing

92 *Fostering Wellbeing through Collective Writing Practices*

Figure 10.1 The Manna gum tree branches represent the connection, growth, and flourishing found across our virtual SUAW sessions. Students exchange discussions, ideas, and research assets across branches, representing the 'fruit' of new thinking and community supported by our virtual SUAW sessions (© Manna Institute/Bright Pilots).

support and camaraderie (Proulx et al., 2023). Examples include writing retreats or boot camps, where postgraduate students gather over multiple days to write, and Shut Up and Write! (SUAW) sessions, shorter periods of focused writing (Micsinszki & Yeung, 2021). Benefits include increased productivity, the solidarity of shared experiences, growing research networks, and learning from peers and mentors (Proulx et al., 2023; Chakma et al., 2021; Wilson & Cutri, 2021; Kumar and Aitchison, 2018).

To better support rural postgraduate students, we need training and capacity-building systems specifically tailored for rural areas. Manna Institute's Higher Degree by Research student Community of Practice (HDR CoP) answers this call through a peer-led collective of students and mentors supporting and learning from each other, sharing experiences and challenges. Explored in this case study/chapter through iterative reflections by the authors (all members of the HDR CoP) that are contextualised within existing literature, virtual SUAW sessions form a key element of the HDR CoP, providing a range of opportunities for learning, connection, and academic and/or psychosocial support.

Manna Institute HDR CoP: A Case Study of Shut Up & Write! Supporting Wellbeing and Connection

Manna Institute is a virtual institute dedicated to improving mental health and wellbeing in rural Australia. It supports meaningful, place-based research and prioritises the development of rural mental health researchers. Manna Institute includes ~27 affiliated rural postgraduate students within an HDR CoP led by postdoctoral fellows (early career researchers; ECRs). CoP ownership is shared by students (peer-led), and offerings include SUAW sessions, monthly seminars, and a virtual space, with minimal face-to-face opportunities.

Students can join two-hour virtual SUAW sessions twice-weekly, via an online video conference platform. These sessions were proposed by a CoP student who expressed a desire for connection during a university holiday period. Originally scheduled to run for six weeks, sessions were integrated as a regular offering, with ~100 sessions in the first 12 months.

Facilitated by early-career postdoctoral fellows, the CoP's SUAW sessions are less structured than traditional SUAW approaches. This deliberate flexibility is designed to accommodate rural students across their postgraduate journeys, and the diversity of disciplines represented. Unlike conventional SUAW, which primarily prioritises writing, our sessions encourage active participation. Student-members led this change from traditional, shaping sessions in which they can connect with peers, seek feedback, and exchange knowledge, insights, and experiences. While our sessions usually allocate time for structured writing, the primary focus lies on fostering a collaborative and connected learning community.

Rural Postgraduate Student Reflections

The chapter's eight rural postgraduate student authors reflected on their experiences within the CoP's SUAW sessions, providing all quotes within this case study. Three student authors analysed these reflections and identified commonalities and unique perspectives, which were agreed by all authors and contextualised within literature. Reflections highlighted observations across four common areas that impact student wellbeing and academic growth: *i) Isolation, ii) Community and belonging, iii) Knowledge-sharing,* and *iv) Support*.

Isolation

Isolation in the PhD journey was common for our rural postgraduate students, evident in reflections such as: "my uni has very low numbers on campus, and no other psychology HDRs on campus at all. I've met one or two HDRs in other disciplines, but nobody who I've really felt has been sharing my journey" and "studying via distance in a regional location means I am several hours away from campus, so all my interactions have been online". SUAW sessions like those offered here provide rural postgraduate students with opportunities to address feelings of isolation by supporting regular connection with like-minded and relatable peers (Chakma et al., 2021).

Community and Belonging

Students commonly felt a sense of community and belonging from our SUAW sessions, recognising a "ready-made community to connect with" and appreciating "making connections with some amazing emerging researchers, who are just as passionate about what they do as I am, has been a highlight". Many reflected on the psychological safety and personal support provided to them in SUAW sessions, recognising these sessions as "my safe space to talk about things I am finding difficult, get advice and support" that "reduces feelings of isolation being a postgraduate student at a regional university". By providing opportunity to learn from peers and mentors through the solidarity of shared experiences in this way, SUAW sessions enable a strong postgraduate student community (Chakma et al., 2021; Wilson & Cutri 2021).

Knowledge-Sharing

The variety of perspectives from emerging researchers at different stages of their careers, and ensuing opportunities to learn from and share knowledge with each other, was an appreciated characteristic. Students appreciated "learning from the experience of postgraduate students at varying stages of their candidature" and having a place to "cheer on my colleagues through their wins". Such opportunities for knowledge sharing with peers and mentors are an established benefit of SUAW (Chakma et al., 2021.

Support

Leadership and support from mentors facilitating sessions was commonly recognised, for example, "a very personable and encouraging ECR leadership team is what has kept me coming back" and "when I share about some confusing or sometimes frustrating stages I am facing, they always have solutions and give me positive feedback". Students reflected on "share[ing] commonalities in our interest. When one shares one's ideas; presents the proposal, or research findings, other members can consolidate his/her learning which can be useful for them." They also acknowledged autonomy within the group, stating "we get to make the sessions what we need most, because it's entirely about us and supporting our progress through our PhDs". The group diversity, coming from six of the seven Australian regional universities and spanning multiple disciplines with shared research interests (rural Australian mental health), was also recognised as an important factor in making our SUAW sessions effective.

Other Benefits

Other notable student reflections included opportunities for collaboration, such as the development and writing of this case study/chapter, motivation to keep working on tasks, and accountability for getting work done.

Finally, the flexibility of our peer-led SUAW sessions was praised. Members valued the blend of social connection, focused writing, presentation practice sessions, and collaborative writing tasks such as this case study, combined with voluntary attendance and free choice in which parts to participate. Interestingly, the virtual nature of SUAW sessions was more attractive than a face-to-face group for some, with one student stating:

> I love that it's entirely online – there are days when I 100% would not have turned up to an on-campus, face-to-face meeting because I wasn't feeling up to it, but I was ok to throw my hair in a messy bun, blur my background and "turn-up" from home. It has kept me engaged even at times when I would normally have procrastinated a day away and not achieved anything.

Practical Application

Our experiences in this case study highlight the potential of virtual SUAW sessions to connect disparate groups of rural postgraduate students, previously isolated by geographic distance and/or disciplinary context. Our reflections provide a framework for other virtual SUAW sessions aiming to support and build the capacity of rural postgraduate students.

When considered within socio-emotional aspects of online learning (Delahunty et al., 2014), we recognise ways in which virtual SUAW sessions may provide synchronous opportunity for interaction, belonging, community, and identity formation. We subsequently present the following strategies for how this blend can be achieved by SUAW approaches prioritising i) Psychological safety, ii) Flexibility, and iii) Collaboration.

Psychological Safety

By providing a *psychologically safe environment* that celebrates wins and shares problems, virtual SUAW sessions not only fill a support void often resulting from distance-based study (Drury et al., 2006), but do so in a peer-based, nourishing, and supportive manner that enhances belonging. This recognised determinant of student wellbeing, self-efficacy, and success is a feature of collaborative, welcoming, and innovative research environments (Petridis, 2015; Gaynor et al., 2022). Such environments can help normalise unhealthy imposter thoughts and perfectionism standards common in postgraduate students (Mills et al., 2024). This is important for all postgraduate students, for whom loneliness is a strong and consistent social determinant of poor mental health (Mills et al., 2024), but especially so for rural postgraduate students who are markedly more vulnerable due to a lack of belonging, community, and support (DeSouza et al., 2020; Brownlow et al., 2023).

We achieved this by offering virtual SUAW sessions within a welcoming, supportive, and friendly peer-led environment, protecting against the illusion of companionship often observed in online groups (Turkle 2011). Prioritising and modelling such environments early in career journeys can embed positive values in HDR students, empowering them to support others as they grow into research leaders.

Flexibility

In offering low-commitment *autonomy and variety in activities and perspectives*, virtual SUAW sessions can provide pathways for engagement and interaction with peers, mentors, and supervisors. Learning from peers and mentors through the solidarity of shared experiences is an established benefit of SUAW sessions (Chakma et al., 2021; Wilson & Cutri 2021), whilst student–supervisor guidance and communion are important predictors of mental health (Mills et al., 2024). Peer-led SUAW sessions delivered through broad CoP models present opportunities for mentors and peers, often outside a direct supervisory team, to provide feedback and guidance in ways that allow for high levels of agency and communion, positively impacting student mental health (Mills et al., 2024).

In our case, the flexible frequency, timing, and focus of SUAW sessions are student-led, and the voluntary nature of attendance and engagement is reinforced by virtual delivery and a peer-led approach. Absences are not critiqued but instead acknowledged by checking in with absentees who are usually present, fostering collective accountability and belonging. Together, these deliver a low-pressure support environment enabling autonomy, agency, and communion, supporting positive mental health, and contributing to student success (Brownlow et al., 2023).

Collaboration

We present this case study/chapter as an example of a *shared collaborative task* that has increased engagement with, and a sense of belonging across our HDR CoP through self-actualisation, empowerment, and visibility (Gaynor et al., 2022). Shared tasks provide not only autonomy, purpose and meaning, but also opportunities for skills development, fostering a burgeoning academic identity (Verneert et al., 2021). By adopting an approach prioritising collaboration, relationships, and mutual autonomy, rather than traditional supervisor control, shared tasks embedded within SUAW sessions can foster inclusive and supporting structures and leaders (Brownlow et al., 2023).

We collaboratively produced a first draft of this work during a focused one month of SUAW sessions, following four key steps: 1) Discussion around the focus of the piece and methods/approach, 2) Collaborative literature review, 3) Drafting and peer review of allocated sections, and 4) Collective edits and approval of final version. This collaborative writing task created a true 'buzz' and togetherness across the CoP, providing opportunity for academic skills-development and helping to cement the identity and profile of our group.

Conclusion

This case study/chapter was conceptualised and written by rural postgraduate student members of Manna Institute's HDR CoP during our SUAW sessions. Our collective experiences highlight the value of peer-led virtual SUAW sessions to connect and support rural postgraduate students previously isolated by geographic distance and/or disciplinary context.

References

Alston, L., McFayden, L., Sen Gupta, T., Payne, W., & Smith, J. (2023). Creating a sustainable and supportive health research environment across rural and remote Australia: A call to action. *Medical Journal of Australia*, 219, S27–S30. https://doi.org/10.5694/mja2.52027

Australian Institute of Health and Welfare. (2024). Rural and remote health. Retrieved from https://www.aihw.gov.au/reports/rural-remote-australians/rural-and-remote-health

Brown, J. & Duguid, P. (2000). *The social life of information*. Harvard Business School Press.

Brownlow, C., Eacersall, D. C., Martin, N., & Parsons-Smith, R. (2023). The higher degree research student experience in Australian universities: A systematic literature review. *Higher Education Research & Development*, 42(7), 1608–1623. https://doi.org/10.1080/07294360.2023.2183939

Chakma, U., Li, B., & Kabuhung, G. (2021). Creating online metacognitive spaces: Graduate research writing during the COVID-19 pandemic. *Issues in Educational Research*, 31(1), 37–55. https://search.informit.org/doi/10.3316/informit.748747335200300

Delahunty, J., Verenikina, I., & Jones, P. (2014). Socio-emotional connections: Identity, belonging and learning in online interactions. A literature review. *Technology, Pedagogy and Education*, 23(2), 243–265. https://doi.org/10.1080/1475939X.2013.813405

Department of Education (2019). Student equity in higher degrees by research statistical report, August 2019. Australian Government. https://www.education.gov.au/download/4829/student-equity-higher-degrees-research/7200/document/pdf

DeSouza, R., Hendry, N., Stevens, R., Gomes, C., Harris, A., Hjorth, L., Richardson, I., & Kokanovic, R. (2020). In a time of uncertainty: Supporting belonging and wellbeing for HDR students. RMIT University.

Drury, V., Francis, K., & Chapman, Y. (2006). Walking the void: Being a rural PhD candidate. *The Australian Journal of Rural Health*, 14(5), 233. https://doi.org/10.1111/j.1440-1584.2006.00816.x

Gaynor, K. M., Azevedo, T., Boyajian, C., Brun, J., Budden, A. E., Cole, A., Csik, S., DeCesaro, J., Do-Linh, H., Dudney, J., Garcia, C. G., Leonard, S., Lyon, N. J., Marks, A., Parish, J., Philips, A. A., Scarborough, C., Smith, J., Thompson, M., ... Fong C. R. (2022). Ten simple rules to cultivate belonging in collaborative data science research teams. *PLoS Computational Biology*, 18(11): e1010567. https://doi.org/10.1371/journal.pcbi.1010567

Kumar, V., & Aitchison, C. (2018). Peer facilitated writing groups: A programmatic approach to doctoral student writing. *Teaching in Higher Education*, 23(3), 360–373. https://doi.org/10.1080/13562517.2017.1391200

Micsinszki, S. K., & Yeung, L. (2021). Adapting "Shut Up & Write!®" to foster productive scholarly writing in graduate Nursing students. *The Journal of Continuing Education in Nursing*, 52(7), 313–318. https://doi.org/10.3928/00220124-20210611-05

Mills, L., Read, G. J. M., Bragg, J. E., Hutchinson, B. T., & Cox, J. A. (2024). A study into the mental health of PhD students in Australia: Investigating the determinants of depression, anxiety, and suicidality. *Scientific Reports*, 14(1), 22636. https://doi.org/10.1038/s41598-024-72661-z

Napthine, D., Graham, C., Peter Lee, P., & Wills, M. (2019). National regional, rural and remote tertiary education strategy final report. Australian Government. https://www.education.gov.au/access-and-participation/resources/national-regional-rural-and-remote-tertiary-education-strategy-final-report

O'Kane, M., Behrendt, L., Glover, B., Macklin, J., Nash, F., Rimmer, B. & Wikramanayake, S. (2024). Australian Universities Accord Final Report. https://www.education.gov.au/australian-universities-accord/resources/final-report

Petridis, H. L. (2015). *Thriving in graduate school: The role of department climate, student faculty interaction, family-friend support, and a psychological sense of community.* ProQuest Digital Dissertations.

Proulx C. N., Rubio D. M., Norman M. K., and Mayowski C. A. (2023). Shut Up & Write!® builds writing self-efficacy and self-regulation in early-career researchers. *Journal of Clinical and Translational Science* 7: e141, 1–7. https://doi.org/10.1017/cts.2023.568

Turkle, S. (2011). The tethered self: Technology reinvents intimacy and solitude. *Continuing Higher Education Review*, 75, 28–31.

Verneert, F., Nijs, L., & De Baets, T. (2021). A space for collaborative creativity. How collective improvising shapes 'a sense of belonging'. *Frontiers in Psychology*, 12, 648770. https://doi.org/10.3389/fpsyg.2021.648770

Wilson, S., & Cutri, J. (2021). Novice academic roles: The value of collegiate, attendee-driven writing networks. *International Journal of Doctoral Studies*, 16, 149–170. https://doi.org/10.28945/4700

11 The Therapeutic Power of Writing

Exploring the Mental Health Benefits for Writers and Readers

Reagan Fleming

Introduction

Writing allows us to safely turn our pain, joys, and ever-evolving understanding about the world into readable art. Through it, we are able to express whatever we're thinking about and get it out on to paper or a Word document on our laptops with the hope that others will connect with our words and feel seen by it. Writing is a way to purge any and all healthy and unhealthy thoughts and feelings, and it can be an incredibly healing act. However, with busy schedules and personal doubts about one's talent, writers can find themselves in a period where they are not writing at all. For me, it was a combination of the two that held me back from writing creatively for a time, even though it is something that brings me joy. I found Shut Up & Write! (SUAW) at a time when I was entering my first semester of graduate school while also working a full-time job and feared that my creative writing would end up on the backburner due to the extensive amount of required academic writing. I work a typical 9–5, read my required texts for class, attend lectures, and write numerous papers throughout each semester, so I don't have much free time for other things. Even though I am quite busy each day of the week during the school year, I choose to schedule out an hour each week to attend my Shut Up & Write! group for my mental wellbeing and to meet with other like-minded individuals and see what we all can get accomplished. I am able to use that time to write whatever I feel like working on that day, which is usually my novel that I'm working on. It is so refreshing to take a break from writing term papers about 19th-century authors or certain themes hidden within Shakespeare's works and simply write for me. SUAW provides both a community and an opportunity for me to work on any creative writing project that I want to work on that week. I chose to include a photo of a stack of books that represent what I write and what I hope to finish writing by being in this group. By talking about what I'm working on with the members of my SUAW chapter and hearing about how they are writing their own trilogies, children's books, or articles about climate change, I am inspired to continue with my own ideas.

Figure 11.1 Books.

Busy Schedules

We all have busy schedules. They're unavoidable. There are ways to carve out thirty minutes of your day to write a little snippet of something interesting that could happen next in your book, or maybe you can carry around a small notebook like I used to in high school and write down lines for future poems, or maybe you take a few minutes before bed and read something inspiring that will spark something in you to write the following day. When I was in high school, I toted a small Five Star notebook and completely filled it by the end of semester with thoughts I had throughout the day or ideas for images I could use in future poems. I don't carry around a notebook with me anymore. Instead, I attend my SUAW meetings each Saturday at 10:30 a.m. We grab our cups of coffee, talk about our days and previous week, and we share what we hope to work on during our upcoming hour. Each and every one of the members of my SUAW chapter bring something special to the group and bring a different outlook on the world. For example, one of the members who uses the hour to write poetry served in the military for many years, and he brings something to the poetry world that I cannot bring. We each write completely different things based on our own personal lived experiences; without our writing, the world would never know things from our points of view.

SUAW provides a great opportunity for people of many different backgrounds and lived experiences to come together for one hour each week and simply shut up and write. And while I do believe that it's helpful to fit writing in your busy schedules, it's also important to do things that build creativity in your daily life. Keeping your head down and only writing day in and day out prevents you from taking in any new experiences that are around you. Yes, it's possible to hunker down in your bedroom and write for hours on end, but there's something life-giving about going outside and opening yourself up to new experiences. Whether you're writing fiction or non-fiction, taking life by the horns and experiencing it for yourself adds *realness* to your writing.

Why We Write

There is something to be said about those books that when you read them, you think, *I understand what the writer is trying to get across, and I feel seen.* Writing is simply a tool for the reader to feel seen as a human being or is an avenue for the reader to make some type of connection to the work.

While it's difficult to do this with my academic writing, I do strive to achieve this in my creative writing. I am currently working on a novel that I hope to get published one day, as almost all authors do. I want to create something for my future readers that they will not only enjoy, but which will also make them feel more connected to the human race. This is a very tall order, and it's a duty that I do not take lightly. My goal in writing realistic fiction and poetry is to allow readers to learn things about themselves and see things from another perspective other than their own. When I was in elementary school and times were incredibly tough for me and my family, I turned to books. Specifically, I turned to classics like *Pride and Prejudice* and young adult books such as *Divergent*. I wanted to escape, and with the long-winded romance and exciting action scenes, I was able to remove myself from the reality I was facing and just have fun for a little while. I would climb up the big maple tree out in the front of our yard and sit in the crevice of intersecting branches and simply read for hours. Some people read for pleasure, some read to understand a new topic better, some want to read something that makes them feel less alone, and some read because they need an escape. I read for all of these different reasons. Just like it's unfair to judge a book by its cover, we can't judge a person by what kind of book they're reading.

Writing as a Student

No student is a stranger to writing, whether it be a term paper, writing prompts from an English professor trying their best to encourage non-English majors to enjoy writing, or writing numerous cover letters to a slew of jobs or internships they're applying for. It's a necessary evil for some and a delightful pastime for others. For me personally, it's my favorite part about being back in school. I'm currently getting my master's in English at the University of Tulsa, and the group discussions, term papers, and weekly blog posts/writeups we do for each class make for stressful, yet exhilarating weeks during the semester. As a student, this is where I see the most benefit to SUAW. The one hour a week I take to sit down, speak with others about what I'm about to write, and actually write something of my choosing (which, for me, is non-school related) allows my school brain to shut off for a sliver of my Saturday morning and focus on something that lets my creative juices flow. Even as I'm writing this, in January of 2025, I'm thinking about how I need to get ahead of the game and start reading certain books for school before the semester starts. However, I keep reminding myself that the writing I do during SUAW is just as important. It's just important in a different way.

Creativity is a Muscle

In "Creative Writing: Embracing Unfamiliar Knowledge," Laura Otis states that as a literary scholar themselves, they believe that "one can build knowledge by writing creatively" (Otis, 2023, para 2). Otis continues,

> For many human brains, straining one's imagination to create a story-world or to enter a story-world that another writer has created counts as experience. Readers respond to literary works in unique ways depending on their life contexts, neural variations, and cognitive habits.
>
> (paras 2–3)

The written word is a fascinating medium; while it presents one product, whether it be a poem, article, book, or essay, its meaning can resonate in a different way for each reader. When a writer is wracking their brain on what should come next in their fantasy novel or testing out different lines for the ending of their poem, it gets those creative juices flowing in their brain. Creativity to me is like a muscle. Everyone has it, but it's up to each person to work on strengthening it. Writing is healthy not only for your brain, but also for physical and mental health. For example, James W. Pennebaker writes, in "Telling Stories: The Health Benefits of Narrative," that through his studies, he and his colleagues found that:

> ...when people put their emotional upheavals into words, their physical and mental health improved markedly. Further, the act of constructing stories appeared to be a natural human process that helped individuals understand their experiences and themselves.
>
> (2000, para. 2)

In said studies, Pennebaker asked the participants to write about something traumatic that happened in their lives. Then, he asked another set of participants to write about unemotional topics. More of those who wrote about extremely emotional topics later decreased their visits to the doctor for mental health checkups compared to those who wrote about everyday topics (pp. 4–5). While there are benefits to writing anything, whether creative or not, this study shows that writing from the heart and tapping into your emotions helps you process those memories and possibly heal from them as well.

Just Shut Up and Write Something

I have heard from numerous authors that it is incredibly important to try and write every day. Whether it be something little or something that turns out to be lengthy and complex, writing something every day encourages inspiration and keeps you in the writing headspace. Even if it's a terrible first draft or a poem that rhymes way too much, get it down on paper (or Word document). I'm not a huge fan of journaling, but approaching my own form of journaling – simply getting my emotions and thoughts out and down on paper, no matter how few words I actually write – is easy. So, I simply jot down ideas and thoughts I have just to get whatever I'm feeling down on paper and out of my brain. The beauty of my particular SUAW group that meets every Saturday is one that I am sure other groups share: encouragement. Before we write, we each explain what we hope to accomplish, and after the hour-long timer sounds, we share if we met those goals and tell the table what we actually wrote. Whether I share that I finished an entire poem or got distracted and applied for a new job instead, the other members of my group never judge; they simply listen and often say how what I did was actually useful in some way. I find that I want to show that I've accomplished something within the hour that I devote to my group; being a part of the group and the group members themselves encourage me to get down to business and write.

Necessary Skill

Writing is a necessary skill to function successfully in this world. Without it, our ideas and concepts would die with us, unable to be passed down to those who come after us. Many famous writers, including Emily Dickinson and Franz Kafka, only gained notoriety posthumously. They had no idea that their books would reach the success that they have today; they just wanted to take the time to write something that *they* would enjoy reading. In addition to writing being used creatively, it is something that professionals use in some way every day, whether it be in writing memos to the staff, emailing coworkers, or simply creating a resume in order to be hired in the first place. You need to learn how to write well in order to be taken seriously in a professional setting. I currently work as an editor for a large nation-wide company where I edit training videos and documents before they go out to the rest of the company. I know the importance of error-free documents, because when I read something with incorrect grammar, which happens more often than I'd like, I don't want to read any further or give my money to that company. It's up to

What You Write Matters

I was once told in a writing class I was taking during my undergraduate years that I was too young (I was 23 at the time) to write a memoir. The professor who told me this was well into his 70s, so I partly understand what he was saying – as one gets older, they experience more life than someone who is, say, half their age. What he said really stuck with me and also bothered me, because up to that point, I had written personal essays here and there so I could turn it into a book one day. I still have those essays, and out of defiance, I continued to write essays about my life. Yes, I was young at the time, but that doesn't mean that I didn't have – and still don't have – anything to say. If Anne Frank was discouraged to write about her life because she was young, we wouldn't have *The Diary of a Young Girl*, which is, I will argue, one of the best books ever written. Simply because you are a living, breathing human, you have a right to write, and what you have to say matters to someone. This "someone" might be yourself, but most authors choose to write things that they themselves would want to read anyway. Just because you are young, have a career in a completely different field, or don't think you're creative enough, you can be a writer. All you have to do is set aside some time and actually write. Each member of my Shut Up & Write! group works in different industries and vary in age. However, we come together one day a week for a common goal – to sit down and simply write whatever we want for an hour. Shut Up & Write! provides the opportunity for people in all walks of life and all stages of life to come together and simply write.

Conclusion

At the end of the day, it's up to you to decide how much, or how little, you want to write each day, if anything at all. We can always come up with excuses on why we can't write that day or psych ourselves out into thinking that what we have to say is unimportant and unoriginal. To simplify things, we are all alike in that we are nothing alike. We are all human beings who can connect in many ways, including, but not limited to, the written word, pieces of art, movies, and television shows. In addition to our ability to connect with these mediums, each person connects to them in different ways. That is one of my favorite things about Shut Up and Write! – every single person who arrives is working on a different thing, something that they love. This group not only allows different types of writing but actually encourages it. We all have our niche, and Shut Up and Write! is a wonderful representation of that.

References

Otis, L. (2023). Creative writing: Embracing unfamiliar knowledge. *Configurations* 31(4), 343–350. https://doi.org/10.1353/con.2023.a912114

Pennebaker, J.W. (2000). Telling stories: The health benefits of narrative. *Literature and Medicine* 19(1), 3–18. https://doi.org/10.1353/lm.2000.0011

12 Academic Identity Development in the Context of Online Writing Groups
Increasing Resilience and Wellbeing

Jason Murphy and Lisa Hodge

Introduction

Higher education is a contested space where acute demands are often endured as researchers move through their journey to become an academic (French, 2020). These demands include extreme pressure to publish and secure funding; engage publicly; and teach (Cannizzo, 2018; Hammond, K. et al. 2022). This can be experienced with a backdrop of toxic work cultures, poverty, unhealthy supervisor arrangements, and isolation (Coates, 2024). Further, there is a gender-based imbalance in how these pressures are experienced. This was exacerbated during COVID-19 lockdowns, as gender inequalities worsened for women with children in higher education (Yildirim and Eslen-Ziya, 2021), representing significant obstacles for researchers seeking to develop their academic identities.

Universities are sites of immense social, symbolic, and cultural capital (Bourdieu, 1984). Paradoxically, this capital can be locked within institutional hierarchy, administrative bureaucracy, managerialism, and organisational structures (Gallagher and Lamb, 2023). Hierarchy may represent a barrier for junior academics accessing the knowledge of their established and experienced peers. Moreover, a spirit of managerialism, positioned within a neoliberal framework (Mula-Falcón and Caballero, 2022), often prevents the exploration of new knowledge and approaches that cannot immediately be shown to be economically profitable. Contradictorily, universities are measured with regard to their effective engagement with communities, but their own internal structures can act as obstructions and deterrents to wider engagement (Collier, 2021).

Writing groups, often emerging from the margins of institutions (Wilmot and McKenna, 2018), can ameliorate some of the harmful aspects of university cultures and have demonstrated profound benefits for researchers at all stages of their careers (Haas et al. 2020; Özdemir, 2021; Pais Zozimo et al. 2023). This has been manifested through reducing feelings of loneliness, anxiety, and other stress-related health issues; increasing scholarly productivity; and providing collaborative environments (Cannell et al., 2023; Hodge & Murphy, 2023). Previously conducted face-to-face, writing groups pivoted overnight to online in response to COVID-19 lockdowns (Freya and Cutri, 2023; Hammond et al.

2022). In this chapter, we explore the role of online groups in developing both academic and writerly identity, and in increasing resilience. We present the results of interviews conducted with writing group attendees during the pandemic and provide valuable insights into the online writing experience, including the ways exchange might differ between group modalities.

Theoretical Framework

We drew on Bourdieu's conceptual devices, capital and habitus. as explanatory concepts that explore the individual's position within social structures, while allowing for individual agency (Pretorius & Macaulay, 2021). These concepts – often considered in isolation – are situated within Bourdieu's practice theory (Bourdieu, 1990), which dialectically analyses practical life as it plays out between structure and agency (Harker et al., 1990). We consider educational institutions as sites of contradictions where the reproduction of inequality is manifest (Bourdieu & Passeron, 1990). Bourdieu's (1986) forms of capital are concepts that describe the social, cultural, symbolic, and economic capital that social agents inherit, amass, and exchange through their individual lived experience and social interactions. The informal field of the writing group and its comparatively flat hierarchy, where researchers of multiple experiences interact while engaging in the act of writing, contrasts with the formal university from which such groups emerge and provides a novel space for capital's exchange. The image in Figure 12.1 makes use of light and shade and the angle of the building to powerfully symbolise universities as sites of immense capital, yet at the same time dark clouds muster encapsulating a moment of natural defiance, where land and sky are locked in a grandiose standoff, emphasising how this exchange can be obstructed by hierarchy and rigid structures. The writing group, however, is a space where capital can be freely exchanged.

While the primary reason for attending online writing groups may be the production of writing texts and other research artefacts, we explored through qualitative interviews whether the existence of, and access to, the group's social and other forms of capital continued to be an aspect of attendance in online modalities.

Methodology

We conducted 19 in-depth semi-structured interviews of approximately 60 minutes in duration, via the online platform Zoom. Participants were based internationally and were from a range of experience levels and disciplines, from doctoral students through to late career researchers. Participants were selected based on their attendance of writing groups during the pandemic period. Writers who volunteered to participate in an interview were from a range of writing groups, including: female-only Vietnamese PhD scholars who were also mothers; large mass writing groups; and groups organised with a pedagogical framework, based on providing writing feedback. All interviews were recorded and transcribed verbatim. Following Braun and Clarke (2019), we

108 *Fostering Wellbeing through Collective Writing Practices*

Figure 12.1 The contradiction of universities (Photo credit: Benjamin Lehman).

used reflexive thematic analysis to analyse the data and generate themes. Braun and Clarke (2019) point out, reflexive thematic analysis is not about 'accurate' coding, but about the researchers' reflective and thoughtful engagement with their data. Both authors are academic scholars who inhabit privileged spaces as white bodies, while at times gender, class, and ethnicity all challenge this privilege. We understood our role in knowledge production as a "continual bending back on oneself" (Braun & Clarke, 2019, p. 594), where we read the transcripts separately and then came together to compare, challenge and negotiate a more nuanced reading of the data (Hodge & Murphy, 2023).

Our research asked the following questions:

- How do online writing groups support the development of academic identity for emerging scholars?
- What motivates scholars to take advantage of informal writing groups beyond institutional contexts?

Results

The benefit of writing as a social activity has been conceptualised as a 'community of practice.' Yet the traditional notion of 'community' relies on the metaphor of physical space and the process of outsiders gradually gaining insider status (Subedi et al. 2022). The sense of 'community' that online writing groups offer is a flexible space in which to enact writing and as a pleasurable academic activity, where feelings of loneliness and stress-related health issues are reduced (Wilson & Cutri, 2019). Three key themes were identified from the data, where over one-third of participants' experiences related to these themes: security, support and wellbeing; online group dynamics; and the exchange of capital in online groups. Bourdieu's theoretical concepts were used to analyse these themes to explore the relationship between the practices of writing group participants and individual agency (Pretorius & Macaulay, 2021).

Security, Support, and Wellbeing

Participants consistently revealed that online writing groups fostered wellbeing by providing psychological support. Indeed, a sense of 'security and support' was a common experience, which had a positive impact on participants' mental health. For example:

> I initially expected the writing group would predominantly just motivate me to be more productive…I have found that the group has also given me a real sense of security and support…it is also really comforting to interact with other people that understand the challenges that are associated with research, and academic writing…So, there's that real connection as well…and they have a lot more expertise and help and guidance and advice that they can offer me.

Thus, the exchange of expertise and ideas, or capital, with other 'group members,' and the 'real connection' that formed, suggests online writing groups can enhance the participants' confidence as researchers and writers. Moreover, at a period where isolation was exacerbated due to lockdowns, the following quote suggests attending online groups helped reduce feelings of depression.

> I don't think I would have progressed that much on my first article if it wasn't for the writing group…I wasn't really doing much because I was too depressed at being at home and the rest of it. But, on attending them my productivity went up quite a lot.

The 'companionship' found through online writing groups was important to contributing to wellbeing, as the following quote explains:

> Suddenly a PhD student…it takes a great deal of adjusting because suddenly you're writing alone…It can feel very isolating…I just basically feel very much alone at times, but not at all since attending the writing groups…It's quite surprising the kind of sense of companionship it offers.

Online Group Dynamics

The transformation of writing groups to an online format during the pandemic reduced physical barriers to attendance, as researchers could join groups from any location. Some attendees relocated overseas, but could maintain established relationships with peers in Australia. Further, the shift to online groups was also found to be a positive experience for persons with disabilities. This finding exemplifies the capacity for inclusivity that writing groups engender. The following quote illustrates this:

> The group of academics that we were meeting for months…one of them is severely, had like severe disabilities. So, she couldn't attend the face-to-face groups, but she could attend the virtual ones. And she made comments a few times that it was really great how this was happening online because it meant she could attend…I never thought about it from an accessibility point of view.

The 'strict regime' created by the Pomodoro structure of 25-minute singularly focused periods of writing itself reduced 'anxiety' for several participants, as highlighted here:

> The first Pomodoro maybe I don't feel like working or writing but the fact that you have to be there…then the anxiety goes away and then you start doing something and then the second Pomodoro is better and then sometimes there are Pomodoros that you don't even want to stop working…That's why I think it is amazing, this pressure of the people, confinement in a single place. The Pomodoros' strict regime is the perfect combination to write.

Participants still felt accountable regardless of modality, but with online groups, cameras were seen as a proxy for engagement and other distractions could impede participation, as the following participant suggests:

> Just turning off your camera is like leaving the room… I consider it rude, even though I did it as well,…it's what I call the hypocrisy of zoom…I'm in a meeting at the same time I'm cooking and doing a million other things, but I'm paying attention…if you see everybody typing in their computers, you feel that peer pressure of doing the same.

Online groups may be more susceptible to disengagement, highlighting the importance of effective facilitation.

The Exchange of Capital in Online Groups

We found that despite groups being run online, they continued to act as a platform for the exchange of social and cultural capital (Bourdieu, 1990), such as writing strategies and communication skills. This aligns with previous research that found writing groups nurture academic and writerly identities (Hodge & Murphy, 2023), as the following quote reveals:

> I feel a bit more…confident to ask the other writing group members questions about writing, than I am my supervisors. I think it's because I feel my supervisors might question to themselves as to why I'm asking them certain questions…she should know better than that. So, I kind of feel more relaxed around the other writing group members.

Feeling comfortable to seek advice about writing from group members supports both the exchange of cultural capital that occurs within these groups, and the accessibility of this exchange and support through the nullifying of hierarchy. Aligning with our theoretical use of Bourdieu, it was apparent that this continued to occur for other attendees of online groups, as the following participant describes:

> I started to see myself as an academic because I'm within a group of other academics. So now I start thinking I'm an actual academic; this is where I'm heading. So, it motivates me to work a lot more on my writing. A lot more on my Twitter identity and opening up to whatever is needed, to get me into that group of academics.

This exchange takes place at the margins of groups and more senior academics can share experiences about writing and the formation of academic identity.

> I think one of the major benefits above and beyond just getting words on the page is the conversations that happened…it's this cross-pollination of all this information from academics at different levels…and being able to bounce ideas off…And other doctoral students saying: 'I've got this issue around my methodology',…and then everyone in the room going: 'Oh, I've got an idea.'

Future Directions

COVID-19 lockdowns significantly changed the way researchers interacted and accelerated a transition to online groups. Some positive aspects of face-to-face groups translated online, with significant advantages for those with accessibility and/or geographical constraints. The exchange of capital that occurs in face-to-face groups remained an important feature, coupled with the alleviation of hierarchy that is typically present in university contexts. The role of the facilitator appears an intrinsic element of success with online groups and warrants further investigation, with implications for institutions that seek to support researcher wellbeing. Future research could also consider the composition of writing groups along the lines of gender, including the bias toward female participation. Moreover, while academic writing groups – particularly doctoral writing groups – are widely researched in the literature, there is little published about non-academic writing groups.

Acknowledgements

The authors acknowledge and thank the research participants for their participation in the study and the organisers and attendees of the *Community in Writing* Symposium, Cambridge University, November 2024 for their valuable feedback and discussion.

Disclosure Statement

No potential conflict of interest was reported by the authors.

References

Bourdieu, P. (1984) *Distinction: A social critique of the judgement of taste.* Routledge.
Bourdieu, P. (1986) The forms of capital, in J. Richardson (ed.) *Handbook of theory and research for the sociology of education* (pp. 241–258). Greenwood.
Bourdieu, P. (1990) *The logic of practice.* Stanford University Press.
Bourdieu, P. and Passeron, J.-C. (1990) *Reproduction in education, society and culture.* 2nd ed. SAGE Publications.
Braun, V. and Clarke, V. (2019) Reflecting on reflexive thematic analysis, *Qualitative Research in Sport, Exercise and Health, 11*(4), 589–597. https://doi.org/10.1080/2159676X.2019.1628806
Cannell, C., Silvia, A., McLachlan, K., Othman, S., Morphett, A., Maheepala, V., McCosh, C., Simic, N., & Behrend, M. B. (2023). Developing research-writer identity and wellbeing in a doctoral writing group. *Journal of Further and Higher Education, 47*(8),1106–1123.https://doi.org/10.1080/0309877X.2023.2217411
Cannizzo, F. (2018) Tactical evaluations: Everyday neoliberalism in academia, *Journal of Sociology, 54*(1), 77–91. https://doi.org/10.1177/1440783318759094
Coates, T. K. L. (2024). Academic abuse: A conceptual framework of the dimensions of toxic culture in higher education and the impact on the meaning of work. *Higher Education Quarterly, 78*(4), 1–21. https://doi.org/10.1111/hequ.12536
Collier, A. (2021). Locks on our bridges: Critical and generative lenses on open education. In M. Bali, C. Cronin, L. Czerniewicz, R. DeRosa, & R. Jhangiani (Eds.), *Open at the margins: Critical perspectives on open education* (pp. 99–110). Rebus Press.
French, A. (2020) Academic writing as identity-work in higher education: Forming a "professional writing in higher education habitus", *Studies in Higher Education, 45*(8), 1605–1617. https://doi.org/10.1080/03075079.2019.1572735
Freya, A., & Cutri, J. (2023). "Memeing it up!": Doctoral students' reflections of collegiate virtual writing spaces during the Covid-19 pandemic. In B. Cahusac de Caux, L. Pretorius, & L. Macaulay (Eds.), *Research and teaching in a pandemic world: The challenges of establishing academic identities during times of crisis* (pp. 455–468). Springer Nature. https://doi.org/10.1007/978-981-19-7757-2_30
Gallagher, M. & Lamb, J. (2023) Open education in closed-loop systems: Enabling closures and open loops, *Distance Education, 44*(4), 620–636. https://doi.org/10.1080/01587919.2023.2267475

Haas, S., De Soete, A. & Ulstein, G. (2020) Zooming through Covid: Fostering safe communities of critical reflection via online writers' group interaction, *Double Helix*, *8*, 1–10. https://doi.org/10.37514/dbh-j.2020.8.1.01

Hammond, K., Trafford, J., Hassouna, A., Jowitt, L., Lees, A., Lucas, P., Power, N., & Stretton, C. (2022). "Ding!" Co-creating wellbeing in a Friday online research writing group. In *Reflections on valuing wellbeing in higher education*. Routledge.

Harker, R., Mahar, C., & Wilkes, C. (Eds.). (1990). *An introduction to the work of Pierre Bourdieu: The practice of theory*. Palgrave Macmillan UK. https://doi.org/10.1007/978-1-349-21134-0

Hodge, L. & Murphy, J. (2023) Write on! Cultivating social capital in a writing group for doctoral education and beyond, *Educational Review*, *77*(1), 117–133. https://doi.org/10.1080/00131911.2023.2184772

Mula-Falcón, J. & Caballero, K. (2022) Neoliberalism and its impact on academics: A qualitative review, *Research in Post-Compulsory Education*, *27*(3), 373–390. https://doi.org/10.1080/13596748.2022.2076053

Özdemir, O. (2021) A case study regarding the comparison of collaborative writing in digital and face-to-face environments, *International Journal of Psychology and Educational Studies*, *8*, 246–258. https://doi.org/10.52380/ijpes.2021.8.2.425

Pais Zozimo, J., Sotejeff-Wilson, K. & Baldwin, W. (eds) (2023) *Women writing socially in academia: Dispatches from writing rooms*. Springer International Publishing (Palgrave Studies in Gender and Education). https://doi.org/10.1007/978-3-031-44977-2

Pretorius, L., & Macaulay, L. (2021) Notions of human capital and academic identity in the PhD: Narratives of the disempowered, *The Journal of Higher Education*, *92*(4), 623–647. https://doi.org/10.1080/00221546.2020.1854605

Subedi, K.R., Shrma, S. and Bista, K. (2022) Academic identity development of doctoral scholars in an online writing group, *International Journal of Doctoral Studies*, *17*, 279–300. https://doi.org/10.28945/5004

Wilmot, K. and McKenna, S. (2018) Writing groups as transformative spaces, *Higher Education Research & Development*, *37*(4), 868–882. https://doi.org/10.1080/07294360.2018.1450361

Wilson, S., & Cutri, J. (2019). Negating isolation and imposter syndrome through writing as product and as process: The impact of collegiate writing networks during a doctoral programme. In *Wellbeing in doctoral education: Insights and guidance from the student experience* (pp. 59–76). Singapore: Springer Nature Singapore.

Yildirim, T. M., & Eslen-Ziya, H. (2021). The differential impact of Covid-19 on the work conditions of women and men academics during the lockdown. *Gender, Work & Organization*, *28*, 243–249. https://doi.org/10.1111/gwao.12529

Part IV
Technology and Innovation

13 Times to Shut Up, Times to Sing Out
How Technology Fosters Productivity and Wellbeing

Yvonne Wood and Alison Talmage

Introduction: About our SUAW Community

In becoming a self-sustaining, virtual Shut Up and Write! (SUAW) community, *Research Accelerator* adopted both a flexible approach and a range of technologies, to meet the needs of a discipline-diverse and geographically dispersed group. In *Research Accelerator* community SUAW sessions, writing is more than just writing. The writing process is more than putting words on the page, and SUAW is more than writing in silence together. The solitary experience of writing is instead often transformed into a collective social event (Lavery & George, 2025).

Virtual sessions, a necessity during the COVID-19 pandemic, remain an intentional choice for our geographically dispersed members, thanks to contemporary software development (Vargo et al., 2021). From a few online meetings per month, led by *Research Accelerator*'s founder, to an international group with daily, member-hosted SUAW sessions on Zoom, the use of other platforms (Welo, WhatsApp, Spotify) has developed collaboratively. With independent access to virtual office space, small group ad hoc sessions, and occasional in-person meetings, the creative use of technology – both during and between periods of writing – has enhanced the development of our community.

Over four years, *Research Accelerator* has grown into a vibrant community of practice (CoP). Members report a strong sense of belonging, mutual support, and increased confidence – the key elements described by recognised champions of the CoP concept (Webber, 2016; Wenger et al., 2002; Wenger et al., 2023). How has this happened, and how has technology fostered such community-building?

In this chapter we describe our community's approach by integrating two explanatory models that theorise the functioning of CoPs and the decision-making process when selecting and adopting new technologies, to illuminate our uniquely collaborative, open, and flexible SUAW community.

Explanatory Models of Practice

To understand the success of our community, we first considered the Community of Practice Maturity (CoPM) model (Webber, 2016). This proposes five stages in CoP formation: (1) Potential: identifying people with shared interests; (2)

Forming: building relationships and a common purpose; (3) Maturing: shared practices and sharing knowledge; (4) Self-sustaining: functioning autonomously with active members and valued activities; and (5) Transformation: adapting to members' changed needs (or alternatively ending the group). Writing during the pandemic, Wenger et al. (2023) acknowledged the shift to virtual communities, but advocated for collective decisions about choice and the use of alternative platforms, as was seen in the *Research Accelerator* community, which has reached self-sustaining Stage 4, heading to transformational Stage 5.

Secondly, we explored the Social Construction of Technology (SCOT) model (Pinch & Bijker, 1986). This framework suggests three stages in how people use and shape technology: (1) Relevant Social Groups, who learn to use specific technologies; (2) Interpretive Flexibility, a collective exploration of alternative ways of using the technology; and (3) Closure and Stabilisation, with *closure* meaning people settle into a purposeful use of technology (not closure as an ending) and *stabilisation* describing agreed ways of using the selected technologies in practice.

In line with recent research that encourages combining SCOT with other models for enhanced rigour (Basu, 2023), we purposefully combined the SCOT and CoPM models to map the integration of relational, informational, and technological aspects of our SUAW sessions (Table 13.1). We hope this will inspire others to build enduring virtual communities. The CoPM model suggests the *why* of the *Research Accelerator* community, while the technology provides the *how*. In the following sections we explain how this has worked in practice.

Forming: Relevant Social Groups

Both the CoPM and SCOT models start with people: convening a group with either a common field of interest (CoPM) or a shared technology goal (SCOT). For *Research Accelerator*, our collective focus is research: our parallel research journeys in varied disciplines. At this initial Forming stage during the pandemic, the community's focus, as for many other groups, was video-conferencing via the Zoom platform. However, the availability of technology alone was not sufficient: "Build it...and they will not come" (Wenger et al., 2023, p. 187). For example, chapter co-author Alison's mixed prior experiences of online SUAW groups with an inconsistent membership made her hesitant to join *Research Accelerator*. The difference she found was the fostering of community and peer support, and operating as a *slow-open* group (i.e., remaining open to new members joining session by session throughout the year, but with care taken to ensure members were oriented to how sessions and technology worked).

Maturing: Interpretive Flexibility

Technology (Zoom) enabled the forming of our CoP and the initial SUAW routines. At the Maturing stage, we collectively explored an additional platform (Welo) and a widely used messaging service (WhatsApp). This stage of

Table 13.1 Mapping the Integration of Webber's (2016) Community of Practice Model and the Social Construction of Technology Model (Pinch & Bijker, 1986) in *Research Accelerator* Shut Up and Write! Sessions

Community of Practice Maturity model →

	Forming	Maturing	Self-sustaining
Relevant social groups	Beginning with geographically dispersed graduate researchers wanting to connect (Zoom).	As a *slow-open* group, new members have joined later, with video resources provided to support orientation to both the group structure and the technologies used.	
Interpretive flexibility		Establishing a format for online sessions: verbal introductions, setting intentions, timed writing with breaks (Zoom); exploring new ways of engaging through additional platforms (Welo, WhatsApp).	
Closure and stabilisation			People connecting, conversing, and wellbeing activities during writing breaks (Zoom, Welo). Technology used for scheduling member-hosted daily groups (Zoom), alongside autonomous individual use of space and ad hoc groups (Welo), and informal messaging (WhatsApp). Openness to potential new technologies (e.g. Spotify playlist), i.e. looping back to Interpretive Flexibility.

Social construction of technology model →

the SCOT model – Interpretive Flexibility – can be grounded in how technologies are used (Bijker, 2010). Ultimately, it is about the people, who "are not passive, they are capable of interacting with technologies in ways the designers may not have predicted" (Meyer & Avery, 2010, p. 158).

For example, virtual SUAW meetings accommodate an international membership and continued engagement during leave and conferences overseas. These opportunities build and strengthen supportive peer relationships. Sharing research and self-care activities encourages positive and constructive feedback from the group and expands our collective ideas about professional and personal opportunities.

Self-Sustaining: Closure (Focus on People) and Stabilisation (Focus on Technology)

The final stage of the SCOT model – Closure and Stabilisation – is often referred to as two sides of the same coin, focusing on people and technology, respectively (Bijker, 1997). Closure is the process of the Relevant Social Group (our CoP) reaching a consensus about how the technology is used and stabilisation is about how the technology is understood and defined (Basu, 2023; Bijker, 2010; Pinch & Bijker, 1986). In contrast to the SCOT model's assumption of consensus about technology, our community has endorsed individual choice among various options, such as member-hosted SUAW sessions (on Zoom) during daytime, evenings, or weekends to accommodate work schedules. This approach has produced a more distributed leadership model for hosted SUAW sessions. The desire for greater connectivity prompted the introduction of an unhosted open space, the Welo platform, which adds autonomy. Open 24/7, a member can send a message to the WhatsApp Notifications group, to say they are "going to Welo", and then choose a virtual space that suits them in either the open plan office, a private booth or the garden. Some members regularly arrive into Welo at 5 a.m. for a brief period of focused work, in the silent no-camera zone, encouraged by seeing the avatars of fellow early-bird members hard at work.

From a CoPM perspective, technology has allowed connections, information-sharing, and common practices to thrive. The power of setting intentions at the start of each SUAW session encourages accountability to self in the company of others; that is, there is a brief opening round (cameras on) at the start of a 3-hour Zoom session where each attendee states their goal for the session; the timer runs for 50 minutes x 2, with breaks where members can chat, sing, dance or keep working; and at the end of the third 50-minute block, everyone reports on progress made. Importantly, this process sparks curiosity, resource-sharing, and vicarious experiences of struggles and triumphs with research landmarks, such as the ethics approval process, handling feedback, or finally getting to thesis submission. Social breaks provide a space for celebration, commiseration, encouragement, and physical activity.

The tasks of sustaining our practice, productivity, and wellbeing, individually and collectively, within these varied environments, have encouraged diverse creativity. Wellbeing strategies include music, movement, and playful exploration of digital effects (e.g., backgrounds, emojis, campfire seating arrangements...). Social breaks provide a space to share news, celebrate wins, and address barriers to writing progress, with each SUAW host developing their own style. More surprising elements include energising Sunday Zumba, a thematic analysis parody song, and a motivational Spotify playlist, all fostering positive emotions and dynamic interplay between individual motivation and connection. These periods are often infused with humour, a great resource for sustaining wellbeing (Savage et al., 2017). For example, "Coding-coding-coding" is a jocular expression of a common intention, drawn from a song parody. Additional songs and sayings have infiltrated community conversations.

Our CoP has settled into a consistent way of speaking about, using, and defining the technologies chosen (Bijker, 2010), with their use now taken for granted (Rosen, 1993). We have a shared lexicon and ways of interacting within diverse platforms, with the corresponding distributed technical know-how and problem-solving of a mature community. The membership model uses the *Research Accelerator* website (https://www.researchaccelerator.nz/) as the central information hub for scheduled Zoom sessions, and Welo (open 24/7) for unscheduled sessions, with invitations posted via WhatsApp. As a space for sharing, WhatsApp activity may stray from the original research intent, with news and banter contributing to community-building (or to some members turning notifications off – again, flexibility is key). Our mature, stabilising CoP demonstrates the value of "research culture and community" (McChesney et al., 2024, p. 137), particularly for postgraduate students and early career researchers.

Our productivity, relationships, and sense of wellbeing have been enhanced by these periods of shutting up and singing out, in a community enabled by technologies. A recent *Research Accelerator* survey investigated members' experiences of the community (Roache et al., 2025). One member commented: "I love that it's a community and that we have developed supportive relationships. It's not just a quiet space to get your work done in silence and then go." Another member reflected on the importance of community: "PhD research, particularly since COVID, can be a long and lonely experience. [...] The Research Accelerator sessions have become my study group, my research community, my tribe."

Self-reflection (Yvonne)
Who am I — who am I able to be in community
Writing now a part of my identity, identity reaffirmed virtually
Now engaged, engaged with my writing self, live streaming with my writing peers

Technologies shift and change subtly over time, as does the community membership, yet our CoP prevails. Key phrases and songs are used to strengthen community bonds; for example, the classic answer, "It depends ...", is given when a member seeks reassurance as to whether 30 participants is "enough" or 35 themes are too many ... Bruun and Hukkinen (2003) suggested that closure is never truly reached, because technology continually evolves. We continue to re-define our use of technology and adapt to using technology in new ways.

In line with the SCOT philosophy, the ability to experiment and make changes and suggestions is vital. Interestingly, although the Welo space was welcomed, the new technology and its quirks were adopted only slowly, until the pivotal implementation of the community WhatsApp messaging group. On the surface, the Zoom and Welo technologies serve similar purposes as immersive spaces for virtual co-location. In reality, subtle differences significantly affect community activity, such as hosted or unhosted SUAW sessions; a Zoom gallery of faces versus visuals of a virtual office, complete with meeting rooms, silent spaces, and social spaces; and the capacity to customise individual avatars and visual backgrounds. To streamline communications, a second WhatsApp group was created for the daily SUAW hosts, specifically to support or change hosting responsibilities, enhancing the group's autonomy. Zoom is also used to invite members to share live thesis submissions or to virtually attend presentations or graduation ceremonies.

Self-reflection (Yvonne)
Through the technology
    We care
        We grow
            We share
Return to silence
    Within the space
        Feeling nurtured
            Being heard

Discussion

Technology – while not a panacea for community-building (Wenger et al., 2023) – has enabled and enhanced the Forming, Maturing, and Self-sustaining stages of our CoP. *Research Accelerator* has stabilised as a broad community with multiple SUAW sessions. The use of technology to connect for meetings, whether scheduled or ad hoc, and in varied constellations of members, has become commonplace.

The *Research Accelerator* community's approach to both SUAW and technology has proved a good fit for individual members and for our growing membership, sustained over many years. The consistent timetable of facilitated Zoom sessions, and the ad hoc WhatsApp invitations to join the Welo space continually strengthen our bonds with the CoP. Testament to *Research Accelerator*'s intertwined scholarly and relational values is that long-term members engage post-PhD and overseas members juggle international time zones to attend.

Times to Shut Up, Times to Sing Out 123

Individual research and writing priorities remain central to our SUAW meetings. However, these are enriched through scholarly and social conversations and supportive activities that enhance wellbeing, focus, and productivity. When we refer to song parodies ("Coding-coding-coding") and quote unique community idioms ("It depends..."), we reinforce our relationality and set the scene for increased research productivity and sustained periods of writing, depicted in Figure 13.1.

Figure 13.1 The threads and thoughts that connect our community of practice in action.

Conclusion

In conclusion, we recommend innovative approaches to SUAW initiatives, to maximise support for community members. The shared values and habits fostered in our community are factors that promote both productivity and wellbeing. These are important considerations, particularly for those off-campus with looser ties to their university community.

Combining the CoPM and SCOT models has provided greater insights than either model would independently highlight. Specifically, we note the intersection of SCOT's technologically supported functions and a CoP's purpose and collective benefits. We suggest that technology options should be explored collectively throughout the lifespan of a SUAW community, rather than assuming a "one-size-fits-all" approach.

The relational aspects of our practice – our use of video-conferencing, virtual office, shared songs/song lists and messaging platforms (Zoom, Welo, Spotify and WhatsApp), together with occasional in-person meetups – foster productivity. Most importantly, this SUAW approach safeguards realistic aspirations and personal wellbeing, as a result of members experiencing a sense of belonging in their group, their research community, their tribe – both when shutting up and singing out.

References

Basu, S. (2023). Three decades of social construction of technology: Dynamic yet fuzzy? The methodological conundrum. *Social Epistemology*, 37(3), 259–275. https://doi.org/10.1080/02691728.2022.2120783

Bijker, W. (1997). *Of bicycles, bakelites, and bulbs: Toward a theory of sociotechnical change*. MIT Press.

Bijker, W. (2010). How is technology made? – That is the question! *Cambridge Journal of Economics*, 34(1), 63–76. https://doi.org/10.1093/cje/bep068

Bruun, H., & Hukkinen, J. (2003). Crossing boundaries: An integrative framework for studying technological change. *Social Studies of Science*, 33(1), 95–116. https://doi.org/10.1177/0306312703033001178

In Lemon, N., Bolzle, A., Santa Cruz, M., & Saunders, R. (2026). *Cultivating wellbeing and community through writing in academia: Shifting the culture with shut up & write!* (pp. 71–83). Routledge.

In Lemon, N., Bolzle, A., Santa Cruz, M., & Saunders, R. (2026). *Cultivating wellbeing and community through writing in academia: Shifting the culture with shut up & write!* (pp. 221–233). Routledge.

McChesney, K., Burford, J., Frick, L., & Khoo, T. (2024). *Doing doctoral research at a distance: Flourishing in off-campus, hybrid, and remote pathways*. Routledge.

Meyer, D. Z., & Avery, L. M. (2010). A third use of sociology of scientific knowledge: A lens for studying teacher practice. *Studies in Science Education*, 46(2), 153–178. https://doi.org/10.1080/03057267.2010.504546

Pinch, T., & Bijker, W. (1986). Science, relativism and the new sociology of technology: Reply to Russell. *Social Studies of Science*, 16(2), 347–360. https://doi.org/10.1177/0306312786016002009

Rosen, P. (1993). The social construction of mountain bikes: Technology and postmodernity in the cycle industry. *Social Studies of Science*, 23(3), 479–513. https://doi.org/10.1177/0306312793023003003

Savage, B. M., Lujan, H. L., Thipparthi, R. R., & DiCarlo, S. E. (2017). Humor, laughter, learning, and health! A brief review. *Advances in Physiology Education*, *41*(3), 341–347. https://doi.org/10.1152/advan.00030.2017

Vargo, D., Zhu, L., Benwell, B., & Yan, Z. (2021). Digital technology use during COVID-19 pandemic: A rapid review. *Human Behavior and Emerging Technologies*, *3*(1), 13–24. https://doi.org/10.1002/hbe2.242

Webber, E. (2016). *Building successful communities of practice: Discover how connecting people makes better organisations*. Tacit.

Wenger, E., Wenger-Trayner, B., & Bruderlein, C. (2023). *Communities of practice within and across organizations: A guidebook* (2nd ed.). Social Learning Lab. https://www.wenger-trayner.com/wp-content/uploads/2024/03/24-02-21-CoP-guidebook-second-edition-final-2.pdf

Wenger, W., McDermott, R., & Snyder, W. M. (2002). *Cultivating communities of practice: A guide to managing knowledge*. Harvard Business School Press.

14 'We are All in this Together'

The Role of Collaborative Writing Sessions in Developing Doctoral Candidates' Confidence to Engage in the Academic Publication Process

Lucy Hall and Paula Villegas

Introduction

Navigating the complexities of academic writing and publication is a significant challenge for many doctoral candidates, yet an increasing requirement in the competitive higher education landscape. In response to these challenges, this chapter presents the collaborative efforts of two practitioners working in the third space (Whitchurch, 2008) in St Andrews. Lucy, a learning developer specialising in postgraduate research (PGR) support, and Paula, who oversees the in-sessional program, Academic English Service (AES). Together, they established an online collaboration to deliver a series of workshops aimed at equipping PGR students with the skills and confidence needed for successful academic publication. The novelty of these workshops lies in the inclusion of a collaborative writing space in every session.

The workshops were designed with an emphasis on fostering a communicative, collective, and safe learning environment. Drawing on the principles of writing retreats and collaborative learning, the initiative aimed to enhance participants' sense of belonging and mutual support, recognising the social and cultural dimensions of the writing process. By combining structured input with opportunities for peer interaction, the sessions sought to scaffold autonomy while encouraging a shared commitment to the challenges and triumphs of academic writing.

This chapter provides an overview of the key challenges faced by our PGR cohort in their publication journey, ranging from navigating disciplinary expectations to managing the pressures of academic scrutiny. We then explore the structure and content of our workshops, outlining the pedagogical and methodological approaches that informed our practice. Central to this discussion are the voices of the participants, who reflect on their experiences and the impact of the collaborative space on their academic development.

Finally, we conclude with a reflection on the lessons learned throughout this initiative, highlighting the importance of institutional support in fostering collaborative writing spaces. We advocate for the adoption of similar initiatives across higher education institutions to enhance the doctoral experience and empower students as active contributors to their academic communities.

DOI: 10.4324/9781003633327-18

Our Challenge

Doctoral candidates often encounter significant challenges in their academic writing journeys, including feelings of isolation, lack of confidence, and the intricate demands of scholarly publication. The solitary nature of research can lead to social isolation, adversely affecting wellbeing and motivation (Forbes & Bowers, 2019). Additionally, many students grapple with limited exposure to disciplinary writing conventions and insufficient academic literacy, further hindering their progress. These obstacles can result in heightened anxiety and diminished productivity (Calle-Arango & Ávila Reyes, 2022). These challenges are familiar to our learners who are also under increased pressure to publish, yet no specific support was provided for doctoral candidates to successfully navigate this challenge.

Our Approach

To address the above-mentioned challenges, we came together with a proposal to deliver a series of workshops that would take our PGR researchers through the writing-for-publication process. We came together in our third-space roles (Whitchurch, 2008) to deliver provision which advocated the creation of a genuine research community. We position our workshop within the third space not only due to the nature of our roles but also based on the nature of the provision. This is open to all St Andrews students as part of their doctoral journey; however, this provision is not income-generating which can lead to complex dynamics when requesting resources to develop it. In our specific case, we aimed to promote a sense of "dignity" in research by fostering practices that prioritise and respect researchers' rights to share their narratives (Smyth, 2018, p. 141). To achieve this, our workshops offered key linguistic frameworks and resources while providing a clear and transparent understanding of the publication process.

Our sessions were designed to combine collaborative input on the writing for publication process with individual writing output. This provided participants with initial guidance informing their writing sessions while establishing a horizontal dialogic space where exchange of ideas and experiences was at the

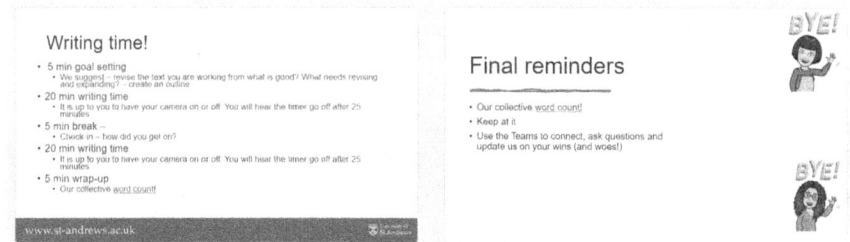

Figure 14.1 Structure of the individual writing output.

forefront of the input. To identify the key aspects informing the writing for publication process we followed Belchers' (2009) didactic syllabus outlined in *Write your Journal Article in 12 Weeks*. However, our 12 workshops expanded over two semesters, allowing for a longer time to work through the program, thereby meeting the needs of our cohort. The output part of the session was grounded in collaborative writing practices such as 'Shut Up and Write' (SUAW) sessions. Originating in the San Francisco Bay Area, SUAW involves writers gathering (virtually in our case) to write in focused, timed intervals. The Pomodoro technique is used to provide structure to each session and to allow for breaks in which participants can discuss their progress and any challenges they experience with their peers. We adopted this approach as it fosters a sense of community and accountability among participants. By dedicating specific times for writing and sharing goals, participants benefit from mutual support, increased motivation, and reduced procrastination (Mewburn, 2013). The social aspect of these sessions helps alleviate feelings of isolation, while the disciplined structure enhances productivity. They are often recommended to doctoral candidates in popular outlets such as the Thesis Whisperer and many institutions host student-led SUAW groups with no specific writing aim, theme, or target demographic.

At their core, these workshops are grounded in a pedagogy of care. As Walker-Gleaves (2019) emphasises, this approach does not prioritise a nurturing environment at the expense of academic rigor. Instead, it leverages our community as a foundation to effectively and sustainably support learners' autonomy while enhancing their social and cultural capital. Our ultimate goal is to empower learners to actively participate in the academic writing, publication, and peer review process. Our interpretation of a pedagogy of care aligns with the perspectives of Walker-Gleaves (2019), as we engage in meaningful academic inquiry (Walker-Gleaves, 2019, p. 109) while critically examining the scope and limitations of care within higher education teaching.

To explore our program's impact, we adopted a Mixed Methods Research (MMR) approach, combining quantitative questionnaires and qualitative focus groups. Thus, MMR integrates data collection, analysis, and inference within a single study (Tashakkori & Creswell, 2007), enabling triangulation, complementarity, and the expansion of findings (Ivankova & Greer, 2015). These strengths make this research method ideal for exploring complex phenomena such as confidence in the writing-for-publication process. A feminist lens allows us to identify the liminal status of our work while providing strong pedagogical principles to inform the development of our inclusive community. Firstly, empowering learners to acquire disciplinary discourses can be traced back to hooks (2000) and Fisher (2000). We specifically strive to free our learners (hooks, 2000) and raise their consciousness (Fisher, 2000) while embracing feminism as an accessible theoretical framework for learners to better understand not only texts but also power relations within their discipline and the broader academic field (Cerda, 2022). The intersectionality of our approach in relation to the third space and feminist pedagogy is crucial to understanding our ethos in developing our joint venture and contextualising the data generated to evaluate the implementation of our collaboration, as it also informs our positionality as researchers.

At the beginning of every session, we ask learners to briefly report on their goals for the session. We generated 128 responses over the course of the 12 workshops. Towards the end of our series of workshops we held a focus group, attended by five participants. It was designed and organised by us to provide learners with a welcoming space to articulate their writing for publication journey. The data discussed in this chapter comes from both the questionnaires and the focus group. This textual data was analysed following Braun and Clarke's (2016) six steps to thematic analysis and was subjected to an inductive approach to generate themes exploring participants' perceptions of the workshops.

Our participants were mostly in the final year of their doctoral journal or were part of a doctorate by impact program (Carver, 2023) which requires them to have tangible research outputs before submitting their reflective portfolio. In line with good research practice, we obtained ethical approval from our home university and sought consent from our participants to gather and disseminate their experiences.

What Did We Learn?

Doctoral Candidates' Voices

Data generated from questionnaires highlights the value of the collaborative writing sessions with learners citing advancing their writing as a key goal to attend the sessions with the idea of 'support' and 'motivation' frequently appearing in their responses. The second key reason for engaging with our sessions was to gain clarity on the process of writing for publication. Our third most frequent code refers to developing the language and organisational structures and characteristics of academic articles.

Table 14.1 What do you hope to gain from today's session?

Table 14.1 Hopes gained

Theme (in order of frequency)	Selected participants' answers
Advancing their writing	Get back into the swing of writing (Session 5) Support in writing (Session 5) Keep focusing on my writing (Session 8) Motivation (Session 4)
Understanding the publication process	Secure a coherent structure of a journal article (Session 9) How to study the information I have to build a coherent argument (Session 7)
Academic writing for publication literacies	Creating a good abstract! (Session 3) Learn how to deal with reviewer's feedback (Session 12)

It is worth noting that, for our participants, the collaborative writing sessions address complex needs such as motivation, ability to gain momentum, and receiving the support which ultimately translates into words on the page.

These themes were echoed in the interviews with participants which highlighted how the input part of the session allowed them to better understand the process and gave them the confidence to work towards publication. *'It has been helpful to understand, sort of, like, behind the scenes if I should call it, and it has increased my…I think it's like the idea that I can'* (Participant 1). Similarly, the collaborative atmosphere of the writing part of the session allowed them to put the ideas into practice and *'just write'* (Participant 1).

Data also shows the power of peer-to-peer interaction. '*So, during the breakout rooms, we got the chance to, to talk to other people coming from very different backgrounds and, and so it was really, really, like, productive*' (Participant 4). '*I feel so productive with everyone writing at the same time as me*' (Participant 5). This collaborative approach was highlighted as positive compared to some other group writing sessions experienced by participants which lacked opportunities for discussion.

Yeah, I attended a couple of well, two types of writing retreats, let's say at St Andrews. I've attended. Shut Up and Write sessions every time they come up. So, and they are very useful. And they're, they're kind of focused time to write. Unfortunately, I find those sessions a bit, like, I say, I don't want to be a rude or anything, but a bit depressing because you just, you know, you're standing (…) Because there's no kind of exchange between the participants and…

But of course, yes, it's a focus time, but yes, I find them a really depressing thing (Participant 4).

The perceived caring role of the facilitators, who were frequently described as '*supportive*', '*caring*' and '*so friendly*', with learners feeling they can '*ask all the questions even if they are stupid*' (Participant 3) routinely appeared in the focus groups and questionnaires.

From a feminist perspective, as discussed by Tuck (2018), this kind of emotional labour is often feminised and undervalued in academic contexts. The value of this to participants demonstrates the tutors' roles being deeply tied to notions of care and nurturance, even when specific pedagogical practices are hard to pinpoint. The tutor's approachability seems to have significantly enhanced students' confidence and engagement. Taken together, these codes show how essential the collaborative, supportive nature of the sessions was for the learners. In line with our ethos, they provided a safe space to unpick the hidden writing for publication process and just write.

Our Own Take

Reflecting on our experience facilitating these workshops, we were deeply impressed by the openness and enthusiasm of our participants. Their willingness to candidly express their fears, share their achievements, and ask insightful questions fostered a truly collaborative and supportive environment.

The commitment they demonstrated to writing in collaboration was both inspiring and affirming of the importance of creating such spaces within higher education.

It became evident that having dedicated time to discuss their writing was immensely valuable to the participants. This was reflected not only in the qualitative data gathered throughout the research process, but also in the dynamic and engaged atmosphere during the workshops. Participants actively contributed to the collaborative writing sections, setting personal goals, tracking their progress, and offering encouragement to their peers. Witnessing these interactions underscored the power of a collective approach where shared experiences and mutual support contributed to a heightened sense of motivation and accountability.

Ultimately, our experience reinforced the notion that fostering a safe and communicative space for PGRs can significantly enhance their writing journey. It highlighted the importance of institutional recognition and support for such initiatives, which empower students to navigate the challenges of academic publication with confidence and a sense of belonging.

As we presented our context, we candidly addressed the challenges of operating these workshops, which are not income-generating and have a liminal status in the academic space. Before concluding this section, it is worth noting how Tuck (2018) also addresses the disproportional number of women performing these roles. For us, specifically, this was the case as both of us are women.

We were able to introduce a more gender-balanced approach by having a male guest speaker at one workshop. Although we reached out to an academic who is sympathetic to our approach and champions the value of this type of provision, he was only present for the input part of the session and not the collaborative writing session. For academics not working in a researcher development space, tensions can arise in managing time and prioritising contracted responsibilities. We were sympathetic to this, and we clarified that we were not expecting him to join the collaborative writing session. This decision reflects the liminal space our collaboration occupied within the institution while echoing Tuck's (2018) critique of how such work, though pivotal to student success, often remains unacknowledged as professional expertise, reinforcing the marginalisation of the practitioners performing it. In a similar vein, in our roles as practitioners and researchers, we reject the perception of our workshops as mothering (Tuck, 2018) but rather as a radical approach foregrounding the needs of our learners as individuals and as part of the academic community while unpacking and questioning the very rules that inform writing for publication through rigorous engagement with research and practice.

Towards a Model for Collaborative Writing in Doctoral Education

The findings from our workshops highlight the transformative potential of integrating collaborative writing practices into doctoral provision. Participants reported increased confidence in their academic writing, a stronger sense of community, and the development of practical skills crucial for navigating the publication process. The opportunity to share challenges, celebrate progress, and receive peer support fostered a safe and inclusive environment where students could thrive academically and emotionally.

These sessions benefited not only the participants, but also us. The workshops provided structured time to write, constructive feedback, and a platform to develop autonomy in our doctoral candidates' writing journey while giving us the opportunity to engage meaningfully with them. This dual benefit underscores the value of such initiatives in bridging gaps between students and educators.

We advocate for collaborative writing sessions to become a staple in doctoral education. Institutions should prioritise these practices by adapting them to fit their unique contexts and by investing in resources that support their implementation.

As higher education continues to evolve, it is essential to reimagine how we support academic writing. By embracing collaborative approaches, we can transform the often-isolating experience of doctoral research into a shared journey of growth, learning, and achievement. The call to action is clear: institutions must adopt and adapt these practices to enrich the doctoral experience and better prepare candidates for the demands of academic publication and beyond.

References

Belcher, L.W. (2009). *Writing your journal article in 12 weeks: A guide to academic publishing success.* Sage Publications.

Calle-Arango, L., & Ávila Reyes, N. (2022). Obstacles, facilitators, and needs in doctoral writing: A systematic review. *Studies in Continuing Education, 45*(2), 133–151. https://doi.org/10.1080/0158037X.2022.2026315

Carver, M. (2023). Why do a doctorate? From 'PhD by publication' to 'PhD by impact'. *Research Intelligence, 34*–35.

Cerda, Y. (2022). Feminism: Affordances and applications for EAP. In A. Ding & M. Evans (Eds.). *Social theory for English for academic purposes: Foundations and perspectives* (pp. 199–219). London: Bloomsbury Academic.

Clarke, V., & Braun, V. (2016). Thematic analysis. *The Journal of Positive Psychology, 12*(3), 297–298. https://doi.org/10.1080/17439760.2016.1262613

Fisher, B.M. (2000). *No angel in the classroom.* Rowman & Littlefield Publishers.

Forbes, C., & Bowers, J. (2019). Emotional silos: A review of doctoral candidates' isolating experiences and the role for academic librarians in campus-wide support networks. *Informationr.net.* https://informationr.net/ir/24-1/isic2018/isic1823.html

hooks, b. (2000). *Feminist theory: From margin to center.* New York: London Routledge. (Original work published 1984)

Ivankova, N., & Greer, J. (2015). Mixed methods research analysis. In B. Paltridge & A. Phakiti (Eds.), Research methods in applied linguistics: A practical resource (63–83). Bloomsbury.

Mewburn, I. (2013). Shut up and write! *The Thesis Whisperer.* https://thesiswhisperer.com/shut-up-and-write/

Smyth, J. (2018). *Toxic University: Zombie leadership, academic rock stars and neoliberal ideology.* Palgrave Macmillan.

Tashakkori, A., & Creswell, J.W. (2007). Editorial: Exploring the nature of research questions in mixed methods research. *Journal of Mixed Methods Research*, *1*(3), 207–211. https://doi.org/10.1177/1558689807302814

Tuck, J. (2018). I'm nobody's mum in this university: The gendering of work around student writing in UK higher education. *Journal of English for Academic Purposes*, *32*, 32–41. https://doi.org/10.1016/j.jeap.2018.03.006

Walker-Gleaves, C. (2019). Is caring pedagogy really so progressive? Exploring the conceptual and practical impediments to operationalizing care in higher education. In P. Gibbs & A. Peterson (Eds.), *Higher education and hope: Institutional, pedagogical and personal possibilities* (pp. 93–112). Palgrave Macmillan.

Whitchurch, C. (2008). Shifting identities and blurring boundaries: The emergence of *Third Space* professionals in UK higher education. *Higher Education Quarterly* 62(4): 377–396. https://doi.org/10.1111/j.1468-2273.2008.00387.x

15 A Luxurious Commodity

Reflections on 'Shut Up and Write!' for Part-time, Taught, Postgraduate Students

Mark Widdowfield

Introduction

In 1934 J.B. Priestley published *English Journey*, a fascinating travelogue through an England that was going through the aftermath of the great depression. It provides an illuminating insight into how the working class lived, worked, and played during this time. In Nottingham, he stays at a hotel where his sleep is continuously interrupted; he blames the newfangled motor car for this: 'It will not be long before quiet is the most luxurious commodity in the world...' (p. 177). This chapter is about the power of quiet. A quiet that I believe is missing in modern life, and one in which we should, occasionally, try to place ourselves and our students.

The importance of quiet goes hand in hand with the increase in technological developments and their wider impact (a theme also developed in Priestley's work). Digital developments have brought solutions to many problems and also introduced new challenges. The ubiquitous nature of information technology has infiltrated every aspect of our lives (Perrin & Atske, 2021). This has resulted in such terms as 'digital availability', creating an 'urgency culture' along with the expectation of always being 'switched on'. This individual availability can increase anxieties that are associated with this constant state of alertness. This has coincided with a marketisation of higher education, particularly in the UK (Wong & Chiu, 2017). There are ways of managing this availability and marking clear boundaries between one's digital availability and other tasks. Using Shut Up and Write! (SUAW) in a taught educational context has the potential not only to increase effective work but also of managing wellbeing through reflection, reducing anxiety, and the creation of a safe, shared space.

Context

The context of this chapter is focused on an often-overlooked student cohort: the part-time student. These SUAW sessions were delivered within taught, post-registration, Health Professions programs. All the students are healthcare professionals (e.g., nurses, podiatrists, etc.) who were undertaking professional development in their current role, working either in university or clinical

Figure 15.1 A representation of the interplay between time, Shut Up and Write!, space, and reflection.

practice. These students work full-time with numerous responsibilities that jostle for their attention (such as families and other commitments).

Salient to this discussion is that these cohorts also contain a proportion of internationally educated healthcare professionals. Whilst these health professionals are working within educational roles, one must be cognisant of potential intersectionality with these students, as this may be their first time studying at postgraduate level within the UK. They may also have had very different life, and especially educational, experiences. Through this discussion I hope to show that integrating SUAW into our teaching practices can help to alleviate study-related anxiety and create a sense of wellbeing within our students, and ourselves, as we engage with writing tasks.

Literature

A shared experience of all students is that of assessment (albeit in different guises). It is already established that students feel a sense of anxiety around assessment. Numerous commentaries, empirical research, and educational self-help books attune educators and students to the factors that impact, and in some cases drive, assessment anxiety (e.g., Cramp et al., 2012; Pereira et al., 2016). It is notable that time is a particular focus when students suffer from anxiety around their assessment tasks (Sotardi & Dutton, 2022) – something which was echoed within these cohorts.

Along with assessment anxiety, part-time learners often feel marginalised or sidelined by the way in which traditional academic study is organised (Butcher, 2015). The traditional lecture, seminar, and other learning and teaching activities are usually undertaken within prescribed spatial and temporal parameters (Race, 2020). Whilst full-time students have traditionally had time to be able to dedicate to undertaking assessments, part-time students (and, at present, some full-time students) have other commitments such as work, caring responsibilities, etc. that are to be accommodated within the times outside of the classroom (Butcher, 2015). Part-time students often study in this manner due to having a full-time role (Delaney and Brown, 2020); these students are usually 'released' from their normal working day or through changing their off-duty/shift work. This therefore requires students to undertake the assessment activities through sacrificing their own free time, fitting it in around those wider commitments (Ho et al., 2012).

This traditional mode of delivery is reflected in how universities organise their modules. The time devoted to learning, teaching, and assessment is normally split up into various activities, such as lectures, seminars, etc. The other hours associated with the modular learning are often defined as 'self-directed': these include engaging with, and preparing for, the assessment (Huntley-Moore and Panter, 2015). The control of the time to be devoted to the assessment is therefore passed from the educator to the student, which then introduces the possibility for extraneous factors to have a further effect on the student's ability to engage.

Curriculum approaches such as Universal Design for Learning afford the students an opportunity to engage with materials on their own terms (Tobin & Behling, 2018). However, an argument can be made that learning predominantly occurs in the application of the learning materials (i.e., engaging in the assessment). Personally, I found engaging with assessment using mobile phones or tablets 'on the move' incredibly difficult. To invoke Priestley once again, I needed that luxurious commodity: quiet. I needed my own interpretation of a safe space; a place of calm in which to organise my thoughts and develop focus. This led me towards SUAW as a potential process for myself and then for harnessing this with students. Engaging with materials *may* be usefully undertaken on the bus or train (e.g., podcasts, reading) and mobile technology affords us the opportunity to do this, but is this really an optimal time and space to engage with assessment? Whilst this may increase engagement with learning materials, given that that some student's private lives may not be amenable to traditional delivery, the creation of an effective space for students to engage with assessment is required. Thus, the students (and staff) may be able to use the contact time to afford an opportunity to address anxieties around *assessment engagement* with activities that they would otherwise not be able to do.

The SUAW approach has been used extensively within postgraduate research degrees; normally where substantial writing is part of the process (Dalton, 2020; Mewburn et al., 2014; Sutherst, 2021). Using the approach within this context brings the assessment from the 'out-there' (something you do outside of the classroom environment) to the 'in-here' (within the classroom environment). We may therefore use SUAW to help students manage the many tasks that compete for their attention. The tasks defined here are not just those related to the wider educational program, but also those extraneous tasks mentioned above. If SUAW is implemented then the dreaded spectre of *time* does not compete, as it is now entwined with the assessment and the classroom space. Space no longer competes with the assessment as it too is now entwined within it. Therefore, we may consider the SUAW space as being devoted solely to student engagement within a defined space and time.

The following discussion is a commentary on how the approach has helped the students (and me!) who have engaged with it. These are my reflections on the evaluation of the sessions that we have undertaken together, across several cohorts.

Shared Commitment to Scholarly Activity

A provocative element of SUAW as a process is the element of shared consciousness and shared experience within the sessions. The sessions begin as timetabled activities for the students and include other study strategies, such as the Pomodoro technique[1] (Wong et al., 2025), which are showcased during the first session. The inclusion of a discussion around digital distractions is also useful in attuning the students to effective writing strategies. They are advised to alter the settings on their phones and not to engage in other activities such as checking social media (Flanigan et al., 2023). Prior to the session, the students are also advised to draw up a plan for the SUAW session. This helps everyone to stay task-focused and prevents wandering to other tasks, such as searching databases for literature or checking emails.

Given the wide variety of previous educational experiences within the cohorts, one of the key elements of the SUAW process is the opportunity for feedback on work. As well as anxiety related to time, there is also anxiety on the suitability of the structure and content of the student's writing. The integration of SUAW here affords the students ringfenced time to engage in formative assessment. This means that they can receive dedicated feedback on their writing style, referencing, etc. without the worry of finding time/space to engage this process. This is an important element when students have not studied in a part-time mode previously.

These sessions, though timetabled for the students, were also part of my own Research and Scholarly Activity rather than my teaching. This meant that, particularly when using the activity with dissertation students, there was a shared experience (I was writing up my PhD at the time). This approach was mutually beneficial but also had the effect of bringing together the educator and the student through addressing hierarchy. These were often full writing days and there was a coffee and a catch-up to be had between myself and the students. This 'in it together' approach has been employed in previous research with master's students (Caldwell et al., 2016). The difference here is that I was not a supervisor for these students, as they were supervised by other academic members of staff. I was simply a facilitator of the session, setting some (very) provisional ground rules, being present in the same space, and doing, ostensibly, the same task.

There is a relational element to the approach, as a firmer relationship developed between the students and me. The informal discussions during the small breaks in the sessions afforded the opportunity to get to know each other as more than simply a student and teacher. The relationship during the SUAW sessions altered from a traditional hierarchy to a more collegiate one, akin to those developed within communities of practice (Zihms and Mackie, 2023). We were simply a group of people engaged in a difficult and challenging task, but with mutual support. The task appears to be become more enjoyable as it becomes clear that this is not an insurmountable mountain up which we scramble, but a genuine learning opportunity which is enhanced through the act of collective writing and a shared experience.

The focus of teaching academic writing has been on the knowledge and skill of writing, whereas the emotional elements have been neglected (Wellington, 2010). I believe that employing a consistent approach to SUAW within the taught space can help in alleviating some of the anxieties that relate to finding the time and space to engage with writing. This is especially apparent when there is a shared goal within the classroom. Students have often commented that the approach allows them to see others working, and that this is motivational for them. Students have also commented that they wish that these sessions were more a regular part of the timetable. This is something that needs to be balanced across the wider student experience and leads us towards how SUAW may be expanded across the programmes.

Expansion of Activities

The SUAW process was further expanded in the sessions following feedback from students. It evolved into running an online approach, allowing synchronous mode of engagement which helped in terms of holding collective accountability and also being able to promote inclusivity. The quiet spaces that are attempted within the in-person approaches are not always as quiet as one first thinks. The constant tapping of the keyboard, the person who has a sneezing fit, someone who leaves the room for whatever reason – all can be a barrier to some people's ability to concentrate. The merging of the online and in-person approaches may allow further inclusivity. The online approach allows the muting of the room, along with showing those who are at home (or elsewhere) that there are others who are engaging in writing within the session. Whilst there is the loss of the communal feel afterwards, this must be weighed up by the individual as to the part of the shared experience that they need the most. This could be, for example, the human engagement or the accountability.

In future iterations of SUAW the hope is that a mix of in-person and on-screen approaches is applied synchronously. I hope to improve the shared experience through the opportunity for students to chat through both modes of engagement, utilising technology to create opportunities for social, as well as writing, engagement.

Concluding Reflections

Whilst we may think that we have moved on from Priestley's time, I would argue that, to paraphrase an old adage, what we have is the same play but with different (technological) actors. If anything, these actors are now more invasive than ever before, and it can feel that they are consistently vying for our attention. As an educator, first and foremost, my role is to ensure that the students are afforded the opportunity to succeed. Part of this opportunity creation must be focused on the removal of barriers so that students are able to meaningfully access the opportunity. Those barriers that cause anxiety in our learners must be dealt with first before they can meaningfully engage with the new learning. The implementation of SUAW within these cohorts has afforded the opportunity for this. Students who previously would have to engage with *less-than-ideal* technologies, in *less-than-ideal* spaces, at *less-than-ideal* times, now have those opportunities *built into* the learning programme. These opportunities can also take different modes, whether those modes are virtual or in-person. The preferences of the students do not necessarily matter – only that they are given the opportunity to engage with the process.

Furthermore, the implementation of SUAW also affords me, as the educator, specific opportunities to feed back on students' work. It is also a driver for the student to engage in these sessions, safe in the knowledge that there was the opportunity to get some timely feedback on work produced. The opportunity to engage with the assessment and knowledge that feedback will be provided (and timely) help to reduce the anxiety that students face, both within their performance and in finding the time/space/technology to engage and complete their allotted tasks. It also afforded me personally the chance to engage with the same activity as the students and to build meaningful relationships with them through the shared experience. Therefore, we all benefit from that luxurious commodity: quiet.

Note

1 The Pomodoro technique is an approach to splitting up a task into a defined timeframe. Focus on a single task for approx. 20 minutes and then takes a short break (3–5 minutes), before returning for another 20-minute focused period. Normally, this cycle is carried out 4 times before breaking for a longer period.

References

Butcher, J. (2015) *'Shoe-horned and sidelined'? Challenges for part-time learners in the new HE landscape*. York: Higher Education Academy.

Caldwell, G. A., Osborne, L., Mewburn, I. & Nottingham, A. (2016). Connecting the space between design and research: Explorations in participatory research supervision. *Educational Philosophy and Theory*, 48(13), 1352–1367.

Cramp, A., Lamond, C., Coleyshaw, L. & Beck, S. (2012). Empowering or disabling? Emotional reactions to assessment amongst part-time adult students. *Teaching in Higher Education*, 17(5), 509–521.

Dalton, S. (2020, October 16) *'Shut up and Write'* – online. https://studenteddev.leeds.ac.uk/news/shut-up-and-write-online/

Delaney, L. & Brown, M. (2020). Many happy returns! An exploration of the socio-economic background and access experiences of those who (re)turn to part-time higher education. *Irish Educational Studies*, 39(1), 83–100.

Flanigan, A. E., Brady, A. C., Dai, Y., & Ray, E. (2023). Managing student digital distraction in the college classroom: A self-determination theory perspective. *Educational Psychology Review*, 35(2), 60.

Ho, A., Kember, D. & Hong, C. (2012). What motivates an ever increasing number of students to enrol in part-time taught postgraduate awards? *Studies in Continuing Education*, 34(3), 319–338.

Huntley-Moore, S., & Panter, J. (2015). *An introduction to module design*. AISHE Academic Practice Guides, 6–18. Available at: https://www.aishe.org/wp-content/uploads/2016/01/3-Module-Design.pdf (accessed 11/12/24).

Mewburn, I., Osborne, L., & Caldwell, G. (2014). Shut up & Write!: Some surprising uses of cafés and crowds in doctoral writing. In *Writing groups for doctoral education and beyond* (pp. 218–232). Routledge.

Pereira, D., Flores, M. A., & Niklasson, L. (2016). Assessment revisited: A review of research in *Assessment and Evaluation in Higher Education*. *Assessment & Evaluation in Higher Education*, 41(7), 1008–1032. https://doi.org/10.1080/02602938.2015.1055233

Perrin, A. & Atske, S. (2021). About three-in-ten U.S. adults say they are 'almost constantly' online. *Pew Research Center*. 26 March. Available at: https://www.pewresearch.org/short-reads/2021/03/26/about-three-in-ten-u-s-adults-say-they-are-almost-constantly-online/ (Accessed 11/12/24).

Priestley, J. B. (1934; 2023) *English Journey*. HarperNorth.

Race, P. (2020). Lectures, seminars and academic advising. in Marshall, S. (Ed) *A handbook for teaching and learning in higher education: Enhancing academic practice*. (pp. 49–60) Routledge.

Sotardi, V., & Dutton, H. (2022). First-year university students' authentic experiences with evaluation anxiety and their attitudes toward assessment. *Assessment and Evaluation in Higher Education*, 47(8), 1317–1329. https://doi.org/10.1080/02602938.2022.2059445

Sutherst, J. (2021, January 25). *Shut up and Write*. https://sites.exeter.ac.uk/doctoralcollege/2021/01/25/shut-up-and-write-2/

Tobin, T. & Behling, K. (2018). *Reach everyone, teach everyone: Universal Design for Learning in higher education*. West Virginia University Press.

Wellington, J. (2010). More than a matter of cognition: An exploration of affective writing problems of post-graduate students and their possible solutions. *Teaching in Higher Education*, 15(2), 135–150.

Wong, B., & Chiu, Y. L. T. (2017). Let me entertain you: The ambivalent role of university lecturers as educators and performers. *Educational Review*, 71(2), 218–233.

Wong, W. Y. A., Caughers, G., Saifullah, A. D., Galeotti, M., Kemp, B. J., Cooper, C., Matthews, M., & Wilson, C. B. (2025). Key considerations when developing academic writing support for nursing and midwifery doctoral students: A scoping review. *Nurse Education Today*, 144, 106399. https://doi.org/10.1016/j.nedt.2024.106399

Zihms, S. G., & Mackie, C. R. (2023). The power hour of writing: An empirical evaluation of our online writing community. *Journal of Academic Writing*, 13(1), 22–34.

Part V
Maximising Impact and Effectiveness

16 Shut Up and Write!, Not Work

Personal Reflections and Strategies Towards Maximising SUAW Wellbeing Benefits

Stephanie Richey and Caylee Tierney

Introduction

Shut Up and Write (SUAW) is at its heart a simple concept – you join a group and write in silence for an agreed amount of time (Proulx et al., 2023; Mewburn, 2017). But as simple as this seems, we found ourselves questioning the boundaries of what constitutes 'writing' in a SUAW session and grappling with the range of tasks we could be doing, or felt we should be doing. We began reflecting on types of writing – for example, more creative work that involves sharing our ideas compared to largely administrative writing tasks. We also considered the validity of using SUAW sessions for activities related to writing, such as reading or preparation work, and the impact such uses of time ostensibly committed to writing could have on self-worth, engagement, and the sense of community SUAW offers.

Reflecting on our own SUAW practices, we realised that we personally were using some SUAW sessions simply for accountability of completing a task, which might have been urgent, but was unrelated to a writing goal. This was affecting our academic wellbeing and negatively impacting our SUAW experience, as we were squandering dedicated writing time on 'menial' tasks that were not progressing our goals, leading to stress, frustration, guilt, and unflattering comparisons with peers. This is unsurprising given the neoliberal higher education 'edufactory' context, an 'unprotected' space which is fast-paced, competitive, and performance-driven (Troiani & Dutson, 2021). For us, academic wellbeing is feeling achievement in all areas of our role, yet this context means we often get entangled in urgent demands like administration and teaching, compromising researching and writing time despite having a 'balanced' workload on paper. Following these realisations about wasting SUAW time, we each sought to develop a suite of strategies to help us maximise the potential wellbeing benefits of SUAW by promoting feelings of belonging and like purpose, and creating traction towards goals and passion for writing. Understanding what SUAW means to us has been a core part of our development of this chapter. We both started to reflect on our individual engagement with SUAW, questioning our broad and easy-going approaches. By working through our thinking around SUAW and with help from the strategies shared in this chapter, we now honour true writing time in SUAW.

Our Context and Visual Narrative

This chapter explores the personal experiences of the authors with SUAW in higher education and creative practice contexts, from the perspective of our roles as academic staff (Stephanie Richey) and casual academic, professional staff and creative writer (Caylee Tierney). Our examination of the various online SUAW experiences in which we have participated focuses on four practical strategies that have helped us to improve our wellbeing by honouring conscious and effective engagement with SUAW. These strategies address urgency versus importance, pre-work, accountability, and SUAW leadership roles. We recognise that our strategies and conclusions may not fit all people or approaches, but offer our perspectives in the hope of encouraging reflection and experimentation where it could maximise the potential of SUAW for generating positive experiences and wellbeing benefits.

Figure 16.1 represents the myriad 'urgent' work it is necessary to consciously detangle ourselves from so we can focus on the 'important' work of writing (for a discussion of urgency and importance see Covey, 1989). In busy workplaces and lives, what is personally important is often forced into the background (Burkeman, 2021; Troiani & Dutson, 2021) and therefore requires intentional foregrounding to bring the wellbeing benefits and satisfaction that come from working on what we value.

We see in Figure 16.1 a metaphor of the process by which we unravelled the knotty tension between allowing the 'W' of SUAW to denote 'work' and holding SUAW time for 'true writing' within ourselves (as seen in the tangled figure on the right of the image) and arrived at the single, smooth path of clarity angling up toward betterment in our wellbeing. For us, drawing out the simplicity of SUAW occurred via thinking through our approach to sessions with the below four strategies. This visual reflects the journey of our thinking and the juxtaposition between 'urgent' work tasks and 'important' writing in SUAW sessions.

Figure 16.1 Finding the write path (created by Caylee).

Strategies

Knowing What is Important Versus What is Urgent for Us, So We Can Honour the Important

So many work tasks feel urgent, and it is easy to prioritise those where others are relying on us – for example, a collaborative article rather than our own solo authored one. Even if we are writing, we can be focusing on things that do not hold the importance we would like, such as teaching materials, procedures and guidelines, research plans – all essential tasks in our roles, but not what is important for us in our own writing. It is key for our academic wellbeing to prioritise our own creative work as much as work we do with others, and to be accountable to ourselves. Therefore, a core idea of this strategy is to treat yourself like you would another team member and have the same expectations of progress on solo projects.

This strategy is key to our newfound philosophy that the 'W' denotes 'write' not 'work'. This means honouring SUAW sessions with our idea of 'true' writing tasks, where we are focused on creating personally meaningful output within our research role and creative writing goals, respectively. Such focus results in feeling a sense of achievement from core writing activities.

As a strategy, knowing what is important halts the powerful momentum associated with the completion of urgent tasks (Bodell, 2016; McKeown, 2014). Developing a practice of intentionally pausing to look up from the frantic motion of the 'urgent' every time we enter a SUAW session re-orients us to the importance of true writing tasks. Sometimes, the simple act of stopping and being conscious in a moment rather than continuing in a disconnected state of doing whatever is in front of us is enough to shift focus for the session. Invariably, we come away from sessions where we have prioritised 'important' work feeling satisfied that we have achieved something meaningful to us, and thus boosting our academic wellbeing, even if we proceed to dive back into the never-ending stream of 'urgent' tasks.

Ensuring We Complete the 'Pre-work'

It is demotivating and distracting to start a SUAW session searching for the latest file version or deciding which task to complete. To disentangle ourselves from the 'urgent' and start writing immediately, we have found that it is best to enter a session knowing exactly what the goal is – and it is a micro goal! Not 'work on that paper' but 'write 500 words of the literature review in section X'. To be able to write that, we are likely going to need some reading completed. Having the awareness to plan and execute any necessary pre-reading before the SUAW session is a valuable lesson we have learnt to boost productivity and honour the writing process. While reading is linked to writing, if we intend to honour the 'W' of SUAW, then it is key to have done necessary work that enables us to do the writing.

In addition to getting us organised for a quick start, preparing and planning in advance can reduce the chance of planning becoming a form of procrastination. We are prone to experiencing a sense of unreadiness to write, despite knowing that beginning what Mewburn (2017) terms 'generative writing' will facilitate the development of ideas. The practical 'doing' of writing is at a certain point of the process more beneficial than continued preparation or thinking (Becker, 2007; Emerson, 2015). Nonetheless, it can feel comforting to stay in the planning stage of a project. SUAW sessions have served us as a circuit breaker for this kind of procrastination – earmarking the time as unequivocal writing time means that we have an endpoint for our planning, even if it causes us to set aside seemingly necessary preparation in favour of seeing what eventuates. From this perspective, our approach of being strict on ourselves by honouring SUAW time as writing time does not preclude experimentation. Dedicated writing time that is exploratory has moved us beyond the hurdle of thinking without action and given us the satisfaction of progressing toward our goals.

Generating Accountability by Visible Intention Setting and Goal Tracking

In our experience, intention setting, either verbally or in the Zoom chat at the start of a SUAW, can assist in identifying and maintaining focus on our 'important' writing task and can create accountability when we share progress at the end of the session. Goal tracking via shared documents (for example, a group spreadsheet for recording goals and word counts) provides additional accountability and motivates us by showing our progress. As Costello et al. (2024) suggest, online SUAW formats lend themselves to this kind of beneficial record keeping. In our SUAW groups, we find sharing aims and progress heightens the identified sense of belonging, community, and motivation generated via SUAW (Costello et al., 2024). Similarly, doctoral students found that setting session goals kept them motivated, but not meeting them enabled collaborative discussion of how to progress with the goals, and in a less guilty manner due to the supportive online SUAW environment (García Marrugo & Anson, 2024). As a group, we encourage, strategise, celebrate, and commiserate. For us, this mutually supportive environment is enhanced when SUAW groups comprise members with different levels of experience, adding an element of mentoring to the group dynamic. Some research on the higher education context suggests that such dynamics can feel 'threatening' for those earlier in their journeys (Aitchison, 2009; Chihota & Thesen, 2014; Costello et al., 2024). However, when this has been us, we have felt welcome and appreciative of the support received in relation to intentions and goals, as well as writing processes more broadly – an experience shared by participants in Wilmot's (2016) study of writing groups. Furthermore, the online mode enables more diversity of experience levels than what might be found in-person, especially for participants with a smaller or no local campus. For participants in García Marrugo and Anson's (2024) study, the online mode promoted accessibility, creating a sense of community, and wellbeing for those previously excluded.

In cases where we have been the 'senior' members, such as Stephanie's experience with doctoral students, entering a mentoring role and offering advice and support also promoted positive feelings of wellbeing. Being of value to 'junior' participants and receiving their valuable contributions to the SUAW in the form of their experiences or advice from their supervisors generates reciprocal sharing and learning during check-ins that can bookend sessions to discuss aims, achievements, and difficulties (Mewburn et al., 2014). Solutions to the challenges we face in achieving our writing aims can and do come from anywhere, making visibility and checking-in valuable for progress at any experience level.

Taking on a Leadership Role

The experience of having a leadership role in a SUAW group elevates the commitment, engagement and belonging SUAW creates. For us, simply being part of the organisation of the group leads to higher personal engagement in and commitment to the sessions. We have turned up to every scheduled session and recorded progress appropriately as an example to others when participating as organisers or hosts. However, the more noteworthy personal shift in these scenarios is a heightened inclination to encourage and celebrate the successes of others in the group when they chose to engage and share, which in turn improves our individual sense of belonging and wellbeing.

In particular, the role of hosting ensures that we show up, turn our camera on, and have a session goal ready to share, which means we arrive already de-tangled from the 'urgency' mess. As hosts, we feel more engaged in the session, and more connected to colleagues as we interact with them at the start and end check-ins. SUAW leadership roles in a large cross-discipline group meant we got to know others and they got to know us from the host and organiser roles. This created a sense of connection and belonging within our university organisational division that we had not previously felt and opened our eyes to the range of disciplines and research around us, as also experienced by Mewburn et al. (2014) and Richardson et al. (2024) in the context of online groups and their capacity to connect across physical distance.

As a host of smaller, less formal groups, it can be disheartening when others fail to attend. However, we turn this around to see the positives of solo sessions to honour the SUAW time regardless of external accountability. Committing to the time and staying in the Zoom call alone has the added advantage of preventing other calls during writing time. Sometimes, late participants will join, allowing the end check-in to occur, which is another benefit of staying in the Zoom call even if you appear alone at the beginning. When viewed this way, the responsibility of hosting is rewarding and of benefit to our own writing practice across the wide range of scenarios that can arise in busy lives and workplaces.

Conclusion

Reflecting on our participation in SUAW sessions and how we can maximise our sense of productivity, self-worth, and belonging has led to some core strategies which inform our engagement in SUAW. As expressed in our image, we have both struggled to break free of 'urgent' but personally unimportant tasks to honour true writing that focuses on our priorities. The strategies shared in this chapter have helped us shift from the tension of using SUAW sessions to complete 'work' and feeling accomplished only in ticking jobs off 'to-do' lists, to honouring the 'W' of SUAW and actually *writing* in these sessions, with the focus on personal writing tasks that are important for our goals. Our collective strategies of 1) putting ourselves first, 2) completing preparation work before SUAW sessions, 3) setting visible session intentions, and 4) having a SUAW leadership role enable us to use sessions to our best ability, boosting productivity and leading to increased wellbeing from a sense of achievement and reduced pressure.

Our shift in thinking encapsulated in the idea that 'it is shut up and *write*, not *work*!' has enabled us to create positive participation in SUAW where we focus on core writing tasks that provide personal meaning and satisfaction, encouraging us to continue working on our writing outside of sessions, and/or return to them in a positive mindset ready to further progress tasks. Our final message is that even in sessions where these strategies are less effective, honouring the SUAW time and stopping the endless cycle of 'urgent' task completion to decompress is valuable in itself, and sharing in others' successes can provide a positive boost to refocus and reset. In exploring our own SUAW experiences and tensions, and the resultant strategies, we have highlighted core practices that increase our wellbeing through self-focus and sustained habits.

References

Aitchison, C. (2009). Research writing groups. In J. Higgs, D. Horsfall & S. Grace (Eds.), *Writing qualitative research on practice* (pp. 253–263). Sense.

Becker, H. S. (2007). *Writing for social scientists: How to start and finish your thesis, book, or article* (2nd ed.). University of Chicago Press.

Bodell, L. (2016). *Why simple wins: Escape the complexity trap and get to work that matters*. Routledge.

Burkeman, O. (2021). *Four thousand weeks: Time management for mortals*. Penguin Random House.

Chihota, C., & Thesen, L. (2014). Rehearsing 'the postgraduate condition' in writers' circles. In L. Thesen & L. Cooper (Eds.), *Risk in academic writing: Postgraduate students, their teachers and the making of knowledge* (pp. 131–147). Multilingual Matters.

Costello, M., Nyanjom, J., Bailey, S., & Ireson, D. (2024). Care in the academy: How our online writing group transformed into a caring community. *International Journal of Educational Research, 127*, Article 102441. https://doi.org/10.1016/j.ijer.2024.102441

Covey, S. R. (1989). *The 7 habits of highly effective people*. Free Press.

Emerson, R. W. (2015). Editor's corner: Preparation, procrastination, production, and perfection. *American Business Law Journal*, 52(4), v–x. https://doi.org./10.1111/ablj.12057

García Marrugo, A. I., & Anson, D. W. (2024). The impact of an online doctoral writing group: Increased confidence, feedback literacy, and wellbeing. *Australian Review of Applied Linguistics*, 48. https://doi.org/10.1075/aral.24012.gar

McKeown, G. (2014). *Essentialism: The disciplined pursuit of less*. Currency.

Mewburn, I. (2017). *How to be an academic: The thesis whisperer reveals all*. NewSouth Publishing.

Mewburn, I., Osborne, L., & Caldwell, G. (2014). Shut up & write! Some surprising uses of cafés and crowds in doctoral writing. In C. Aitchison & C. Guerin (Eds.), *Writing groups for doctoral education and beyond: Innovations in practice and theory* (pp. 218–232). Taylor & Francis.

Proulx, C. N., Rubio, D. M., Norman, M. K., & Mayowski, C. A. (2023). Shut Up & Write!® builds writing self-efficacy and self-regulation in early-career researchers. *Journal of Clinical and Translational Science*, 7(1), Article e141. https://doi.org/10.1017/cts.2023.568

Richardson, S., Krueger, L., Richardson, A., Coleman, E., Ogilvie, S., De La Fosse, K., Tobita, I., van der Wath, A., Mondejar-Pont, M., Mitterdorfer, A., & de Ruiter, H.-P. (2024). Collaborative international nursing writing group: A nonpatriarchal approach. *Creative Nursing*, 30(4), 299–307. https://doi.org/10.1177/10784535241276558

Troiani, I., & Dutson, C. (2021). The neoliberal university as a space to learn/think/work in higher education. *Architecture and Culture*, 9(1), 5–23. https://doi.org/10.1080/20507828.2021.1898836

Wilmot, K. (2016). Designing writing groups to support postgraduate students' academic writing: A case study from a South African university. *Innovations in Education and Teaching International*, 55(3), 257–265. https://doi.org/10.1080/14703297.2016.1238775

17 Unlocking Writing
Using Creative Tasks to Prepare the Ground

Claire Saunders

Introduction

> This calm moment breathes
> and gently renewal dawns,
> 'til hurry invades

As the convenor of Writing Kitchen, this image, and the haiku poem it inspired, captured my sense that 'calm moments' feel few and far between in the current higher education climate. The persistent narrative of metrics-driven, competitive cultures and shifting priorities makes it difficult to "navigate normative demands" (Nästesjö, 2023, p. 657). Alongside growing fears about job security, the result is a negative impact on academics' wellbeing (The Wellcome Trust, 2020).

Writing Kitchen is an online writing group established to respond to this challenging context. Its structure reflects Shut Up and Write! (SUAW)'s 'gather, write, repeat' pattern: an introduction, focused writing time and end-of-session check-in. The rather unconventional name derived from a colleague's passing comment at the end of our first meeting that it felt like we had gathered around a virtual kitchen table. As we played with the metaphor, we imagined the kitchen as the heart of the home, a sociable, creative, and nourishing space. Our 'kitchen table' is where writing happens.

Although some members (me included) have moved into different roles since Writing Kitchen began, at its inception we all acknowledged an often-fragile sense of academic identity further exacerbated by the challenges both of finding space and time to write, and the legitimacy of even doing so. Our academic contracts were somewhat unique. As part of the UK's largest distance learning university, our primary responsibilities were managing a widely dispersed body of Associate Lecturers and contributing pedagogic expertise to module and qualification development. This pedagogic activity resembled that of academic developers in more traditional universities. Even in those contexts, that work can be ambiguous and contested (Manathunga, 2006); in our

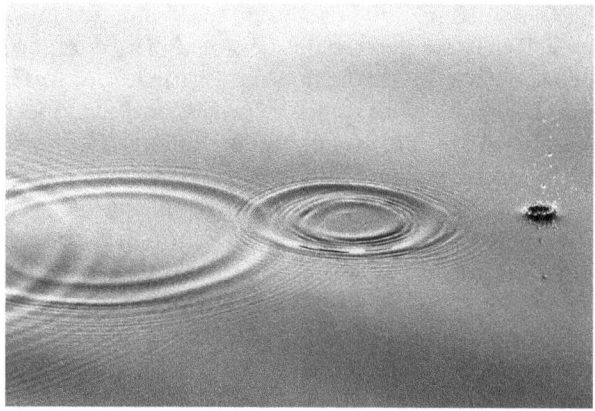

Figure 17.1 Water Ripple by Linus Nylund on Unsplash.

institution, with the label implied rather than explicit, the extent to which it was valued often felt uncertain. Time for writing felt scarce and its legitimacy tenuous:

> You don't feel qualified enough to be in a room with certain people. Or you don't feel that you fit a particular image of what you know, what is a writer or what's an academic? You know, I've always felt well, I don't fit into those images the way that you know it's been portrayed.
>
> (Ayomide)

This chapter argues that regular use of creative tasks as part of SUAW strengthens the connection between writing and identity (French 2020), positively impacting both the individual and the writing process. None of us has links to creative writing disciplines, yet we employ creative tasks in Writing Kitchen. This demonstrates their potential to enhance SUAW as a space for "identity-work" (French, 2020, p. 1605), simultaneously enabling community (Saunders, 2024). Both are essential to an institutional environment that genuinely values and enables writing.

A Theoretical Frame

Barriers to writing are widely acknowledged in academia. Competing institutional demands erode writing time (Gale, 2011). These can be compounded by the often-solitary nature of writing (Dwyer et al., 2012) and a series of negative emotions associated with the process, including low self-confidence, anxiety, and fear of criticism and rejection (Grzybowski et al., 2003; Morss & Murray, 2001; Pololi et al., 2004).

French (2020) argued that higher education is "saturated in academic writing practices which facilitate the core business of higher education, that is, processes of academic knowledge production and exchange" (p. 1607). Therefore, to some degree academics work out their professional identities through the types of writing they undertake and the audiences they choose. However, this is not straightforward, given the institutional pressures outlined above; the personal and the institutional intertwine in shaping academic identities.

The negative impact of this higher education landscape on academics' wellbeing is, therefore, hardly surprising. But there is hope. 'Spaces of Wellbeing' (Fleuret & Atkinson, 2007) is a four-dimensional model, drawing on the physical, social, and relational to propose the need for spaces of capability, integrative spaces, therapeutic spaces, and spaces of security. Beasy et al. (2020) used this model to demonstrate how a writing group can develop doctoral students' "capability" or "agency and freedom to achieve desired outcomes" (p. 1094). Writing Kitchen demonstrates the same potential and the creative tasks are instrumental in building the network of social relations that facilitate a supportive and affirming space, helping both to sustain motivation and to "nourish the capacity" (Beasy et al., 2020, p. 1094) for managing the cognitive and emotional labour of writing. In their work on writing for wellbeing, Smith and Jones (2024) explored how we bring ourselves to the writing space and subsequently to the writing itself. In a context where performativity and competition remain rife, opportunities to bring ourselves and to be vulnerable with others feel rare. But if writing is identity-work, fragile academic identities can have a profound effect on our writing.

Poetic Playfulness

The introduction of creative tasks is an adaptation to the traditional SUAW format.[1] They draw deliberately on aspects of poetry and figurative language. Poetry offers an antidote to the pace of change and sometimes relentless demands of the "sprint towards employability, standardisation, and quantitative benchmarks" (Illingworth & Jack, 2024, p. 8). Metaphor makes room for thinking differently, offering us "an invitation to hear the world anew…to encounter the world with fresh perceptions, exciting us with novel perspective, provoking new thoughts" (Hiley, 2006, p. 563).

Writing Kitchen began in 2020 and we came together at the end of 2024 to participate in a semi-structured discussion, reflecting on the role it has played in our academic lives. A thematic analysis of that discussion identified two key roles that the creative tasks play in the Kitchen:

1 **Getting ideas going** to move beyond the blank page, building momentum for writing.
2 **Thinking about ourselves as writers**, digging beneath the surface to acknowledge and address the barriers we experience.

Below you will encounter our own voices, heard through these tasks and our reflections, which I use as a stimulus for exploring their deep connection to our writing identities and their impact on our writing practices and wellbeing.

Getting Ideas Going

Our initial intention was to use creative tasks to move us beyond the fear of a blank page. Some were poetry, but we tried other things too, always with a creative emphasis. For example, we tried:

- Choosing a number between 8 and 12 and writing four lines of text containing that number of syllables, capturing the essence of what we would write about that day.
- Writing a short paragraph on the theme of our writing, but in an alternative genre – as a detective novel, a piece of romantic fiction, a travel journal.
- Capturing the main argument of our writing in a 'tweet' – no more than 280 characters.
- Writing a paragraph about a mundane household object in the style of our academic discipline.

These tasks and countless others flexed our writing muscles. We played around with form and genre to unlock the ideas that we subsequently shaped into more traditional 'academic' pieces. They served this purpose well. But it transpired that they also functioned as a means of shifting negative writing emotions:

> But the free writing I found really, really kind of loosened it up because I never do something like that. Because, I mean, you've all heard me say a million times. I hate writing.
>
> (Penny)

They also served as a valuable transition from the other spaces we inhabited into the writing space:

> I can't just switch into that. I need to do something to help me transition into writing as I want to write…the bit that you do before you put pen to paper or type is as important as what comes [next].
>
> (Rebecca)

Thus, whilst these were initially intended as tasks to 'get writing going', we recognised that they played another important role in creating the kind of space where we could shift our attention from the competing priorities of other work and begin to write.

Thinking About Ourselves as Writers

However, the tasks did more than enable the writing itself; as Writing Kitchen became more established, our creative responses captured shifts in our writing identities.

> **Then** I was a branch.
> Broken and low hanging,
> sitting apart,
> from the tree of my colleagues.
> At risk of snapping, falling,
> being blown by the wind,
> away from the tree
> I was supposed to grow from.
> **Now** I am more rooted.
> Stronger,
> a part of the canopy.
> Reaching for the light,
> I spread my leaves.
> They don't always flourish,
> Some dry, crisp and drop.
> But always there are more,
> Fresh, green and growing
> New promise of possibility and future.
> (Penny)

Through this 'Then and Now' poem (Illingworth & Jack, 2024) we explored how we saw ourselves as writers when we first attended Writing Kitchen and the changes we had observed. Penny's 'then' speaks of fragility, a sense of not belonging to the 'academy'. She prefaced her reading of the poem:

> I thought…what is a poem? Am I going back to childhood? Does it have to rhyme? Does each line have to be a certain length…But I thought, OK, I'll just have to. I have to do something…[My poem] tells something and it says something and it's quite emotional and I would never have had that confidence to do that by myself, ever.
> (Penny)

Penny traces her lack of confidence back to her early education. The 'identity-work' evident here is profound; the second verse sees her rooted in a community, willing to let some ideas go, hold onto others and embrace a hopefulness that was absent from verse one.

Other colleagues experienced similar revelatory moments:

> [It was] really emotional and personal...one of the few spaces I think within HE where I have written or thought about things from my childhood and how they impact. So yeah, it kind of sticks out as different, very different.
>
> (Rebecca)

For both colleagues, the creative tasks took them not just beyond their writing, but beyond even their adult lives. This connection with the past highlights the complexity of our identities and for these colleagues, surfacing this in the safety of Writing Kitchen helped them acknowledge the lasting impact on their writing practices. In this sense, Writing Kitchen was something of a therapeutic space; we recognised that we were increasingly prepared to be vulnerable and even sometimes to sit with some discomfort:

> I think, for some people, it takes us to a bit of an uncomfortable place to see what are our strengths potentially.
>
> (Bex)

> I think any creative activity you gave me to do beforehand would get me focused and start me writing. But I think there's something about the activities that we've done that probably had a bit more of a profound effect, whether consciously or unconsciously, on thinking about some of the deeper identity work.
>
> (Iain)

Iain's reflection was particularly poignant. Some weeks before we began the session with an 'I am from' poem to "capture...our own story, our own voice, our own complexity and history" (I am from project, FAQ, n.d.). Iain's poem reduced some of us to tears:

> I am from the smell of freshly brewed coffee
> I am from the taste of disappointment for never quite being what they wanted
> I am from the sound of finally hearing those words, "we're proud"
> I am from the movement of a rock accelerating down the hill, destination undefined
> I am from the feeling of the narrow beam under my foot as I move forwards
> I am from the sight of the faint light on the horizon
> I am from the place I am yet to define.
>
> (Iain)

The connection between writing and identity is stark; surfacing this connection allows us to examine it and to move beyond some of the deeper barriers to writing that we may not otherwise have allowed ourselves to acknowledge.

From the start, Writing Kitchen was a social, relational space. Participants willingly shared the outcomes of their creative tasks, expanding on them and responding to the contributions of others. For example, Harriet reflected on the value of community in creating a context for writing:

> So if I was in my writing closet by myself I wouldn't be able to do that. I need to be in the kitchen where there's, you know, knives and dangerous stuff happening in order to get me in the zone.
>
> (Harriet)

There is a paradox here. The space is secure, but rather than complete safety, we can live a little dangerously. Vulnerability co-exists with courage; there is space for taking risks, exploring new writing identities, and testing out different ways of writing. Furthermore, the creative tasks often surface our writing emotions, both positive and negative, which can have a liberating effect on the writing that follows. For example, we explored our experience of the writing process in the form of Haiku:

> Like leaves thoughts tumble,
> for a moment, still – before
> They blow away.
>
> (Claire)

> Falling full perfect,
> raindrops of inspiration,
> complete replete. Gone.
>
> (Harriet)

We were struck by the similarity of our emotions, the sense of thoughts captured and then escaping. It was our collective reflection that we shared many writing emotions as part of the process, despite our hugely varied experiences of academia and writing for publication. We all acknowledged a healthy dose of impostor syndrome in some of the spaces we find ourselves inhabiting. In Writing Kitchen, we have noticed its absence:

> But when you come into the [Writing Kitchen] room…there's no airs of arrogance in the room. You know, nobody's going, "Oh, I've written 20 papers since last year, and all that kind of stuff".
>
> (Ayomide)

For us all, sharing our writing processes legitimised the challenges we encountered as we recognised they were shared – and could be overcome:

> Claire, you have created a 'tribe' which is enabling and without ego.
>
> (Bex)

It is clear that the creative tasks play a significant role in building the positive relationships that underpin the Writing Kitchen; whilst they enable us to surface conflicting priorities and tensions, they also capture perspective shifts and moments of hope.

A Final Word

Writing Kitchen has taken SUAW and added an ingredient. In doing so, we have created a 'space of wellbeing' (Fleuret and Atkinson, 2007). Creative tasks unlock not just our writing, but a deeper awareness of writing as identity-work. As we reflected on the role of Writing Kitchen, we noticed that some of what we do there has seeped beyond its edges into our wider academic lives. In practical terms, we have seen the value of blocking out even short periods of time in our calendars to write. But we have also given ourselves permission to play, sometimes using creative tasks to ease our way into solitary writing. We are not the finished article or necessarily the most accomplished writers in our fields:

> **I used to be** the laundry basket,
> Little things and heavy things and nice things and work things and sticky things and heavy things and everyday things.
> All mixed up together
> Crumpled and tangled and needing to be sorted.
> Somewhere you delve with caution and trepidation,
> Only when absolutely necessary.
> **Now** I'm halfway through the ironing,
> Smoothing out wrinkles, turning things over and around and inside out.
> Gradually seeing things as they should be
> Aware there is still tricky stuff lurking
> Knowing I'll get to it – when I'm ready.
>
> (Harriet)

We do not produce polished pieces week in, week out, but we have gone somewhere on the journey together; our identities are more secure and our writing is the better for it.

Note

1 Sources of the creative tasks are varied – some we devise ourselves; others are adapted from activities we have encountered elsewhere. Where tasks mentioned in this chapter are sourced from other authors, these have been acknowledged.

References

Beasy, K., Emery, S., Dyer, L., Coleman, B., Bywaters, D., & Garrad, T. (2020). Writing together to foster wellbeing: Doctoral writing groups as spaces of wellbeing. *Higher Education Research & Development*, 39(6), 1091–1105. https://doi.org/10.1080/07294360.2020.1713732

Dwyer, A., Lewis, B., McDonald, F., & Burns, M. (2012). It's always a pleasure: Exploring productivity and pleasure in a writing group for early career academics. *Studies in Continuing Education*, 34(2), 129–144. https://doi.org/10.1080/0158037X.2011.580734

Fleuret, S., & Atkinson, S. (2007). Wellbeing, health and geography: A critical review and research agenda. *New Zealand Geographer*, 63(2), 106–118. https://doi.org/10.1111/j.1745-7939.2007.00093.x

French, A. (2020). Academic writing as identity-work in higher education: Forming a professional writing in higher education habitus. *Studies in Higher Education*, 45(8), 1605–1617. https://doi.org/10.1080/03075079.2019.1572735

Gale, H. (2011). The reluctant academic: Early-career academics in a teaching-orientated university. *International Journal for Academic Development*, 16(3), 215–227. https://doi.org/10.1080/1360144X.2011.596705

Grzybowski, S. C., Bates, W. J., Calam, B., Alred, J., Elwood, M., Andrew, R., & Rieb L. (2003). A physician peer support writing group. *Faculty Development*, 35(3), 195–203.

Hiley, T. J. (2006). Finding one's voice: The poetry of reflective practice. *Management Decision*, 44(4), 561–574. https://www.emerald.com/insight/content/doi/10.1108/00251740610663081/full/html

I am from project. (n.d.). FAQ – I Am From Project.

Illingworth, S. & Jack, K. (2024). *Poetry and pedagogy in higher education: A creative approach to teaching, learning and research*. Oxford University Press.

Manathunga, C. (2006). Doing educational development ambivalently: Applying post-colonial metaphors to educational development? *International Journal for Academic Development*, 11(1), 19–29, https://doi.org/10.1080/13601440600578771

Morss, K., & Murray, R. (2001). Researching academic writing within a structured programme: Insights and outcomes. *Studies in Higher Education*, 26(1): 35–52. https://doi.org/10.1080/03075070020030706

Nästesjö, J. (2023). Managing the rules of recognition: How early career academics negotiate career scripts through identity work. *Studies in Higher Education*, 48(4), 657–669. https://doi.org/10.1080/03075079.2022.2160974

Pololi, L., Knight, S. & Dunn, K. (2004). Facilitating scholarly writing. *Innovations in Education and Clinical Practice*, 19, 64–68.

Saunders, C. (2024). One writing group's story: Using an ethnographic case study to investigate the writing practices of academics. *Studies in Higher Education*, 49(7), 1194–1207. https://www.tandfonline.com/doi/full/10.1080/03075079.2023.22610.1

Smith, A. M., & Jones, K. (2024). "Catch it, drop it, leave it there": Writing for Wellbeing as a tool for compassionate practice in higher education. *Prism*, 1(1), 35–45. https://openjournals.ljmu.ac.uk/prism/article/view/1206/1263

The Wellcome Trust (2020). *What researchers think about the culture they work in*. https://wellcome.org/reports/what-researchers-think-about-research-culture

Part VI
Identity, Care, and Resistance

18 Nurturing Academic Mothers
Reconstructing Academic Identity During and After Career Interruptions through a Writing Community

Belinda Paulovich, Emma Fisher, Emma Grace, Abirami Thirumanickam, and Julie-Ann Hulin

Introduction

Academic mothers who take parental leave are required to navigate constant reconstruction of their identities and work practices. Often returning to academia on a part-time basis post-leave, academic mothers can experience isolation and confusion as they attempt to re-establish their careers. Despite parental leave being an Enterprise Agreement entitlement, it is well-known in academia that taking lengthy – or multiple – periods of leave can be considered detrimental due to the 'interruptions' these periods create in an individual's academic track record (Bowyer et al., 2022, p. 15). Furthermore, when women return to work after a career break, they are likely to do so "within the constraints of their competing responsibilities for households, partners, children and possibly other family members" (Stone & O'Shea, 2019, p. 98). This significant lifestyle adjustment inevitably results in having less time available to complete academic tasks and requires academic mothers to do more with less.

The impact of time pressure and competing demands on academic mothers cannot be underestimated. In recent years, academics have been required to adapt and increase their productivity due to the heightened demands of academic work, the reorganisation of teaching, research, and service roles, and the growing emphasis on metrics for productivity, efficiency, quality, and accountability (Lipton, 2020). While this evolution impacts all academics, mothers returning from parental leave experience these demands in a magnified way as they attempt to find where they belong within a landscape that has changed significantly while they were gone.

To cope with the challenges of time pressure, adjustments to new motherhood, and the desire to advance an academic career, many academic mothers "[seek] shelter in conversations with other mothers" (Yoo, 2020, p. 3179). This sentiment aligns with the views of Gavin et al. (2024), who introduce the concept of 'collective collegiality' as a counter-space to institutionalised collegiality. This concept allows academics to learn from each other how to navigate, survive, and thrive in the neoliberal academy. It involves socially constructing collegiality to prioritise group wellbeing and collaboration (p. 388). This process is facilitated through acts of care and specific spaces or times, creating a 'bubble' outside the neoliberal hierarchy (p. 397).

We view our Shut Up and Write! (SUAW) group as a counter-space that offers an opportunity for academic mothers to re-connect with their academic identities while receiving peer support to focus on writing productivity. The counter-space offers a safe environment for members to express their hopes and fears as they navigate the process of integrating two separate identities: mother and academic.

Experiences of Academic Mothers in SUAW

This chapter turns a mirror on the experiences of five academic mothers who participate in a multi-institutional SUAW group called Academics Down Under SUAW. Academics Down Under is a professional networking group that was launched by Dr Belinda Paulovich and Dr Julie-Ann Hulin in January 2024. The core members will describe the impact that the Academics Down Under SUAW group has had on their academic identity and work practice, and how this intersects with the demands of being an academic parent.

Dr Belinda Paulovich – Lecturer in Communication Design

As a mother to two young children, I have experienced a significant recalibration of my work and home life over the past six years. Following the birth of my daughter in 2019 I took 12 months parental leave. I returned to work part-time in 2020 during COVID-19 lockdown. University campuses were closed, and we had to work from home. Access to childcare was extremely limited, so my daughter remained at home with me for 6 months while I worked. In 2022 I took parental leave again, following the birth of my son. I was on leave for 16 months, and returned to work part-time, this time on-campus.

Upon returning to academia, I was keen to pursue a leadership opportunity. However, finding something that aligned with a part-time academic career proved challenging. I started to explore self-generated leadership opportunities that would complement what I was already doing in my career, as well as align with the rhythm of part-time work and the demands of motherhood. I realised that members of our Academics Down Under network would be engaging in solo writing tasks each week, so I put out a call for academics to join a weekly SUAW group. The five core members that have participated in our SUAW group from its inception are the authors of this book chapter.

Being the facilitator of SUAW has offered a flexible leadership opportunity that I have been able to pursue at my own pace. More importantly, however, our SUAW group has activated friendships across borders, reducing feelings of isolation that occur when re-establishing academic identity after career interruption. It has allowed me to realise a long-term dream of collaborating with Author 5, who is my friend from childhood. I have also reconnected with

Author 4 who I went to university with 20 years ago, deepened my relationship with my on-campus colleague, Author 2, and discovered a new friendship with Author 3.

Through the haze of early motherhood, and all the lifestyle adjustments it has required, I have succeeded at keeping a firm grip on my academic career and identity, which at times felt as though it could slip away. Critical to maintaining my passion and self-belief in academia has been finding like-minded people who understand the nuanced intersection of academic life and motherhood, and who join me each week for two hours to Shut Up and Write!

Dr Emma Fisher – Lecturer in Communication Design

I hold 27 years of experience as a communication designer, starting at a prominent Melbourne studio for 10 years, followed by a directorship in a smaller practice since. I've also taught for eight years in higher education and completed my PhD in 2015 to pursue opportunities in academia. During this time, I took two 12-month periods of parental leave while maintaining minor roles in design practice.

I find publishing to be the most challenging part of my academic role. Self-imposed deadlines are hard to prioritise over competing commitments and, while I enjoy conducting investigations, writing is less enjoyable. This leads to procrastination, fewer publications, and limitations on future promotion opportunities.

For me, our small, hybrid, semi-structured SUAW gatherings have been incredibly useful and supportive for progressing my writing. The sessions offer the perfect amount of structure for productive progress, balanced with flexibility to accommodate my unpredictable availability. More importantly, the conversations, suggestions, and encouragement within our group have helped me enjoy and appreciate the writing process.

Dr Emma Grace – Senior Lecturer in Inclusive Education

Returning to work in academia following a third period of parental leave and adjusting to shifts in my perspective, priorities, and capacity has been harder than I imagined. It may seem obvious that becoming a mother to three children brought significant change to my working life, but that idea seems to be in contrast with academic workplace expectations. Connecting with others has helped me realise that I am not "returning", but redefining what success looks like for me. The community and structure provided by the SUAW group has been invaluable in this process.

The Academics Down Under group has connected me to others who have faced similar challenges in navigating motherhood and academia, offering a shared understanding of these struggles. Our informal chats provide solutions, advice, and encouragement, and our shared experiences remind me that I'm not alone in this. There's a sense of community that comes from managing similar circumstances, like knowing the multitude of tasks that have already been accomplished before the workday begins or juggling unplanned care of children who have become unwell.

The network provides structure with regular uninterrupted time to write, which I've come to view as career-focused work time. Using the Pomodoro technique, sessions create protected space to prioritise writing, sustain momentum, and connect with my academic goals. Coming together with others who understand the personal challenges of protecting this time inspires and strengthens our individual efforts.

Productivity is further supported through celebrating and encouraging each other to set small goals and celebrate achievements each time we meet. The efforts and progress of each community member is a genuine encouragement to me and boosts my motivation and confidence. Keeping a reflective log provides both structure and motivation, enabling us to see our progress and notice how a series of progressive commitments builds momentum in writing. Most importantly, in our shared time, we don't pretend that balancing academia and motherhood is easy or seamless.

Success now means balancing academic growth with the needs of my family and celebrating even small achievements in both areas. This network supports my progress, helping me set and navigate realistic goals. Through dedicated writing and a community that provides sustained support, it is reshaping my career and expectations.

Dr Abirami Thirumanickam – Senior Lecturer in Speech Pathology

My academic career began three years post-PhD, at a Group of Eight (Go8) university (one of the 8 leading, research-intensive universities in Australia). The timing of my career shift presented with unique challenges. I had a delayed start to my research career, having spent the first two of my early career researcher (ECR) years in a teaching-focussed position without research opportunities. Moreover, my transition to a research-active role coincided with the global pandemic and the establishment of three new allied health programs within a new school. Balancing program development, accreditation, curriculum design, and establishing a research profile, while adapting to remote work and homeschooling, was arduous.

Nonetheless, I secured small seed funding, which later led to other competitive external grants and collaborations. However, securing grants was only part of the academic equation. Finding time to write was equally crucial and challenging.

The SUAW sessions were a game-changer for me. The anticipated, weekly structured writing blocks allowed me to re-prioritise and organise other commitments. These sessions provided a focussed time for dedicated writing, which was vital when balancing family life and building a career. During this time, I submitted four manuscripts and one book chapter, which substantially boosted my academic output.

We used the Pomodoro method of writing for 25 minutes and re-grouping for 5. As the group expanded, the re-grouping exceeded the allocated time;

however, I felt that these re-groups were critical in building cross-disciplinary peer networks. I am hopeful that, over time, they will expand to interdisciplinary research collaborations. Most importantly, this online group offered peer networking with other academics facing similar challenges. This sense of community bolstered my confidence and reminded me I was not alone. Over the last year, we have had two in-person social catchups, further strengthening our connections.

Encouraged by my experiences, I advocate for these sessions to other ECRs. As an academic navigating career interruption and rebuilding, I feel a responsibility to mentor and promote a balanced approach to academic work and life. Sharing my experiences and strategies, I aim to shift academic culture towards valuing wellbeing and self-care, particularly for those juggling multiple roles like motherhood and research. Whilst these challenges remain, I believe I now have the tools and support to face them as I commence my new senior role. For me, the SUAW sessions became not only a writing tool, but also a catalyst for career development and personal affirmation in academia.

Dr Julie-Ann Hulin – Researcher in Clinical Pharmacology

In the past five years I have taken two substantial periods of parental leave and reduced my working hours to part-time, to accommodate primary caregiver responsibilities. As a laboratory researcher, balancing the dual roles of a part-time academic and primary caregiver has been challenging, particularly when navigating the demands of research alongside the unpredictability that comes with young children. I have found that during these transition years, reconnecting with a professional identity has felt overwhelming. However, being a part of the SUAW group has been transformative; offering a structured time to write and a renewed sense of belonging within the academic community.

The group has provided a fantastic platform to prioritise dedicated writing time, something that has often felt elusive. Setting aside a focused, uninterrupted block of time, free from the constant pull of domestic or other professional obligations, has had a profound impact on my productivity. More importantly, I have rediscovered the joy of thinking deeply and engaging meaningfully with my research. Carving out two hours of dedicated writing time each week has not just been a practical exercise, but a statement of valuing my intellectual contributions in a life filled with competing priorities.

Beyond productivity, the group has fostered an invaluable sense of connection. It has offered a safe and inclusive space for informal discussions, which often touch on the less visible aspects of academic life. We have shared many triumphs, frustrations, and questions surrounding part-time academia and career goals. These conversations have reminded me that my struggles and successes are shared by others walking a similar path.

Ultimately, our SUAW group has created a supportive environment filled with encouragement, that has helped to dispel feelings of isolation that often accompany fragmented work patterns. Whether discussing the realities of

Figure 18.1 Our SUAW group can be visualised as an organic Venn diagram containing our five group members. We are united by a central link of shared experiences of parenthood and the demands of academic careers, while also being enclosed and supported by our surrounding SUAW community.

juggling caregiving and research or celebrating victories, the group has provided a sense of solidarity that is grounding and uplifting. It has demonstrated the value of community and shared purpose in academic life, proving that even amidst the challenges of balancing motherhood, it is possible to find a meaningful space for connection and growth. It has helped rekindle a passion for research, reminding me why I first chose this career.

Strategies for a Successful SUAW Experience

From reflecting on how and why Academics Down Under SUAW has been so beneficial for us, the strategies we offer to others are to:

1 Create a supportive space with like-minded colleagues who share common life experiences and challenges.
2 Choose a time and duration that is realistic for all members to attend regularly. We have found a weekly session of two hours to be achievable and useful.
3 Block out the writing time in your calendar and avoid moving this for other meetings. Prioritise this time!
4 Offer a hybrid format for in-person or online participation.
5 Provide a level of structure that is aligned with the needs of members. We have found it beneficial to facilitate a semi-structured environment that allows any kind of writing task, rather than strictly for manuscript preparation.
6 Use Pomodoro timing to stay focused and to allow for frequent short breaks for informal, useful discussions which help prevent mental fatigue.
7 Log both the goals and achieved activities for each member at the beginning and end of each session, for personal and group reflection.

8 Set writing times to be first thing in the morning and, where possible, find a working place that offers limited distractions. We suggest closing the office door, finding a different room if you are situated within an open plan office, wearing headphones, and/or using a sign to indicate you are currently unavailable.
9 Use the break time to build networks and interdisciplinary collaborative opportunities.

Conclusion

The journey of academic mothers balancing their careers and parental responsibilities is fraught with challenges, including identity reconstruction, time pressures, and the need to navigate competing demands. Supportive networks, such as the Academics Down Under SUAW group, help them reconnect with their professional identities by fostering productivity, peer support, and community. The experiences of the five core members show the transformative impact of such networks, enabling them to integrate roles, reduce isolation, and maintain academic momentum. The success of the SUAW group demonstrates that with the right support, academic mothers can balance professional and personal responsibilities. This chapter serves as a testament to the resilience and determination of academic mothers and the critical role of supportive networks in their journey.

References

Bowyer, D., Hodgson, H., Hamilton, M., James, A., & Allen, L. (2022). Mid-career challenges in Australian universities: A collaborative auto-ethnographic narrative. In H. L. Schnakenburg (Ed.), *Women in higher education and the journey to mid-career* (pp. 168–200). IGI Global.

Gavin, M., Grabowski, S., Hassanli, N., Hergesell, A., Jasovska, P., Kaya, E., Klettner, A., Small, J., Walker, K. N., & Weatherall, R. (2024). 'Maybe one way forward': Forging collective collegiality in the neoliberal academy. *Management Learning*, 55(3), 386–405. https://doi.org/10.1177/13505076231181670

Lipton, B. (2020). Introduction. In B. Lipton (Ed.), *Academic women in neoliberal times* (pp. 1–20). Palgrave Macmillan. https://link.springer.com/chapter/10.1007/978-3-030-45062-5_1

Stone, C., & O'Shea, S. (2019). My children ... think it's cool that mum is a uni student: Women with caring responsibilities studying online. *Australasian Journal of Educational Technology*, 35(6), 97–100. https://doi.org/10.14742/ajet.5504

Yoo, J. (2020). An autoethnography of mothering in the academy. *The Qualitative Report*, 25(8), 3173–3184. https://doi.org/10.46743/2160-3715/2020.4582

19 Choosing Affective over Effective Collaboration in Academic Writing

Pathways to Mentorship, Collaborative Wellbeing, and Self-Care through Scholarly Personal Narrative

Syed Ali Nasir Zaidi and Finney Cherian

A broken bone can heal, but the wound a word opens can fester forever. Jessamyn West

nulla dies sine linea – never a day without a line. Apelles

Introduction

As teacher educators, we introduce teacher candidates to the grand stories of curriculum theory, and instructional approaches but at the expense of their self-care and wellbeing (Britzman, 1991).

Brookfield (2017) notes that

> First, the syllabus reigned supreme in my kingdom. Classroom discussions would start to ignite as students brought in personal experiences, but I'd constantly have to cut these short in order to get back to the "official" business of covering the designated content. Sometimes when students seemed the most engaged, I had to act as the enforcer of dullness, dragging them back to the study of disembodied content.
>
> (p. 10)

Disembodied content resonates with Ahmed (2004) who states emotions are not simply something 'I' or 'we' have...they have forms of reorientation or a rippling effect. In other words, soulful classroom amalgamates and centers both affective and effective aspects for writers' wellbeing and self-care. That is why in our teaching lives, like Brookfield's, course syllabi kept us away from the stories of our students' lives. However, while smaller in scale and equally important, the anecdotes that have influenced their identities as teachers must be acknowledged. All teaching is filtered through the personhood of the teacher. Examining how lived experiences inform an educator's practice and classroom relationship is critical, especially for those beginning to forge their professional identities for the first time. Our instructional paranoia – fixated on

DOI: 10.4324/9781003633327-25

Figure 19.1 Affective and effective writing practices reciprocate mutual self-care and well-being.

getting through the curriculum and preparing them to survive practice teaching – seemed convenient excuses to avoid the practice of sharing personal narratives of wellbeing that truly centers student's self-care. That is why we believe beginning with *Shut Up and Write! followed by "Don't Shut Up and Share"* fosters both technical expertise as well as the literacy of soulful practitioners.

Making course space to share and analyse personal stories fueled a sense of insecurity compared to topics like assessment and mastery of the mandated standardised curriculum. So, reflective writing and educational autobiographies were squeezed after "big" curriculum, assessment, and instructional stories were covered. We seemed content in our actions until we kept crashing into two realities: First, our hypocrisy was hard to hide, as we consistently preached the importance of developing into reflective practitioners who critique the actions and the incidents of our teaching and living. Second, we could not overlook the lively and charged conversations that emerged when we shared stories about the students and experiences that shaped our identities as educators. These included stories of students who sadly passed away, leaving us devastated, as well as moments when we realised our own teaching dreams alongside our insecurities, such as imposter syndrome. Sharing these experiences allowed our students to see us as authentic and imperfect individuals whose lives were enriched through the pursuit of knowledge and the relationships we nurtured with colleagues and students. Building on these reflections, this chapter explores the significance of effective and affective writing mentorship.

Mentorship: Reflexive Craft-Focused Learning Relationships (RCFLR)

Mentorship is to be a source of inspiration, caring, wisdom, and companionship to novices who are learning to teach the complex craft to others (Sommer et al., 2013). As we believe teaching is a craft demanding intense study and reflection situated in a trusted relationship between mentor and mentee, we term our vision of mentorship as a Reflexive Craft-Focused Learning Relationship (RCFLR). If new teachers don't experience wise, caring, and supportive mentorship, how can we expect them to express these virtues to their students?

As we believe definitions justify practice, the wording for the mentorship framework we define is very purposeful: Reflexive Craft-Focused Learning Relationship. The wording is intended to express the ideological vision and practice of mentorship that helps novice writers and educators come to the fullness of their identity as teachers and develop the intellectual and social competencies needed to support the growth, wellbeing, and self-care, resulting in the learning of all students.

Our Theoretical Framework for Affective and Effective Mentorship in Writing

The RCFLR model integrates affective and effective writing strategies since both run parallel to complement and offset each other. For example, we theorise effective writing strategies around Donald Graves, Nash Viray, and Brian Cambourne whereas affective writing strategies reminds us of Sara Ahmed, Toni Morrison, and bell hooks. Affective is based on dispositions whereas effective is skills- and knowledge-based.

Ideological Pillar: What Effective Writing Should Be?

DeSalvo (2000) offers us a powerful expression of the power of writing to heal and transform: "what if writing were as important and as basic a human function and as significant to maintaining and promoting our psychic and physical wellness as, say, exercise, healthful food, pure water, clean air, rest and repose and some soul-satisfying practice" (p. 6). In the absence of theoretically grounded and craft-orientated curricular visions, writing expectations become adrift, disjointed in their relevance and interest to teachers and students. The preoccupation of teachers to cover the mandated writing expectations is legitimate; it does not become the forfeiture of pursuing the creative ways of making writing personally satisfying for students and helping the development of wellbeing and self-care via critical and creative thinking. Newkirk and Kittle

(2019) summarise the extensive writing research of Donald Graves who identifies six essential elements that writing mentors need to cultivate with their students/mentees to stimulate:

1. Desire to Express Ideas
2. Writing to Stimulate Initiative
3. Democratic Voice
4. Helping Mentees Cultivate Writing
5. Analysis and Synthesis of Information
6. Discovering Answers

As teacher educators, we deeply believe in Parker Palmer's (1998) observation that *we teach who we are*. We teach through our personhood. The shadowy figures and divine angels of our inner worlds manifest themselves in our pedagogy and our writing. This belief fuels our ***desire to express ideas*** which is rooted in lived experience and that speaks to the transformative potential of teaching. We encourage our beginning teachers to engage in deep anecdotal writing as a way to understand how their personal histories shape their professional identities. Writing becomes not only a reflective act but also a tool to ***stimulate initiative*** – prompting pre-service teachers to take ownership of their journeys and act with intention in their classrooms.

We see writing as a ***democratic voice***, one that allows teachers to speak back to hierarchical norms in education with authenticity and agency. Through Scholarly Personal Narrative (SPN), we create a space where our mentees can explore how their experiences, values, and traumas shape the kind of educators they are becoming. Our mentoring thus centers on ***helping mentees cultivate writing*** as a process of self-discovery and empowerment, one that fosters a deeper engagement with teaching and learning.

As we reflect on how we have been shaped by those who raised and taught us – whether through nurture or neglect – we guide mentees ***in the analysis and synthesis of information*** that stems from those formative experiences. In doing so, we emphasise writing not as a final product but as a dynamic process of ***discovering answers*** about themselves and their place in the educational landscape. We argue that such soulful work through writing rehydrates the spirit, heals the silent wounds inflicted by an unforgiving system (Britzman, 1991), and ultimately cultivates a liberatory and emancipatory mindset in our future educators.

As teacher educators, we go to great lengths for students to look at how mentors, and their failures and successes have shaped their motives to teach and enact their vision (Feiman-Nemser, 1998).

To help our students use writing to explore these autobiographical journeys, we looked for a methodological approach that could offer three conditions – ***accessible, soulful, and experiential***. First, it could be accessible to students from various undergraduate degrees with a spectrum of experiences with writing. We wanted a soul-searching rigorous methodology that would not intimidate or require extensive study to honour the orthodoxy of its traditions like academic writing. Finally, a methodological framework could accommodate the complexity of experiences of success, marginalisation, injustice, and alienation while at the same time helping the writer confront these experiences and offering pathways to generalise and validate the theories of social justice through their own lives. SPN accommodates these three conditions offered by Robert Nash and Susan Viray (2013).

Scholarly Personal Narrative (SPN)

We present the ideological and instructional frameworks that guide our approach and highlight the potential of Scholarly Personal Narrative (SPN) as a powerful method to enhance writing, reading, and critical thinking for our students' lifelong wellbeing and self-care (Nash & Viray, 2013).

Our observation is that SPN is more accessible for students as a writing methodology since it establishes rigour, complexity, and possibility over the other rigid narrative forms of writing by meaningfully touching upon teachers' knowledge and knowing (Nash & Viray, 2013; Cole & Knowles, 2000). SPN surpasses other forms of writing such as memoir, autobiography, autoethnography and narrative; its potential lies not in it being a shortcut to complex writing methodology, but in the fact that it offers ideology, structure, and practice guidelines to manage the mining and analysis of heavy themes such as alienation, power, marginalisation, standardisation, conformity, voicelessness, facelessness, and courage.

Ten General Guidelines for Scholarly Personal Narratives

Nash and Viray (2013) outline ten elements that characterise SPN. These elements help explain and model SPN's ideological and genre structures and the guidelines become the criteria for assessing student work. Encouraging students to share intimate thoughts and experiences and grading those confessionals seems unethical. However, the guidelines offer greater objectivity to be used as assessment criteria. They are as follows:

1 Students' central questions should help organise themes and provoke engaging hooks whereas their grand questions should overcome the singularity of an individual experience.
2 Move from the particular to the general, from the theory to the practice, and back again.
3 Storytelling matters for larger-life implications. Connect them to classroom theories and social phenomena, another evidence-based work.
4 A writers' past and present is the gunpowder of their critical scholarship. Do not weaponise the content for petty gains – ignite dormant volcanos for genuine social justice ideals.

5 Use scholarly references whenever appropriate to help generalise and situate personal truths in the literature relevant to the writer.
6 Always tell an honest story.
7 Show some passion but be sure your passion is tempered and not "preachy", not red-hot and humble.
8 Open-mindedness is a key to your audience, rallying around you to reflect on and challenge their own flawed assumptions.
9 Remember that writing is both a craft and an art. Without one, the other is incomplete.
10 Keep language simple, straightforward, and to the point.

SPN Instructional Approach

Brian Cambourne (1988) bases his literacy framework on the importance of a developmental and scaffolded approach to teaching literacy. He asserts that children acquire early oral and written language skills most effectively when specific conditions are designed into the instructional approach of teachers. To this end, Cambourne offers eight conditions to assist students to engage in meaningful ways with literacy. Teachers model resources, skills, and necessary concepts in a manner that scaffolds complexity and does not rush students to independence, forfeiting competence and mastery in a rush to teach and learn, where independence is confused with abandonment.

As instructors, we insist that our teacher candidates integrate the conditions into their lessons and instructional practices. The conditions, in turn, prove effective in teaching the teacher candidates themselves in SPN writing. Cambourne's conditions are described as they pertain to our efforts to teach SPN:

1 Immersion: Expose students to rich, diverse SPN texts and analyses.
2 Demonstration: Model writing by analysing personal and classroom experiences.
3 Engagement: Foster a safe, reflective space for SPN experimentation and sharing.
4 Expectation: Set realistic goals and clear assessment criteria.
5 Responsibility: Encourage gradual independence through scaffolded support.
6 Approximation: Support early drafts with peer/instructor feedback aligned to SPN principles.
7 Use: Promote authentic language use through shared, functional tasks.
8 Response: Provide constructive feedback that supports revision, reflection, and celebration of voice.

Our Affective Writing Strategies

Ahmed and hooks infuse their writing with emotions as they both argue that it is deeply rooted in one's habitual orientations and social contexts (Ahmed, 2017; hooks, 1994). That is why affective writing collaboration between mentor and mentee not only supports, sustains and challenges but also it resists fear, and rigid academic rules, while truly fostering hope through loose writing assessments. These acts strengthen mentee's positive affective valence for better writing. To Ahmed, this positive affective valence, which is attached to bodies, institutions or words, shapes our belonging, and alienation. In other words, mentor should not silence, punish differences, or restrict non-linear thinking; rather, they should allow the mentee to demonstrate openly his/her emotions in fearlessly tackling with writing as an act of wellbeing and self-care rather than following normative scripts, colonial narratives, and sanitised professionalism – a true reflective practitioner must know how to fight the shadow self (Jung, 1969; Newsome, 2023). Here bell hooks' notion of "teaching to transgress" further enriches the discussion by positioning the mentor as a radical educator who prioritises the emotional and psychological wellbeing of the mentees when they are emotionally charged or overwhelmed. For hooks, education is not merely a transfer of knowledge but a political act and a transformative process that should be healing and liberating. Affective mentoring, according to hooks, involves creating a nurturing environment where mentees can engage in self-actualisation, critical thinking, and the development of their unique voices. This approach encourages mentees to view academic writing not as a solitary struggle but as a collaborative and supportive endeavor for development, self-care, and wellbeing.

We are inspired by Sara Ahmed, Toni Morrison, and bell hooks, who position the mentor–mentee relationship as a craft that binds mentor and mentee together in critical scholarships. These seasoned writers were inspired by their mentors; for example, although separated by time, Sara Ahmed found in Virginia Woolf's *Mrs. Dalloway* a form of intellectual and affective mentorship; through Woolf's narrative, Ahmed was compelled to engage in the world with a spirit of direct confrontation and vulnerability (see Ahmed, 2017). In addition, Toni Morrison (see 2019) persuades us to seek care from mentor for future wellbeing. For hooks (see 1994, 1999), her mentoring of black writers is a clear reminder that writing mentorship is to take full charge of their minds, bodies, and souls.

Our Practice Evolution: Collaborative Writing

This chapter explores the mentorship model as a foundation in our future work with pre-service teachers. Initially, the authors began with one-on-one interaction as an education faculty member and a PhD candidate. In this Reflexive Craft-Focused Learning Relationship model, we aimed to establish a wellbeing and self-care in academic writing as practiced by authors where mentor and mentee accompany to achieve affective and effective goals simultaneously. Now we are planning to replicate this mentorship for future pre-service teachers or teacher candidates. However, modeling and demonstration cannot be the sole characteristic; following a critical interaction between mentor and mentee, we aim that the writing course must be critically developed and grounded in the following ideological pillars.

- **Relationships**: The circle needs to be broadened between a mentor and mentee to include a small-group setting of peers. The intimacy of small groups creates the opportunity for discussing writing to receive feedback, as well as broader perspectives (agreeable and non-agreeable feedback). The group writing and discussion can help students to bridge the insular nature of the perspectives.
- **Nurturing Creativity and Critical Reflection**: Small collaborative opportunity offers writers the opportunity to question creative approaches to connect writing with art, music, and other multimodal forms of expressions while also using the group to help members examine the unchecked assumptions and perspectives about lived experiences.
- **Therapeutic Potentials**: While writing about experiences, especially negative ones, can help to sort through emotions of events; this is only one opportunity for cathartic release. Sharing these written expressions with others help to identify the individual lived experiences as well as the common aspects of human experience. These shared expressions of writing can lead to deeper self-awareness and nurturing of the soul through emotional release, healing, personal growth, and empowerment.

The writing of this chapter has helped us to confidently move towards the evolution of these three ideological pillars of collaborative writing opportunities in our courses. Pre-service certification course like ours are highly regulated in terms of mandated learning objectives. However, the opportunity to write about our classroom lives in this chapter invites curricular reform and gives us the courage to move beyond teaching and expressing our teachers solely the technical aspect of the teaching profession (Cochran-Smith & Zeichner, 2006). We believe that beginning with *Shut Up and Write!* followed by *"Don't Shut Up and Share"* fosters both technical expertise and the literacy of soulful practitioners.

Conclusion

Critical writing assures the wellbeing and self-care of our students. The transformative power of writing and mentoring draws on the theoretical insights of Sara Ahmed, bell hooks, and Toni Morrison. It lays the foundations for the wellbeing and self-care of the writer as Kafka said that writing is "descent into the cold abyss of oneself" (Kimmage, 2013, p. 4). Through SPN, the mentee examines the theoretical grounds of how affective (emotional support) and effective (goal-oriented) mentoring foster resilience, belonging, and healing. It bridges the gap of knowing and doing, theory and practice (Connelly & Clandinin, 1985). Academic healing does not happen in a vacuum, it needs theoretical grounds such as those advanced by Donald Graves, Nash and Viray, and Brian Cambourne. Ahmed's concept of "affective economies" explains how emotions circulate between mentors and mentees, forging relational bonds that empower mentees to navigate anxieties and find belonging and becoming. hooks' "teaching to transgress" reinforces the mentor's role as a radical educator who nurtures self-actualisation, critical thinking, and liberation, emphasising the emotional dimensions of academic writing. Writing becomes not only a tool for academic success but also a pathway for healing, transformation, and empowerment, stitching wounds and cultivating resilience. It is the headspace where the subaltern finds peace in writing to learn in a *Room of One's Own* (Woolf, 2019).

References

Ahmed, S. (2004). Affective economies. *Social Text*, 22(2), 117–139. https://doi.org/10.1215/01642472-22-2_79-117

Ahmed, S. (2017). *Living a feminist life*. Duke University Press. https://doi.org/10.1023/B:IHIE.0000048795.84634.4a

Britzman, D. P. (1991). *Practice makes practice: A critical study of learning to teach*. State University of New York Press.

Brookfield, S. D. (2017). *Becoming a critically reflective teacher* (2nd ed.). Jossey-Bass.

Cambourne, B. (1988). *The whole story: Natural learning and the acquisition of literacy in the classroom*. Scholastic, Inc.

Cochran-Smith, M., & Zeichner, K. M. (2006). *Studying teacher education: the report of the AERA Panel on Research and Teacher Education*. Lawrence Erlbaum Associates.

Cole, A. L., & Knowles, J. G. (2000). *Researching teaching: Exploring teacher development through reflexive inquiry*. Allyn and Bacon.

Connelly, F. M., & Clandinin, D. J. (1985). Chapter X: Personal practical knowledge and the modes of knowing: Relevance for teaching and learning. *Teachers College Record*, 86(6), 174–198.

DeSalvo, L. (2000). *Writing as a way of healing: How telling our stories transforms our lives*. Beacon Press.

Feiman-Nemser, S. (1998). Teachers as teacher educators. *European Journal of Teacher Education*, 21(1), 63–74. https://doi.org/10.1080/0261976980210107

hooks, b. (1994). *Teaching to transgress: Education as the practice of freedom*. Routledge. https://doi.org/10.4324/9780203700280

hooks, b. (1999). *Remembered rapture: The writer at work* (1st ed.). Henry Holt.

Jung, C. G. (1969). *The archetypes and the collective unconscious* (Collected Works of C.G. Jung, Vol. 9, Part 1). Princeton University Press.

Kimmage, M. (2013). Fathers and writers: Kafka's "letter to his father" and Philip Roth's non-fiction. *Philip Roth Studies*, 9(1), 27–40. https://doi.org/10.1353/prs.2013.a502683

Morrison, T. (2019). *The measure of our lives: A gathering of wisdom*. Knopf.

Nash, R. J., & Viray, S. (2013). *Our stories matter: Liberating the voices of marginalized students through scholarly personal narrative writing*. Peter Lang.

Newkirk, T., & Kittle, P. (Eds.). (2019). *Children want to write: Donald Graves and the revolution in children's writing*. Heinemann.

Newsome, R. (2023). *Writing-as-shadow-work: An aesthetics of Jungian psychoanalysis*. University of Salford (United Kingdom).

Palmer, P. J. (1998). *The courage to teach: Exploring the inner landscape of a teacher's life*. Jossey-Bass.

Sommer, C. A., Markopoulos, P., & Goggins, S. L. (2013). Mentoring master's level students: Drawing upon the wisdom of Athena as Mentor in Homer's Odyssey. *Journal of Poetry Therapy*, 26(1), 1–12.

Woolf, V. (2019). *A room of one's own*. Ren Kitap. (Original work published 1929.)

20 'Performing' the Good Neoliberal Academic

Using Critical Autoethnography to Interrogate Dominant Higher Education Audit Cultures

Katarina Tuinamuana, Rafaan Daliri-Ngametua, Wade Naylor, Melissa Cain, Luke Rowe, Debra J. Phillips, Jason Y.L Wong, Helen Sheehan, Marie White, Renee Morrison, Christopher Duncan, and Shu Chao

Introduction

Committed academics are often guided by a profound belief in the ethical purpose of teaching and research—work that brings joyful meaning and thrives on collaborative discussion and deliberation (Schriever et al., 2021). They aspire to make a meaningful impact and contribute to the collective knowledge that benefits the common good. However, recent policy changes have introduced significant occupational stress, as academics struggle to manage increasing demands and the growing expectations of their roles (Chamorro-Koc & Caldwell, 2021). Consequently, academic work has become defined by performativity pressures, shaped by audit cultures that evaluate performance through narrow, technocratic metrics. Mountz et al. (2015) argue that these trends have led to widespread self-surveillance, diminishing the quality of life for academics and affecting their communities and colleagues.

Additionally, the relentless push to publish in prestigious academic journals can be overwhelming, often extinguishing the joy of research and eroding intrinsic motivation. Many academics feel compelled to "play the game of academia…playing to be valued as a professional" (Nislev & Cain, 2018, p. 106). These tensions highlight the mixed responses, ambiguities, and ambivalence that characterise the experience of academics as neoliberal policies increasingly reshape higher education.

The authors of this chapter are members of a Shut Up and Write! (SUAW) collective established to foster a positive research culture at an Australian university (see Figure 20.1). Through weekly meetings, we have worked independently-together on our research projects for the past 18 months, regularly welcoming new members. Our group comprises a diverse cohort: a PhD candidate, nine early-career researchers, and two mid-career researchers. This

DOI: 10.4324/9781003633327-26

178 *Fostering Wellbeing through Collective Writing Practices*

Figure 20.1 ACU SUAW group.

Note: An image taken in Teams of our SUAW Group. From top left clockwise, rows top to bottom: Shu Chao, Jason Wong, Debra Phillips, Helen Sheehan. Melissa Cain, Katarina Tuinamuana, Wade Naylor, Luke Rowe, Christopher Duncan, Rafaan Daliri-Ngametua, Marie White & Renee Morrison.

chapter reflects on our individual and collective experiences within the SUAW initiative. We address the following questions:

1 How do academics experience a "Shut Up and Write!" initiative?
2 What conditions nurture and enable relational and meaningful writing for academics working in higher education?
3 How and why might academics resist the performative cultures that detract from an emphasis on purposeful work?

The chapter is organised as follows: We begin by outlining the methodological framework and data-generation processes within a collaborative, autoethnographic approach. We then present Berlant-inspired vignettes, linking them interactively under three themes in a quilt-making fashion. Throughout, we integrate analysis within these vignettes, illustrating the contributions of this study to existing knowledge.

Methodology and Processes

Autoethnography aims to "describe and systematically analyse (graphy) personal experience (auto) in order to understand cultural experience (ethno)" (Ellis et al., 2011, p. 273). This chapter is grounded in a collaborative form of autoethnography (Anderson & Fourie, 2015), which emerged organically as we documented our experiences and connected them to broader socio-cultural debates. Our approach developed relationally and temporally through extended, iterative practices of discussion and writing during and beyond SUAW sessions. Adopting autoethnography allowed us to write with vulnerability, fostering rich analytical connections between our academic work and its wider contexts about a range of matters affecting purpose, personal flourishing, and societal change.

Data Generation

Ellis and Adams (2014) explain that in autoethnography, "everyday experience can serve as relevant data" (p. 19). Within the SUAW collective, our everyday experiences unfolded through weekly writing blocks and the ensuing conversations. After six months, it became evident that a strong camaraderie was forming. We decided to document our thoughts and experiences as a metanarrative accompanying the academic writing produced during SUAW sessions.

To promote a collaborative approach, we initiated the process with an invitation to contribute to a shared Google document:

> Please add any thoughts and comments on what you would like to write about or how you would like to contribute to this work. This can include what SUAW has meant to you, why you came, and any other experiences related to the group that are noteworthy.

Following an initial burst of contributions, a member proposed adopting the "100s" technique described by Berlant and Stewart (2019). This experimental format, which incorporates images and lyrical writing, challenges conventional assumptions about academic writing and elevates everyday observations. We adapted these principles to craft a quilt of interconnected stories. Each story is built upon, and responded to, preceding ones, representing our collective experience. The vignettes were drawn from emails, team chats, and research notebooks. Consistent with autoethnography, these texts were grounded in lived experiences, producing free-flowing and often lyrical expressions of personal subjectivities.

Data Analysis

After producing a substantial body of text, we iteratively read and re-read the vignettes, treating each as a piece of a larger mosaic. Contributors layered their narratives with connections to others' work, developing a cohesive form of inductive thematic analysis (Holman Jones, 2016). One team member initially identified four themes; this was later reduced to three through discussion.

Writing tasks were distributed among small groups to ensure collaboration. Each group interwove descriptive and analytical insights under their assigned themes, sharing drafts with the broader team for feedback. This iterative process

Vignettes: A Quilted Autoethnographic Dialogue

Theme 1. SUAW Reminds Us That We Are Researchers

Initially, the SUAW sessions were conceived as a means to enhance focus and productivity by setting timers and writing in silence for defined periods. However, they quickly became much more than a utilitarian exercise. Beyond writing, these sessions fostered a sense of connection and joy, providing a sanctuary within the broader audit culture of the university. Here, we reclaimed, renewed, and reaffirmed our identities as researchers.

Many of us faced challenges in meeting the expectations of higher education, often grappling with the pressure to produce outputs characteristic of "researchers". SUAW became a supportive space that inspired us to rediscover ourselves as academics.

Melissa reflected on how SUAW addressed the isolation she felt in her previous roles:

> In my prior positions as a sessional academic, I wasn't permitted to engage in research initiatives or apply for grants. Writing on weekends, I muddled through, led by curiosity but without clarity. Joining SUAW here, I found a supportive community and a structured opportunity to connect, learn, and write.

For Shu, SUAW alleviated the overwhelm of her teaching-focused role: "Teaching and service had consumed my time, leaving little for research. My mentor recommended SUAW, and here, I became part of a community of practice – sharing a mutual commitment to research and writing, both individually and collectively."

Jason underscored the affirmation of academic identity SUAW provided: "Research activities affirm our identities as academics, yet they're often deprioritised amidst teaching and administrative responsibilities. SUAW gave us the space to balance these demands while rediscovering our scholarly purpose." Christopher, at the start of his academic journey, found immense value in the collective:

> As a Master of Philosophy student, SUAW was a blessing. It offered a consistent, dedicated time for MY writing and helped solidify my academic identity. I have been able to connect, yarn and learn from academics across the faculty at so many different stages of the academic life cycle.

Many of us battled with imposter syndrome, feeling uncertain about our roles as researchers and SUAW became a refuge of resistance, challenging this narrative. Sharing our journeys and celebrating achievements within the group helped us confront self-doubt, a sentiment reinforced by increasing demands for efficiency and outputs among universities (Mulholland et al., 2023).

Luke shared the transformative impact of SUAW:

> Although I secured a rare, continuing academic position before COVID-19, it came with many challenges. As my role was teaching-focused, my research identity felt fractured. This (SUAW) allowed me to reconcile this conflict and enabled me to advance my research interests despite an intense teaching workload.

Wade shared a similar sense of renewal: "Transitioning between academia and teaching left me feeling detached from research. SUAW reignited my academic curiosity and even inspired collaborative projects with other members." Mulholland et al. (2023) emphasise the role of peer support in strengthening academic identity, particularly for early-career researchers. SUAW exemplified this, reminding us that, despite heavy teaching and administrative loads, we remain researchers capable of meaningful contributions under the right conditions.

Theme 2. Collaborative Relational Purpose

Some of us in this SUAW collective have navigated the challenges of academia during the late 1980s and 1990s, which were shaped by neoliberal and neo-conservative ideologies. These eras brought reductions in government research funding and a growing reliance on student evaluations to measure academic performance, often emphasising quantifiable outcomes (Macdonald et al., 2023; Davidovich & Eckhaus, 2019). These shifts have deeply influenced academic practice, fostering fear and hesitation in questioning workload allocation processes. This environment perpetuates competition among colleagues and intensifies tensions within academic spaces, both physical and virtual. However, as the following vignettes reveal, what is most disheartening is the erosion of collegiality and relational pedagogy – elements central to a supportive academic culture.

Debra highlighted that SUAW sessions became a vital space for fostering collegial relationships and said: "By dedicating time each week, I acknowledged the significance of professional connections. This was especially evident in our discussions about overcoming challenges in research and publishing." Katarina commented:

> I couldn't always attend due to heavy workloads, but whenever I joined, the group's supportive and collegial nature was deeply nourishing. SUAW offered connection, laughter, and shared struggles, easing the isolation of stepping away from the neoliberal academic ideal. It has been invaluable for my growth as a writer, scholar, colleague, and friend.

Debra and Katarina's reflections emphasise the importance of relational connections in resisting the isolating pressures of a performance-driven academic culture. The following vignettes from Melissa, Helen, and Renee illustrate how such collaboration can also be deeply cathartic:

> Melissa exclaimed, "It's fascinating! We all bring depth of knowledge, thought, and experience, yet we also carry doubts and moments of dread. Academia rarely asks us to be honest about what we don't know, which makes such vulnerability humbling. This group includes early career researchers alongside seasoned academics, and together, we have much to learn from one another. It's a cathartic process. Without judgment, we motivate and support each other, becoming catalysts for one another's achievements and celebrating our progress."
>
> Helen continues, "SUAW has been transformative in my journey as a researcher. Despite the persistent demands of teaching and administration, the group has provided a positive, supportive space. It has fostered connections that inspire and nurture – connections among researchers at various stages, sparking new projects, and connections to the broader academic community through shared readings and collaborative publications. These networks have enriched my growth as a scholar."

Renee added that much of her career has been shaped by working from home during the COVID-19 pandemic, often in isolation. Initially, she hesitated to join SUAW, as she did not see the need for structured writing time. However, she realised that, "I was pleasantly surprised to find that the greatest benefits weren't the writing outputs but the sense of being bolstered and truly 'heard' every time I attended."

These vignettes illustrate how connection within SUAW has helped sustain our academic identities. Participation not only enhances research expertise but also reveals abundant ideas and opportunities, reinforcing the value of a supportive academic community.

Theme 3. Resisting and Countering Performativity: Comparing Authentic Scholarship with Performative Scholarship

We have embraced SUAW as both a comforting quilt and a suit of armour, enabling us to resist the pressures of performative academic cultures. This dual purpose encourages us to explore alternative ways of being, persistently crafting and asserting our academic identities. Harré (2018) contrasts 'finite' games (i.e. performative scholarship), which prioritise competition and sameness, with 'infinite' games (i.e. authentic scholarship), which value inclusivity, humanity, and diversity. While performative scholarship focuses on metrics and rankings, authentic scholarship fosters relational, meaningful, and purpose-driven work where everyone benefits.

The following vignettes illustrate how participants resist performative pressures and embrace authentic scholarship:

> Raf shares her thoughts: "Academic work is constrained by neoliberal, performative, and competitive agendas that question the worth of our contributions. I resist by valuing collaboration and shared success. I thrive when others thrive and feel fulfilled when I work in conditions that enable collective engagement and happiness. This resistance is both activism and compassion, showing what academia could look like if we prioritised people over metrics."

For Marie, SUAW embodies collegiality, camaraderie, and even fun – qualities rarely associated with the serious demands of market-driven academic writing, while Melissa added that: "SUAW offers the rare luxury of 'slow scholarship' (Mountz et al., 2015), allowing time to think, write, and resist the relentless administrative and professional demands that stifle intellectual growth and personal freedom."

Concluding Thoughts

SUAW groups are usually set up to encourage uninterrupted, focused writing. There is a sense of responsibility to other members to support their writing through these silent phases of work. We too were quick to adopt these aims initially. However, we soon came to notice that these somewhat utilitarian aims started to expand towards a relationality based within a collective of writers. We had created a dedicated space in our busy schedules to support each other in scholarly writing, share ideas, encourage and help sustain an academic identity.

Our SUAW experience is validated by much evidence suggesting that academic writing groups are effective at making the process of writing more generative in various ways. SUAW groups help make academic writing visible and explicit, and protect time for writing. They reduce anxiety associated with procrastination, offer social-emotional support, help members develop their writing skills, and provide guidance to improve written outputs (Aitchison & Guerin, 2014; Haas, 2014). Moreover, our SUAW community validates findings that suggest such groups can help academics resist the neoliberal view of writing as strictly about product and seldom about process (Aitchison & Guerin, 2014).

Writing groups are also effective in helping academics overcome isolation (O'Dwyer et al., 2017). In our SUAW community, we saw that it allowed us to "come away feeling bolstered and heard" (Renee). Emboldened, we reimagined a different approach to writing within the institution's demands (Bosanquet et al., 2017). As we embark on new writing ventures, we hope to inspire fellow academics and continue the rich tradition of academic collaboration and inquiry. In the end, we did not just "shut up and write"; we forged a path toward a more collegial and resilient academic community.

References

Aitchison, C., & Guerin, C. (2014). Writing groups, pedagogy, theory and practice. In C. Aitchison & C. Guerin (Eds.), *Writing groups for doctoral education and beyond: Innovations in practice and theory* (1st ed.). Routledge. https://doi.org/10.4324/9780203498811

Anderson, T. D., & Fourie, I. (2015, 2-5 September 2014: Part 2). Collaborative autoethnography as a way of seeing the experience of care giving as an information practice. *Proceedings of ISIC, the Information Behaviour Conference*, Leeds.

Berlant, L., & Stewart, K. (2019). *The hundreds*. Duke University Press.

Bosanquet, A., Mailey, A., Matthews, K. E., & Lodge, J. M. (2017). Redefining 'early career' in academia: A collective narrative approach. *Higher Education Research & Development*, 36(5), 890–902. https://doi.org/10.1080/07294360.2016.1263934

Chamorro-Koc, M., & Caldwell, G. A. (2021). Running the academic marathon. Planning and executing as planned. In A. Blackler & E. Miller (Eds.), *How to be a design academic. From learning to leading* (1st ed., pp. 189–207). CRC Press. https://doi.org/10.1201/9780429351693

Davidovich, N., & Eckhaus, E. (2019). Student evaluation of lecturers – What do faculty members think about the damage caused by teaching surveys? *Higher Education Studies*, 9(3), 12–21.

Ellis, C., & Adams, T. E. (2014). The purposes, practices, and principles of autoethnographic research. In P. Leavy (Ed.), *The Oxford Handbook of Qualitative Research*. Oxford University Press. https://doi.org/10.1093/oxfordhb/9780199811755.013.004

Ellis, C., Adams, T. E., & Bochner, A. P. (2011). Autoethnography: An overview. *Historical Social Research/Historische Sozialforschung*, 36(138), 273–290. http://www.jstor.org/stable/23032294

Haas, S. (2014). Pick-n-mix: A typology of writers' groups in use. In C. Aitchison & C. Guerin (Eds.), *Writing groups for doctoral education and beyond. Innovations in practice and theory* (pp. 30–48). Routledge. https://doi.org/10.4324/9780203498811

Harré, N. (2018). *The infinite game: How to live well together*. Auskland University Press.

Holman Jones, S. (2016). Living bodies of thought: The "critical" in critical autoethnography. *Qualitative Inquiry*, 22(4), 228–237. https://doi.org/10.1177/1077800415622509

Macdonald, M., Gringart, E., Garvey, D., & Hayward, K. (2023). Broadening academia: An epistemic shift towards relationality. *Higher Education Research & Development*, 42(3), 649–663. https://doi.org/10.1080/07294360.2022.2087602

Mountz, A., Bonds, A., Mansfield, B., Loyd, J., Hyndman, J., Walton-Roberts, M., Basu, R., Whitson, R., Hawkins, R., Hamilton, T., & Curran, W. (2015). For slow scholarship: A feminist politics of resistance through collective action in the neoliberal university. *ACME: An International Journal for Critical Geographies*, 14(4), 1235–1259. https://acme-journal.org/index.php/acme/article/view/1058

Mulholland, K., Nichol, D., & Gillespie, A. (2023). 'It feels like you're going back to the beginning…': Addressing imposter feelings in early career academics through the creation of communities of practice. *Journal of Further and Higher Education*, 47(1), 89–104. https://doi.org/10.1080/0309877X.2022.2095896

Nislev, E., & Cain, M. (2018). Playing in the corridors of academia. In A. L. Black & S. Garvis (Eds.), *Lived experiences of women in academia. Metaphors, manifestos and memoir* (pp. 98–108). Routledge. https://doi.org/10.4324/9781315147444

O'Dwyer, S. T., McDonough, S. L., Jefferson, R., Goff, J. A., & Redman-MacLaren, M. (2017). Writing groups in the digital age: A case study analysis of shut up & write

Tuesdays. In A. Esposito (Ed.), *Research 2.0 and the impact of digital technologies on scholarly inquiry* (pp. 249–269). IGI Global.

Schriever, V., Elsom, S., & Black, A. L. (2021). Mentoring beyond the finite games: Creating time and space for connection, collaboration and friendship. In A. L. Black & R. Dwyer (Eds.), *Reimagining the academy: Shifting towards kindness, connection, and an ethics of care* (pp. 55–77). Springer International Publishing. https://doi.org/10.1007/978-3-030-75859-2_5

21 Benefits of Shut Up and Write! for Inclusion

Jonathan O'Donnell, Rosemary (Rosey) Chang, and Amie O'Shea

Introduction

These back-less stools inspired this chapter. When setting up a Shut Up and Write! (SUAW) program, Jonathan chose a café that seemed ideal—except for these stools. They did not provide back support, and couldn't be adjusted. After one session, participants cursed them as toadstools and moved to a new venue.

Context

Jonathan set up his first SUAW with Inger Mewburn and Tseen Khoo in 2011 (Mewburn et al., 2014). This program moved online during COVID-19 and continues online each week. He helped to establish #MelbWriteUp, an independent program that runs all Saturday (Hodge & Murphy, 2023). Not all the programs that he has set up have flourished, but most have.

Rosemary first hosted SUAW in 2012 and has hosted and attended programs at four Australian universities. SUAW was particularly valuable during part-time PhD study as a working parent supporting elderly parents. Since 2024, together with Jonathan, Rosemary has managed centrally organised SUAW programs at Deakin University.

Amie participated in both the 2011 SUAW and #MelbWriteUp programs and credits them for the successful completion of her PhD, including her re-integration from two periods of maternity leave. At Deakin University, she co-convenes one of two weekly online SUAW programs for queer Deakin staff and students.

All authors met at SUAW. Our experiences have been positive and we have continued to run SUAW programs for 14 years.

Shut Up and Write! and Inclusion

SUAW is successful because the format is simple. Find a space, invite some people, write, chat, repeat. This flexibility allows programs to run quite

DOI: 10.4324/9781003633327-27

Benefits of Shut Up and Write! for Inclusion 187

Figure 21.1 The toadstool-style stools.

differently. Do you run your sessions in a café, a classroom, a library, or online? On campus or off campus? Are they open to anyone, or organised to support a specific group? These choices matter. Different choices allow different benefits to come to the fore. For example, a SUAW program that is open fosters engagement beyond the university, while a program reserved for a specific group fosters group cohesion (Tang & Andriamanalina, 2016).

Fundamental to our argument is the concept of belonging through inclusion: the "importance of fostering belonging through holistic, contextually sensitive approaches that attend to diverse needs and experiences" (Lemon, 2024, Section 3). When SUAW is inclusive, it creates a place to build community among participants, which builds a sense of belonging.

Positioning SUAW in this way shifts the emphasis to a social model of writing. Through 'troubles talk' in the scheduled breaks, attendees learn from people with varied backgrounds. These backgrounds might span disciplinary boundaries, levels of seniority, and diverse life experience (Mewburn et al., 2014). Our own experience of neurodivergence and caring responsibilities informs our approach. We've not always got this right. We are still learning, being influenced by disability studies, Universal Design for Learning, and inclusive practices (Hasted et al., 2022; Meyer et al., 2014).

Much of the literature positions academic SUAW as a cheap program that can reduce isolation (e.g. Fegan, 2016). But participants enjoy SUAW even if they aren't lonely or isolated. Writing is academic work and can be difficult, but it is also pleasurable. Lisa Hodge and Jason Murphy identified social support, collegiality, and common goals as the beneficial aspects of #MelbWriteUp. Of those three benefits, only 'common goals' was associated with writing (Hodge & Murphy, 2023).

To this end, we sought to examine the who, where, when, how, and why of designing SUAW programs:

- Who can attend? Under what conditions might people be excluded?
- When are programs run, for how long, with what effect on attendance?
- Differences between face-to-face programs and online programs.
- How can physical environments make a difference?
- How might the demeanour of the session leader change group dynamics?
- The effects of rules of conduct and unstated norms.

Who is Included/Excluded?

Some programs are developed for particular (often minority) groups. Jasmine Kar Tang and Noro Andriamanalina limit their program to students of colour because "...race and writing are inextricable: Racial formation cannot be removed from writing program administration in the US nation-state" (Tang & Andriamanalina, 2016, p. 10). They enable wellbeing through a sense of cohesion: "...in a predominantly white university that's the size of a small town, we can offer an intimate writing space" (Tang & Andriamanalina, 2016, p. 13).

Amie is part of a team which co-convenes a program for queer-identified staff and students. It creates a safe and inclusive writing environment. The program aims to counter the experiences of isolation or invisibility which queer researchers may experience. It does this via a supportive and collegiate setting in which collaborations and professional exchanges are also valued.

Some SUAW programs may only be offered to members of a specific discipline, department or centre. By contrast, #MelbWriteUp exists outside any university, with subscribers from multiple disciplines and universities (Hodge & Murphy, 2023). An open group creates opportunities to blur boundaries, so that people from diverse backgrounds can meet and learn from each other (Mewburn et al., 2014).

How a program is advertised shapes who attends. Advertising within a university will limit attendance to that university, whereas advertising through social media brings a cross-section of participants and "...enabled both inter- and intra-group bonding to occur in between and during the sessions" (Mewburn et al., 2014, p. 229). Jonathan and Rosemary have found that listing their programs on the SUAW public site attracts a mix of participants from inside and outside universities.

When and for How Long?

SUAW sessions can vary from one hour to 24 hours/seven days a week. The 'Power Hour of Writing' involves 10 minutes goal setting, 60 minutes writing, and 10 minutes windup. This leads it to becoming a daily practice, while being long enough to enable writing focus, progress and community building (Zihms & Reid Mackie, 2023).

A three-hour session with breaks provides "…for a substantial stretch of writing to promote productivity and is reflective of typical graduate class time" (Micsinszki & Yeung, 2021, p. 315). However extended productivity sits in tension with reduced interaction. To that end, Lisa Hodge and Jason Murphy ran their eight-hour program with extended breaks for morning tea, lunch, and afternoon tea. Their respondents suggested that "…the breaks between writing were 'just as useful' as the writing itself…the pauses between writing sprints facilitated networking and mentoring opportunities, a platform to discuss writing, and an opportunity to identify solutions to research challenges" (Hodge & Murphy, 2023, p. 10).

The program that Jonathan established with Inger Mewburn and Tseen Khoo has run from 9:00 a.m. to 12 noon on Friday since 2011. The consistency of the program allowed people to fit back in after a significant break. Both Amie and Rosemary experienced these programs as a space to identify with and enact their PhD identities, while also connecting with others who understood such experiences.

At the other end of possibilities, Jo Sutherst co-ordinates online SUAW rooms ('PGR Study Space') that are partially facilitated, but available 24 hours/seven days a week. Sutherst notes that the open-ended timing offers flexibility and availability, which is particularly beneficial to neurodivergent researchers (Mewburn et al., 2024).

Samantha Micsinszki and Lily Yeung (2021) survey their participants each semester. They establish the date and time based on the greatest convenience to the greatest number. This is a flexible way to cope with changes in university timetables.

Face-to-Face Versus Online

Jonathan runs his online session from his house. It's very convenient for a session that starts at 9:00 a.m. It is convenient for the participants, too. Academics in Eastern Australia are starting their day. Writers in North America are finishing their day. It makes for a cosmopolitan group, working together.

But convenience should not be the only consideration. Social connections are central to the efficacy of SUAW and may be easier to build face-to-face. Suzanne Fegan writes of an Australian face-to-face group where "…social connection has increased over the two-year period in which the group has met. With this has come a more informal and relaxed sense of community…" (Fegan, 2016, p. A-26). By contrast, online meetings are generally limited to one person speaking at a time. Multiple concurrent conversations take place via written chat. Break-out rooms provide an avenue for multiple conversations, but they require the intervention of the facilitator, which undercuts the spontaneous nature of conversations.

However, online meetings aid diverse participation. Online meetings enable individual choice relating to perception, language, expression, and communication, and self-directed executive function (Meyer et al., 2014). These are all important principles of Universal Design for Learning, through live speech, closed captions, writing in chat, emojis, GIFs, as well as opting out of social interactions, video, or audio. Closed captions can be beneficial for those with limited working memory, those for whom English is an additional language, or those who are hard of hearing. Online can provide accessibility for people who are lipreading, who are using an interpreter, or who need managed social interactions. The choice to opt out of social interactions can be useful for those who like joining the group, but who would rather focus exclusively on writing than social turn-taking. Keeping video cameras on may be preferred by those who value visual accountability. Having the audio turned off may be preferred by participants who find talking a distraction.

It is extremely difficult to create an effective SUAW program that combines online and face-to-face elements at the same time. In most instances, the facilitator is effectively managing two different events simultaneously.

Physical Environment

The toadstools that inspired this chapter epitomise the issues that arise when facilitators do not pay attention to physical elements of SUAW. With no back support and no ability to move closer or further from the table, these stools were unusable for long periods of writing.

Even the choice of a café versus a quiet space can make a difference. Inger Mewburn, Lindy Osborne, and Glenda Caldwell found that the "[r]epurposing of public cafes into work and study areas is not always smooth; and some participants find the noise and bustle of these spaces off putting" (Mewburn et al., 2014, p. 229). Most cafés in Australia are welcoming of writers. However, any expectation that a purchase should be made during SUAW may not be appropriate due to income inequality.

Facilitators aiming to encourage engagement with the community might consider an off-campus location. While academics feel that campuses are welcoming places, they can be alienating for others. Perhaps consider a community centre or local library instead.

Facilitating the Group

While sessions need to work for both facilitators and participants, facilitation is key to the SUAW experience. Facilitators set up, advertise, and run the sessions. They chose when and where the program runs and maintain the tone of the sessions. They welcome the participants, and encourage introductions and intention-setting. They organise the timing and manage the breaks. They encourage discussion during the breaks and steer the conversation if it moves into difficult topics or if one person is too dominant. This involves a degree of reflexive practice, and awareness of potential power imbalances based on academic seniority, race, sexuality, socio-economic class, and other factors. As much as they can, facilitators should be aware of, and acknowledge, the power dynamics within the group. A co-facilitator approach in which two facilitators take the lead can help to manage some of these dynamics.

Facilitators need to commit to attending until the program is well-established. Jonathan believes that, over time, facilitators should encourage the participants to take responsibility for the sessions. An established group should be able to manage themselves when a facilitator is not available. This won't work forever—without facilitation, the group will shrink over time, or choose a new facilitator.

Facilitators should be willing to learn. Jonathan, Amie, and Rosey have tried to improve their programs in response to the needs of the participants. Over time, facilitators can build their understanding and incorporate more inclusive characteristics. At most universities, facilitators should be able to draw upon experienced colleagues and professionals with skills in the areas of inclusion and wellbeing.

Rules and Norms

The facilitator is responsible for maintaining the norms of the group. It can be useful to think about what should be encouraged, and how that might happen. Norms often emerge through the activity of the participants themselves. When Jonathan describes his programs, he mentions that people are free to arrive or leave at any time, that participants can steer the conversation away from topics they find uncomfortable and that Australian universities encourage a diversity of views, but have zero tolerance for aggressive or disruptive behaviour. These guidelines have evolved to deal with difficulties that the programs have encountered. Clear enunciation of norms can be important for some attendees as "neurodivergent individuals often look for clear directions when entering a new…environment" (Hasted et al., 2022, p. 62).

Perhaps unsurprisingly, the queer SUAW programs that Amie co-facilitates have 'queered', or deconstructed, some of the elements of SUAW. Being conscious of their role as perhaps the only place that queer-identified people affiliated with the university can safely bring their whole selves means that the sessions are not strictly timed. Some discussions cannot be interrupted. Collegiate, peer-based support is essential for a minority group to thrive. People cannot write if something is 'on top' of them in a psychological sense, and this may be the only context where that can be safely shared and understood. While some hour-long sessions may involve 2 x 25-minute writing blocks, others may involve differing blocks of time which are flexibly determined when the group is ready to start.

Conclusion

There are excellent case studies on SUAW, describing programs for writing productivity (e.g. Skarupski, 2018); for building culture (e.g. Hodge & Murphy, 2023; Mewburn et al., 2014; Tang & Andriamanalina, 2016); and for writing strategies (e.g. Proulx et al., 2023). Excellent as they are, they rarely document the decision-making progress that led to those programs. One exception is Samantha Micsinszki and Lily Yeung's program to create a sense of togetherness for graduate nursing students. They documented the choices that they made around length of sessions, feedback, inclusion, frequency, and structure (Micsinszki & Yeung, 2021, Table 21.1).

This chapter calls on SUAW facilitators to purposefully build inclusive education into their SUAW programs by considering what benefits they provide for their participants. Facilitators should consider who is invited to participate, what structure the programs have, whether they are face-to-face or online, aspects of the physical and the emotional environment, facilitation, and the norms of operating sessions. These decisions require choices. Amie's group had to decide whether allies could attend. They also require attention to the concerns of the group. Jonathan reminds participants that they control the conversation because a participant approached him after a session with concerns about a topic of conversation.

The chapter seeks to provoke reflection on the purposes of SUAW programs, so that the sessions encourage and reinforce those purposes, while still retaining the flexibility that has made the scheme so successful. Thinking through the varied needs of the participants can go a long way to making SUAW more welcoming and beneficial for all participants, particularly neurodivergent, queer, and minority groups in academia. Designing for choice, in

Table 21.1 Adaptation and implementation strategies for Shut Up & Write!® and Sit Down & Write! (Reproduced from Micsinszki & Yeung, 2021)

Shut Up & Write! characteristic	Sit Down & Write! adaptation strategy	Implementation of Sit Down & Write! adaptation strategies
40- to 45-minute writing sessions	Host longer sessions	3-hour writing sessions
Formal feedback not provided	Discuss achievable and time-sensitive writing goals	Informal conversations before and after the writing session
Open to any writing participants	Included only graduate nursing students	Open to domestic, international, and visiting students affiliated with nursing faculty
Weekly sessions	Obtain informal feedback about schedule preference	Sessions held once or twice weekly
Structured writing sessions	Obtain informal feedback about writing session structure	Unstructured writing sessions

line with Universal Design for Learning principles, creates a more inclusive space. Inclusive and diverse spaces can, over time, create a sense of community and belonging and wellbeing for participants.

References

Fegan, S. (2016). When shutting up brings us together: Several affordances of a scholarly writing group. *Journal of Academic Language and Learning*, *10*(2), Article 2.

Hasted, C., Shores, T., Doğan, E., Healey, O., Moon, L., Gordon, C., & Wood, J. (2022). *Co-Designing a More Inclusive Workplace*. ThinkLab–BBC CAPE. https://www.repository.cam.ac.uk/bitstreams/5ba292e8-0c0b-4aa6-b794-9b3287b7304f/download

Hodge, L., & Murphy, J. (2023). Write on! Cultivating social capital in a writing group for doctoral education and beyond. *Educational Review*, 1–17. https://doi.org/10.1080/00131911.2023.2184772

Lemon, N. (2024, November). *SUAW for and as wellbeing: So times a million more than productivity. Community in writing symposium*, Cambridge, UK.

Mewburn, I., Doğan, E., Sutherst, J., Zihms, S., & Shores, T. (2024, November). Writing for all: Accessibility and neurodiversity in SUAW. *Community in Writing Symposium, Cambridge, UK*.

Mewburn, I., Osborne, L., & Caldwell, G. A. (2014). Shut up and write! Some surprising uses of cafes and crowds in doctoral writing. In C. Guerin & C. Aitchison (Eds.), *Writing groups for doctoral education and beyond: Innovations in theory and practice* (pp. 399–425). Routledge.

Meyer, A., Rose, D., & Gordon, D. (2014). *Universal Design for Learning: Theory and Practice*. CAST Professional Publishing. https://publishing.cast.org/catalog/books-products/universal-design-for-learning-meyer-rose-gordon

Micsinszki, S. K., & Yeung, L. (2021). Adapting "Shut Up & Write!®" to foster productive scholarly writing in graduate nursing students. *The Journal of Continuing Education in Nursing*, *52*(7), 313–318. https://doi.org/10.3928/00220124-20210611-05

Proulx, C. N., Rubio, D. M., Norman, M. K., & Mayowski, C. A. (2023). Shut Up & Write!® builds writing self-efficacy and self-regulation in early-career researchers. *Journal of Clinical and Translational Science*, *7*(1), e141. https://doi.org/10.1017/cts.2023.568

Skarupski, K. (2018). *WAG your work: Writing accountability groups*. CreateSpace Independent Publishing Platform.

Tang, J. K., & Andriamanalina, N. (2016). "Rhonda left early to go to black lives matter": Programmatic support for graduate writers of color. *WPA: Writing Program Administration*, *39*(2), 10–16.

Zihms, S., & Reid Mackie, C. (2023). The power hour of writing: An empirical evaluation of our online writing community. *Journal of Academic Writing*, *13*(1), 22–34. https://doi.org/10.18552/joaw.v13i1.791

For Product Safety Concerns and Information please contact our EU representative GPSR@taylorandfrancis.com
Taylor & Francis Verlag GmbH, Kaufingerstraße 24, 80331 München, Germany

www.ingramcontent.com/pod-product-compliance
Lightning Source LLC
Chambersburg PA
CBHW051611230426
43668CB00013B/2066